FIFTY YEARS OF Q
"TWO DOGMAS"

Grazer Philosophische Studien

INTERNATIONALE ZEITSCHRIFT FÜR ANALYTISCHE PHILOSOPHIE

GEGRÜNDET VON
Rudolf Haller

HERAUSGEGEBEN VON
Johannes L. Brandl
Marian David
Leopold Stubenberg

VOL 66 - 2003

Rodopi

Amsterdam - New York, NY 2003

FIFTY YEARS OF QUINE'S "TWO DOGMAS"

Edited by

HANS-JOHANN GLOCK
KATHRIN GLÜER
GEERT KEIL

Die Herausgabe der GPS erfolgt mit Unterstützung des *Instituts für Philosophie der Universität Graz*, der *Forschungsstelle für Österreichische Philosophie, Graz*, und wird von folgenden Institutionen gefördert:
    Bundesministerium für Bildung, Wissenschaft und Kultur, Wien
    Abteilung für Wissenschaft und Forschung des Amtes der Steiermärkischen Landesregierung, Graz
    Kulturreferat der Stadt Graz

GRAZ

In memoriam Donald Davidson

The paper on which this book is printed meets the requirements of "ISO 9706:1994, Information and documentation - Paper for documents - Requirements for permanence".

Lay out: Thomas Binder, Graz
ISBN: 90-420-0948-9
ISSN: 0165-9227
© Editions Rodopi B.V., Amsterdam - New York, NY 2003
Printed in The Netherlands

TABLE OF CONTENTS

Introduction 1

Herbert SCHNÄDELBACH: Two Dogmas of Empiricism.
   Fifty Years After 7

I. Analyticity Revisited

Paul A. BOGHOSSIAN: Epistemic Analyticity: a Defense 15

Kathrin GLÜER: Analyticity and Implicit Definition 37

Verena MAYER: Implicit Thoughts: Quine, Frege and Kant on
   Analytic Propositions 61

Christian NIMTZ: Analytic Truths—Still Harmless after all these
   Years? 91

Åsa Maria WIKFORSS: An a posteriori Conception of Analyticity? 119

II. Necessity, Synonymy, and Logic

Hans-Johann GLOCK: The Linguistic Doctrine Revisited 143

Peter PAGIN: Quine and the Problem of Synonymy 171

Tyler BURGE: Logic and Analyticity 199

III. "Two Dogmas" and Beyond

Geert KEIL: "Science Itself Teaches". A Fresh Look at Quine's
   Naturalistic Metaphilosophy 253

Donald DAVIDSON: Quine's Externalism 281

INTRODUCTION

2001 marked the fiftieth anniversary of the publication of W. V. Quine's "Two Dogmas of Empiricism". Developing out of intense discussions with Carnap, the paper was first presented in December 1950 at a meeting of the American Philosophical Association in Toronto. It was published in the *Philosophical Review* in January 1951. Only four months later, first symposia on "Two Dogmas" were held, in Boston and in Stanford.

Some may have missed the anniversary, since the article is usually quoted from its reprint in Quine's *From a Logical Point of View*, which came out in 1953. Thus, even 2003 is a good occasion to celebrate fifty years of "Two Dogmas".

"Two Dogmas" is one of the most influential articles in the history of analytic philosophy. But its influence has not been confined to analytic philosophy. The article does not just question central semantic and epistemological views of logical positivism and early analytic philosophy, it also marks a momentous challenge to the idea that conceptual analysis is a main task of philosophy. The rejection of this idea paved the way for a new conception of philosophy which turned out to be relevant to all branches of Western philosophy. The idea that philosophy is an *a priori* discipline which differs in principle from the empirical sciences dominated early analytic philosophy, but similar views are to be found in the Kantian tradition, in phenomenology and in philosophical hermeneutics. In questioning this consensus from the perspective of a radical empiricism, Quine's article has had a sustained and lasting impact across all these philosophical divisions.

In the wake of "Two Dogmas", and of related early articles by Quine such as "Truth by Convention", most contemporary analytic philosophers assume that it is impossible to draw a clear and sharp distinction between empirical propositions and propositions that are true solely because of their meaning. In the same breath, they often repudiate the distinction between a priori and a posteriori knowledge. This repudiation also rules out once dominant positions like the linguistic doctrine of necessary truth, according to which the source of such truth lies in language and meaning, and the analytic theory of a priori knowledge, which explains such knowledge by reference to the analytic nature of its content. Quine himself moves from the abandonment of these distinctions and doctrines to a thoroughgoing naturalism, and many analytic philosophers have followed his lead. They insist that philosophy is part of natural science, or at least continuous with it.

It is beyond dispute that "Two Dogmas" has shaped the philosophical landscape more than any other article of the second half of the twentieth century. The reasons for a philosophical retrospective of fifty years of "Two Dogmas" and its repercussions are not, however, purely or even predominantly historical. For one thing, on closer scrutiny the apparent consensus on what the article has demonstrated proves to be deceptive. Quine employs a number of different formulations of the distinctions he attacks, and he pursues different argumentative strategies in the course of the article. Different suggestions have been made both as to what the overall argumentative dialectic of "Two Dogmas" is and how to evaluate the specific arguments. There does not even seem to be agreement on what the main thesis of the paper is: Does Quine hold that the analytic/synthetic distinction is hopelessly unclear or that there are no analytic statements? Moreover, there is lively controversy on further reaching questions, for instance: How does the rejection of the analytic/synthetic distinction relate to Quine's equally famous thesis of the indeterminacy of translation? And how does it relate to various kinds of semantic holism?

For another thing, ever since Grice and Strawson there have been notable if sporadic attempts to rehabilitate one or the other dichotomy between the analytic and synthetic, a priori and a posteriori, necessary and contingent, conceptual and factual, philosophical and scientific in the face of Quine's arguments. In recent years, such attempts have been made with increasing frequency by otherwise diverse figures like Boghossian, Putnam, and followers of Wittgenstein. These writers question either the cogency of Quine's original arguments, or suggest that there are better ways of drawing these distinctions which are immune to them.

Thirdly, the debate received an important additional stimulus through Kripke's *Naming and Necessity*, which resuscitates the traditional idea of *de re* necessities and thereby challenges both the Kantian analytic/synthetic distinction and its empiricist debunking. According to Kripkean essentialism, some necessary truths, truths about the essence of things, are discovered *a posteriori* by empirical science. Kripke's essentialism has forcefully revived the view, rejected by Quine, that necessity is an intrinsic and perhaps *sui generis* feature of reality, rather than a product of our thought and language.

All in all, the time has come to reconsider the semantic, epistemological and methodological questions raised by "Two Dogmas". The current collection differs from other anthologies devoted to Quine in two respects. On the one hand, it focuses on his attack on analyticity, apriority and necessity; on the other, it considers implications of that attack that far transcend the limits of Quine scholarship, and lie at the heart of the current self-understanding of philosophy. It deals with issues like semantic holism, indeterminacy of translation, recent attempts to rehabilitate the analytic/synthetic distinction and its brethren, the status of philosophy between conceptual analysis, empirical science and essentialist metaphysics, but also with important but hitherto neglected aspects of "Two Dogmas", such as its treatment of Kant's notion of analyticity and its consequences in the philosophy of language and the philosophy of mind, such as Davidson's discussion of its legacy for externalism.

The contributors include both opponents and proponents of the dichotomies attacked by Quine. Furthermore, they include both eminent figures such as Boghossian, Burge, and Davidson, and up and coming younger philosophers. Finally, they combine philosophers from the USA, Germany, Sweden and Britain. The analytic/synthetic distinction was decisively shaped by Germanophone philosophers from Kant to Carnap, and this is reflected by an abiding interest in the Quinean debate among analytic philosophers who read German but publish in English.

The contributions fall roughly into three groups. In the papers of the first group, the case against analyticity is reopened. Paul Boghossian endorses the project of explaining the *a priori* via the notion of meaning. He starts from the notion of *epistemic* analyticity. A sentence is epistemically analytic if grasp of its meaning suffices for justified belief in its truth. In particular, Boghossian defends the idea of implicit definition against objections, and tries to show how facts about meaning can explain entitlements to reason according to certain rules. Kathrin Glüer examines Boghossian's epistemic version of the analytic theory of *a priori* knowledge, arguing that his implicit definition account of the meaning of the logical constants does not meet the challenge of the classical Quinean criticisms. Verena Mayer traces back the notion of analyticity from Quine via Carnap to Frege and Kant. She concludes that the so called Frege-Kant notion of analyticity cannot be attributed to Kant, who had a distinctly pragmatic notion of analytic judgements. Christian Nimtz reconsiders and defends Putnam's semantic approach to the problem of analyticity. He develops a semantics within the two-dimensionalist framework which aspires to explain the genesis of analytic truths, or at least of the harmless ones. Åsa Wikforss addresses the question whether Kripke's revival of a non-epistemic, non-linguistic notion of necessity can be taken one step further in order to free *analyticity* from its epistemic ties. She examines Burge's claim that truths of meaning are a posteriori, depending on features of the external environment, and concludes that Kripke's strategy with respect to necessity is not easily transferable to analyticity.

The papers in the second group deal with further issues raised by Quine's paper: with linguistic necessity, synonymy, and logic. Hanjo Glock takes a fresh look at the linguistic doctrine of logical necessity. He argues that a limited version of it is in line with common sense and that it can be defended against standard objections by reconciling Wittgenstein's claim that analytic statements have a normative role with Carnap's claim that they are true. Peter Pagin addresses what Quine called "the problem of synonymy": the problem of approximating the extension of our pretheoretic concept of synonymy by clear and respectable means. He discusses some difficulties for providing a solution and comes to a skeptical conclusion: it could well be the case that the problem of synonymy cannot be solved at all. Tyler Burge considers the place of logic and mathematics in knowledge of the world. Like Quine, he rejects the view that logic is true independently of a subject matter. Developing a route to rationalism and metaphysics that Quine reopened but did not pursue, Burge argues that full reflective understanding of logic and deductive reasoning reveals apriori relations and requires substantial commitment to mathematical entities.

The two remaining papers put "Two Dogmas" in the perspective of Quine's overall philosophy. Geert Keil takes up one of Quine's preferred phrases, "Science itself teaches", and traces it through his writings, trying to find out what exactly the notorious claim amounts to that philosophy is continuous with natural science. He emphasizes that Quine's job description for philosophers has remarkably traditional features, and concludes that Quine's avowed naturalism is more innocuous than it seems. Donald Davidson celebrates Quine's recognition of the fact that all there is to meaning is what we learn or absorb from observed usage. He argues that this behaviorist approach does not only destroy the myth of meaning, but also entails a powerful form of externalism. According to Davidson, Quine was an externalist from the time of *Word and Object* onwards, despite his reluctance to take the final step from the proximal to the distal stimulus as the relevant cause of a mental state.

With one exception, the essays in this collection were presented at a conference that took place in Berlin, 13.–15. September 2001 under the title "50 Years of Empiricism without Dogmas". We are grateful to the Deutsche Forschungsgemeinschaft and to the Humboldt-Universität Berlin for granting the funds that made the conference possible. Herbert Schnädelbach's paper was delivered as the opening address to that conference. Donald Davidson was prevented from coming to Berlin by the events of September 11; we are grateful to him for nevertheless contributing his paper. Sadly, he will not see the result in print, nor could he proof-read his paper. His sudden death means the loss of one of the greatest philosophers of the 20th century. We dedicate our collection to his memory.

The editors

TWO DOGMAS OF EMPIRICISM.
FIFTY YEARS AFTER

Herbert SCHNÄDELBACH
Humboldt-Universität Berlin

Summary

Quine's "Two Dogmas of Empiricism", a short paper which appeared 50 years ago in the *Philosophical Review*, was a milestone within the development of analytic philosophy. It was more important than many big volumes before and after. This might strike someone not familiar with the analytic tradition as a bit unusual; such impact one might expect from whole books like the *Critique of Pure Reason* or the *Tractatus*, but not from a 16 page paper. In these remarks, which opened a conference on Quine's seminal paper, I would like to indicate why "Two Dogmas" was and still is so important, not only as a standard topic of modern philosophical teaching and as a provocative treatment of the evergreen problem of analyticity, but also as one of the most challenging answers to the question what role philosophy can play in an age of science.

Donald Davidson says somewhere: "In my view, erasing the line between the analytic and synthetic saved philosophy of language as a serious subject". This seems to me to apply to analytic philosophy in general: erasing the line between the analytic and the synthetic saved analytic philosophy as a serious subject. (The question to what extent other types of philosophy can be regarded as serious disciplines should be left open at the moment.) Why would the line between the analytic and the synthetic threaten philosophy in the analytic tradition? In this tradition, science and philosophy were conceived of as complementary, a view shared by German Neokantianism and Husserl's phenomenology. Due to its empiricist origins, early analytic philosophy held that there are no synthetic statements a priori. All synthetic statements a posteriori, however, belong to the empirical sciences. Philosophy not being an empirical science, it thus would seem confined to analytic statements which were thought of as a priori by definition. But at the same time, following Frege and Russell, analytic statements were normally held to exist only within logic and mathematics. But then, what *was* left for philosophers to do—except logic and mathematics?

The answer was: "*applied* logic". But, applied to what? Since the world had been ceded to the empirical sciences the only thing left that philosophers could apply logic to seemed to be scientific *language*. "*Logische Analyse der Wissenschaftssprache*" (Carnap) thus came to be the new password for scientific philosophy, and it was used as the leading slogan in the battle against metaphysics and other symptoms of modern irrationalism. Philosophical analysis, on this reading of 'analysis', was understood as a critical enterprise. Its method consisted in syntactic transformation of allegedly scientific statements into the language of *Principia Mathematica* in order to find out whether they were even candidates for having empirical meaning. Their empirical meaning itself, if any, had then to be determined in accordance with the verification principle after first reducing the statements in question to atomic statements. Both kinds of analysis, syntactic transformation and logical reduction, were supposed to operate within the limits of the analytic.

There was a problem, however, a problem first exposed by G. E. Moore and thereafter extensively discussed from the thirties onwards: the so-called paradox of analysis. This paradox results from supposing that any correct philosophical analysis consists of nothing but analytic statements. For analytic statements can be transformed into logical truths. Logical truths, however, were supposed to be tautologies and tautologies are trivial. So philosophical analysis is correct only if its results are trivial. Thus, rather ironically, it was just within the analytic tradition of philosophy inspired by Russell and Moore that analysis itself came to seem questionable as the very method of philosophy—as witnessed by the title of John Wisdom's famous 1934 paper "Is Analysis a Useful Method in Philosophy?" This seems very doubtful if philosophy is supposed to be nothing but logical calculation trying to reduce everything to logical truths. Analysis does not seem very useful if it reduces philosophical wisdom to insights like 'All bachelors are unmarried men' while all other kinds of knowledge are relegated to science and common sense.

Quine's "Two Dogmas" provided the most effective means of getting rid of the paradox of analysis. Erasing the borderline between the analytic and the synthetic meant releasing analytic philosophy from its self-made prison. To be sure, analytic philosophy had managed to lock itself up by means of pretty good arguments, but Quine's arguments appeared to be even better. Now, linguistic knowledge could be conceived of as intimately connected with knowledge of the world, and this opened up the possibility for philosophy to reach that degree of seriousness which we are ready to grant to our other scientific activities.

But just at this point, it seems to me, analytic philosophy is threatened by an opposite danger: Excluded from the realm of the synthetic, its statements seem to disappear into the trivial, but after the reunification, philosophical statements are in danger to disappear as well, this time into empirical science. If we look at the holistic model of science that Quine lined out in "Two Dogmas", there are logical and mathematical truths, theoretical and empirical statements, but it is really difficult to locate any statements that could be called philosophical in a narrower sense. What the model seems to call for is a radical naturalization of philosophy as a whole. But philosophy continues to exist. And Quine himself did continue to work as a philosopher instead of returning to mathematics or going into natural science. Can facts like these be reconciled with a Quinean model of science? Is there room in such a model for anything distinctively philosophical?

If the answer is yes, we clearly need a new understanding of what analytic philosophy is, however. If it no longer is supposed to consist only of logical analysis and analytic statements, the question is exactly what kind of statements philosophers could make if they refuse to convert to empirical science. It seems to me that from a Quinean perspective the answer has to be something like the following: Doing philosophy is not a matter of a separate *kind* of statements but of a special *use* of statements of *all* kinds. Philosophy is not located in a special region within Quine's universe of science but it is a special way to move or to navigate within this universe.

And what is special about such navigation, I think, can be gleaned from Wittgenstein's hints in the *Tractatus*. In sentence 6.54 we read: "My sentences serve as elucidations in the following sense: anyone who understands me eventually recognizes them as nonsensical, when he has used them—as steps—to climb up beyond them. (He must, so to speak, throw away the ladder after he has climbed up it.)" What we find here could be called the *paradox of elucidation*: How is it possible that nonsensical sentences explain or elucidate anything? We find

Wittgenstein's answer in the well-known sentence 4.112: "Philosophy is not a body of doctrine but an activity. A philosophical work consists essentially of elucidations. Philosophy does not result in 'philosophical propositions', but rather in the clarification of propositions." If we accept this message, we are relieved from any alleged duty to justify the continued existence of philosophy by distinguishing "philosophical propositions" as a special kind of sentences or propositions from others. Any linguistic means could be put to philosophical use as long as it facilitates the clarification of propositions—even if it prima facie appeared to be nonsensical.

Following these lines we may say that after Quine's "Two Dogmas" the 'analytic' in 'analytic philosophy' can only be made sense of if we understand philosophical analysis in a *pragmatic* sense. Philosophy and science do not occupy distinct 'geographical' or linguistic regions; they can only be distinguished pragmatically, that is, by looking at the special features of their discursive practices. As I see it, philosophy finds its true self in what I call "explicative discourse". Such discourse, however, is not confined to those rooms in the building of the sciences that have "philosophy" written on their doors—it is or could be practiced anywhere else, too. And similarly, philosophers are free to make use of any kind of empirical knowledge—provided that they really have and understand this knowledge, of course.

In order to gain a better understanding of what characterizes explicative discourse we should, I think, look at Wittgenstein's *Philosophical Investigations*. Here, the early paradox of elucidation disappears. It is replaced by a therapeutic conception of philosophical elucidation. Such elucidation, as Wittgenstein emphasizes, is by no means to be mistaken for some kind of theoretical or scientific explanation. But what exactly does it amount to? Wittgenstein might easily be misinterpreted here. He presents his own philosophical practice as one of *describing language games*, but what he means by 'description' surely is not anything like the empirical descriptions we find in linguistics. My hunch is that 'description' in Wittgenstein is to be read as a metaphor for something that in German goes by the really ugly name 'Vergegenwärtigung'. In English, one would maybe speak of 'recall', or of 'calling things to mind'. This interpretation would seem to be supported by those passages in Wittgenstein where he describes doing philosophy as calling to mind the familiar in order to gain an overview.

Looking at philosophical analysis as an activity along these lines, modern analytic philosophy can be seen as intrinsically linked to Plato's conception of philosophy as an art of *anámnesis*. And yet another godfather of a pragmatic reading of analysis is Kant. He suggests to call analytic judgments "Erläuterungsurteile" (explicative judgments), in contrast to synthetic judgments which he thought of as "Erweiterungsurteile" (ampliative judgments) (*KrV* B 11). Kant defines analytic judgments as those "in which the connection of the predicate with the subject is thought through identity" (B 10), thus drawing attention to the semantic fact that analytic judgments can be transformed into logical truths or tautologies. (In Verena Mayer's contribution, we are told more about that.) But this is not the whole story. Kant adds: Analytic judgments could be called "Erläuterungsurteile", because they add "nothing through the predicate to the concept of the subject, merely breaking it up into those constituent concepts that have all along been thought in it, although confusedly" (B 11). Thus we can see how the use of *semantically* trivial statements can bring about a non-trivial effect like that of clearing up confusion. Analytic judgments can be used as means of elucidation (Erläuterung) in situations where there is a difference between obscurity and clarity of thinking, between the implicit and the explicit, or even in cases of linguistic ignorance, e.g. if children ask: "Mom, what is a bachelor?" And the situations in question are to be conceived of in *pragmatic* terms. I admit that in Kant himself the relation between the semantic and the pragmatic aspects of the analytic is not very clear, but it seems to me that the pragmatic aspects of analyticity are much more important to his own philosophical practice than the semantic ones. The constructive (or re-constructive) part of his *Trancscendental Logic* is called "Transcendental Analytic", and if we take a closer look at what is done there we are far from finding nothing but analytic judgments. In Kant, there is no paradox of analysis because to him, information of very different kinds, even empirical information, can play an elucidational role within the context of transcendental analysis. I read Kant's "transcendental philosophy" as an explicative discourse based on what was available at the time in terms of everyday and scientific knowledge. It is this knowledge that provides the non-trivial input for his analytic enterprise. In this respect, Kant's project does not differ that much from Wittgenstein's or Quine's, it seems to me; none of them sees a need to abstain from using non-trivial knowledge for "analytic", i.e. elucidational, purposes. Moreover, I suggest that this is the very kind of practice all of us try to engage in—all of us, at least, who do not see philosophy from a purely historical or purely philological perspective.

If all this is even roughly true, analytic philosophy is essentially explicative philosophy. It has its identity in the pragmatics of elucidation, and not in some sort of special knowledge incorporated in special philosophical statements. This is not to deny that there are philosophical statements or even philosophical theories; these arise naturally out of the practice of elucidation as systematic reconstruction. But the point is that calling such statements or theories philosophical cannot be justified by any special semantic feature of these statements. Rather, it depends on the pragmatic role they play in such discourse.

An important question remains, however—the question whether analytic philosophy in this pragmatic sense can do without a sensible understanding of analyticity as a semantic property. I suspect it cannot. Since we do not know of any way of reducing semantic problems to pragmatic ones, or of formulating a convincing theory of meaning in purely pragmatic terms, we might still need the notions of analyticity and synonymy. Even if they cannot really be defined in terms of something else, they do seem indispensable to the philosophical practice of elucidation and clarification.

I.
ANALYTICITY REVISITED

EPISTEMIC ANALYTICITY: A DEFENSE

Paul A. BOGHOSSIAN
New York University

Summary

The paper is a defense of the project of explaining the a priori via the notion of meaning or concept possession. It responds to certain objections that have been made to this project—in particular, that there can be no epistemically analytic sentences that are not also metaphysically analytic, and that the notion of implicit definition cannot explain a priori entitlement. The paper goes on to distinguish between two different ways in which facts about meaning might generate facts about entitlement—inferential and constitutive. It concludes by outlining a theory of the latter.

Epistemic vs. Metaphysical Analyticity

In an earlier paper—"Analyticity Reconsidered"—I attempted to do two things: salvage a notion of analyticity from Quine's widely accepted critique of that notion and show how it might be able to do serious work in the epistemology of a priori knowledge.[1]

Salvaging analyticity, I argued, depends crucially on distinguishing between a metaphysical and an epistemic version of that concept. According to the *metaphysical* notion, a sentence is analytic if it owes its truth entirely to its meaning and without any contribution from the 'facts.' By contrast, I took a sentence to be *epistemically* analytic if grasp of its meaning can suffice for justified belief in the truth of the proposition it expresses.

I believe that Quine was deeply right to insist that there are no metaphysically analytic sentences. However, I argued, first, that the considerations that militate against metaphysical analyticity do not extend to

---

1. See Boghossian 1996. A longer version containing some further discussion of Quine and an appendix on knowledge of meaning appeared as Boghossian 1997.

epistemic analyticity and, second, that it is possible to provide a model of how some sentences might be epistemically analytic.

While I continue to believe that these claims are true, I have also come to think that "Analyticity Reconsidered" was less clear than it needed to be about the exact nature of the relation between meaning facts and entitlement. In particular, at the time of writing that paper, I did not delineate sufficiently clearly the difference between *inferential* and *constitutive* construals of the relation between meaning and entitlement. In this paper, I explain in what that difference consists and how it bears on the project of the analytic theory of the a priori. In the course of the exposition, I attempt to respond to various criticisms that have been made of that project and of my particular way of pursuing it.

Before proceeding, it is worth emphasizing that although I follow tradition in construing analyticity as a property of linguistic items, that feature of the presentation of the view is entirely optional. For example, I will talk of grasp of the meaning of a sentence as sufficing for justified belief in the proposition it expresses; but I could equally well simply have talked about grasp of a proposition p as sufficing for justified belief in p. Thus, too, I will talk about words being synonymous with each other; but I could equally well have talked about concepts being identical to one another. Finally, I will talk of holding some sentences true, as a condition of meaning some specific proposition by them; but I could equally well have talked of believing some propositions as a condition of having some of their ingredient concepts. Although I find it convenient for expository purposes to assume that we think in a language (which I will pretend is in fact English), no central issue hangs on that assumption.

So, playing along with this linguistic picture, and assuming that T's believing that p is constituted by T's accepting a sentence S which means that p, let us ask: Why should it matter whether or not there are epistemically analytic sentences—sentences such that grasp of their meaning can suffice for justified belief in the truth of the proposition they express?

The interest of the epistemically analytic derives from the thought that it might help explain how there could be factual propositions known a priori. To see how this might work, let us first distinguish between three different things that one might mean by the phrase "grasp of meaning."

In one sense, a thinker T grasps S's meaning just in case T means some determinate thing or other by his use of S. Call this notion of grasp "mere grasp of meaning." In a second sense, T grasps S's meaning when he can correctly and knowledgeably *state* what S means. In this sense, it is not enough that T mean something by S—he must also have second-order knowledge of what S means. Call this notion of grasp "knowledge of meaning." In the third and most demanding sense, T's grasping S's meaning implies not only that T is able to state S's meaning knowledgeably but also that he understands that meaning well enough to know whether or not it means the same as some other sentence. Call this "understanding of meaning."

As we shall see, different models of epistemic analyticity employ one or more of these notions of grasp of meaning. And although these notions differ from each other in significant ways, they share the following property: each of them has been thought to be attainable without the benefit of empirical knowledge. Given this assumption, it becomes easy to see how the existence of epistemically analytic sentences might contribute to demystifying the phenomenon of a priori knowledge.

In a minute we shall look in detail about how such meaning-justification connections are to be construed, but I first want to take up an objection to the idea that there could be epistemically analytic sentences that are not metaphysically analytic. The objection has been pressed by Eric Margolis and Stephen Laurence:

> After all, if p really is an independent fact that makes S true, then just knowing that S means that p couldn't suffice for the needed justification; one would also need to be justified in believing that p. In other words, so long as the truth of S isn't merely a matter of what it means, then grasping its meaning can only be (at best) part of the story about why one is justified in holding it to be true. (Margolis/Laurence 2001, 294)

If we try to turn the hunch that Margolis and Laurence are giving expression to here into an argument, we would need to rely on the following epistemic principle:

> So long as the truth of S isn't merely a matter of F, but is also a function of G, then being justified in believing F can only be (at best) part of the story about why one is justified in holding S to be true; one would also need to be justified in believing G.

But this is not in general a sound epistemic principle. The truth of the sentence "This is water" isn't merely a matter of how some substance looks or feels; it is also a matter of its being H_2O. However, it doesn't follow that I could never be justified in holding some stuff to be water without my first being justified in believing it to be H_2O.

At least as far as this particular argument is concerned, I see no reason to doubt that there could be epistemically analytic sentences that are not, per impossibile, also metaphysically analytic.

Explaining Epistemic Analyticity: Synonymy

The real problem with the epistemically analytic lies not in demonstrating its independence from the metaphysically analytic; it lies, rather, in explaining how any sentence *could be* epistemically analytic. How might grasp of the meaning of a sentence S suffice for justified belief in the truth of the proposition S expresses?

Let us start with the chestnut "All bachelors are unmarried males." How might grasp of the meaning of this sentence by a speaker suffice for his being justified in believing the proposition it expresses?

One route from meaning to justification that philosophers have often had in mind, without bothering to spell it out, would imagine our thinker reasoning as follows:

1. "All bachelors are unmarried males" means that All bachelors are unmarried males. (By knowledge of S's meaning)
2. Since "bachelor" just means "unmarried male," "All bachelors are unmarried males" is synonymous with "All unmarried males are unmarried males." (By understanding of meaning)
3. "All unmarried males are unmarried males" means that all unmarried males are unmarried males. (By knowledge of S's meaning)
4. If sentence F is synonymous with sentence G, then F is true iff G is true. (Conceptual knowledge of the link between meaning and truth)
5. Therefore, "All bachelors are unmarried males" is true iff all unmarried males are unmarried males.
6. All unmarried males are unmarried males. (By knowledge of logic)
7. Therefore, "All bachelors are unmarried males" is true.
8. Therefore, all bachelors are unmarried males.

The template that this bit of reasoning instantiates may be represented as follows:

1. S means that P. (Knowledge of meaning)
2. S is synonymous with S'. (Understanding of meaning)
3. S' means that Q, where Q is some logical truth. (Knowledge of meaning)
4. If F is synonymous with G, then F is true iff G is true. (Conceptual link between meaning and truth)
5. Therefore, S is true iff Q.
6. Q (Logic)
7. Therefore, S is true. (Deductive reasoning)
8. Therefore, P. (Deductive reasoning)

Let us call this the "Synonymy Template" and the model of a priori knowledge that it presents the "Synonymy Model." If someone in possession of justification for the premises of this argument actually runs through it, I will say that he is *justified* in believing P; if someone is merely *able* to run through such an argument without actually doing so, I will say that he is *entitled* to P.[2]

Quine, of course, objected that the notion of synonymy on which this model relies is not sufficiently well-defined to do serious explanatory work. However, as I argued in "Analyticity Reconsidered," no Meaning Realist can afford to accept Quine's argument.

I think that the Synonymy model is correct so far it goes: it correctly explains the structure of our knowledge of *some* a priori truths—of those 'conceptual' truths, namely, that are transformable into logical truths by the substitution of synonyms for synonyms (sentences that in "Analyticity Reconsidered" I called "Frege-analytic"). However, the Synonymy model is obviously not a *complete* story about how grasp of meaning might generate entitlement, and this in several respects.

First, it relies on a piece of a priori conceptual knowledge at premise 4—connecting meaning and truth—that it cannot explain.

Second, it relies on a priori knowledge of logical principles that it cannot explain, and this in two ways. First, it relies on the thinker's knowing that a certain principle is a truth of logic; second, it relies on the thinker's being able justifiably to infer in accordance with deductive rules of logic, so that the thinker is able knowledgeably to move from the premises to the conclusion of the Template.

---

2. This invokes Tyler Burge's well-known distinction between justification and entitlement. See Burge 1993.

Finally, it seems quite clear that there will be *other* propositions, beyond the ones mentioned thus far, that the Synonymy Model will be unable to account for. For there do seem to be a considerable number of a priori propositions that are expressed by sentences that are not transformable into logical truths by the substitution of synonyms for synonyms. For example,

- Whatever is red all over is not blue.
- Whatever colored is extended.
- If x is warmer than y, then y is not warmer than x.

If meaning-based explanations of the a priori are to be complete, a meaning-based explanation must be found for the apriority of each of these other types of proposition.

Explaining Epistemic Analyticity: Implicit Definition

As I explained in "Analyticity Reconsidered," one of the central ideas in this connection is that of Implicit Definition (ID). I will look in detail here at the case of logic, postponing to another occasion a description of how ID explanations of apriority might be extended to the other cases we described.

As a first approximation, we may explain the idea of ID, as applied to logic, thus:

> It is by stipulating that certain sentences of logic are to be true, or that certain inferences are to be valid, that we attach a meaning to the logical constants.

For example, one might think that:

> It is in part by stipulating that
>
>> It is not the case that both P and not P
>
> is to be true, that someone comes to mean negation by 'not.'

Or, to pick another example that will feature further below:

It is in part by stipulating that all inferences of the form

> p
> If p, then q
> Therefore, q

are to be valid that someone comes to mean *if* by 'if.'

In considering implicit definitions, we must bear in mind that they come in two varieties: explicit and implicit. An *explicit* implicit definition involves an explicit stipulation by a thinker that a given sentence S(f) is to be true if its ingredient term f is to mean what it does. In the *implicit* variety, it is somehow tacit in that person's behavior with the term f that S(f) is to be true if f is to mean what it does.

Later on I will come back to what it might mean for an implicit definition to be itself implicit. For now, let us operate with the explicit version and ask: how would S(f)'s being an implicit definer for f help explain how grasp of S(f)'s meaning might suffice for justified belief in its truth?

One suggestion, though as we shall see, not ultimately the favored one, would mimic the Synonymy model by supplying an argument template that a thinker will be in a position to perform as a result of grasping the meaning of S(f).[3]

1. S(f) means that P (By knowledge of meaning)
2. If S(f) means that P, S(f) is true (By knowledge of the contents of one's stipulations)
3. Therefore, S(f) is true
4. If S(f) means that P, then S(f) is true iff P (By knowledge of the link between meaning and truth)
5. S(f) is true iff P
6. Therefore, P

Call this the "Implicit Definition Template" and the model of the a priori that it presents the "Implicit Definition" model.[4]

---

3. This seems to me a better representation of the relevant template than what I offered in "Analyticity Reconsidered," but it is not materially different.

4. An example of an a priori that this model might plausibly be taken to explain is the proposition *Vixens are female foxes*.

Knowledge of Meaning and Implicit Definition

Several philosophers have objected to this model of the a priori. The main recurring complaint has been nicely expressed by Kathrin Glüer:

> ... let P be the proposition that S(f) expresses. On Boghossian's account, it seems to me, being justified in believing that S(f) means P *presupposes* being justified in believing P. Of course, it then *follows* from being justified in believing that S(f) means P that I am justified in believing P. However, believing P cannot be justified in this way; for knowledge of the meaning of the sentence already requires such justification and, therefore, cannot provide it. (Glüer, this volume, 57)

Laurence Bonjour makes a similar point when he says:

> Thus, for example, one might stipulate that the sentence '40@8=5' is to count as a (partial) implicit definition of the symbol '@'. This, along with other stipulations of the same kind, might prove a useful way of conveying that '@' is to stand for the operation of long division (assuming that the other symbols in the sentence are already understood). But if this is the right account of implicit definition, then the justification of the proposition that 40 divided by 8 is equal to 5 (as opposed to that of the linguistic formula '40@8=5' is not a result of the implicit definition, but is rather presupposed by it: if I were not justified in advance, presumably a priori, in believing that forty divided by eight is equal to five, I would have no reason for interpreting '@' in the indicated way. (Bonjour 1998, 50–1)

According to Bonjour and Glüer, if S(f)'s expressing P is fixed via the stipulation that S(f) is to be true, one cannot be justified in believing that S(f) expresses P without *first* being justified in believing that P is true. If that is right, then the Implicit Definition Template could not explain how someone could acquire a priori warrant for the belief that P, since warranted belief in P would be presupposed by anyone running an argument of that form.

This is a surprising objection. As I noted towards the beginning of this paper, most philosophers simply assume that meaning facts are first-person accessible in some privileged way, regardless of what the supervenience base for meaning facts is taken to be. For example, many philosophers believe that even if facts about meaning and concept possession were to supervene on facts that are *external* to the mind that

that would have no tendency to undermine our privileged access to first-person facts about meaning.

Now, it is an interesting question whether these many philosophers are right to make this assumption. I, for one, have worried about whether we genuinely understand how first-person access to meaning is possible, especially if meaning is externally determined. I am not a skeptic about such access; I simply believe that we don't really understand how it works.

Bonjour and Glüer, however, write neither as skeptics about privileged access, nor in the service of raising a question about how such access should ultimately be understood. They write as though there is reason to think that in the *special* case where meaning is fixed by implicit definition, there is a problem with the assumption of privileged access. In that case, they assert, someone cannot be said to know that S means that P without first knowing that

a. if S means that P, then S has to be true
and that
b. P is true.

But they have supplied us with no special reason to think that, if S's meaning is fixed via implicit definition, the usual assumption of privileged access must be suspended.

This point is only strengthened when we reflect that the only plausible version of ID is not the explicit one with which we have been working so far, but rather the implicit one.

It is rare for a term to be introduced via some explicit stipulation. And in the special case that interests us—the case of the logical constants—it is not only rare but incoherent. As Quine pointed out, if the logical constants are to be thought of as having their meaning fixed by implicit definitions, that meaning cannot be thought of as fixed by explicit implicit definitions, since the logical constants will have to be presupposed in any statement of the stipulations by which we might seek to fix their meanings (see Quine 1935). Rather, if there is to be anything at all to the idea of ID as applied to logic, it must be that the logical constants have their meaning fixed by our *tacitly* regarding some of the inferences involving them as valid, or by our *tacitly* regarding some of the sentences involving them as true. It's a good question what this sort of tacit stipulation amounts to—many a conceptual role semantics has struggled with that question. But it is a question to which there has to be an answer if, as seems likely, our only hope of explaining how we come to grasp the concepts of the logical constants is through the idea of ID.

But do Bonjour and Glüer really wish to say that if the meaning of 'and' is fixed by a thinker's being disposed to use it according to its standard introduction and elimination rules that he cannot be said to know what 'and' means without first knowing that

'A and B' implies A?

If this particular style of objection is to be sustained, we need to be given a special reason for thinking that where a conceptual role semantics is concerned, there the usual assumption of privileged access must be rejected. But I don't see that we have been given any such reason.

Implicit Definition and Entitlement: The Constitutive Model

However, there are several other difficulties with the suggestion that the ID Template gives a fundamental account of the entitlement that implicit definition is able to provide.

First, there continues to be a reliance on the link between meaning and truth at step 4. Even if we can correctly say that we know that

If S means that P then S is true iff P

because we have stipulated it to be true, we cannot hope to explain *why* the stipulation grounds the knowledge via the Implicit Definition Template, because that template relies on our knowledge of that link.

Second, no such argument template could possibly hope to explain in what our entitlement to *reason* according to certain deductive rules consists, since—once again—it presupposes such reasoning.

Finally, if we are operating with the more promising *tacit* version of implicit definition rather than with the version according to which our stipulations are explicit, there is the problem that we can no longer rely on its following from the fact that S(f) is an implicit definer of f that S(f) is true. On the view according to which implicit definitions are themselves implicit, there is a difficulty seeing how it would follow from S(f)'s being an implicit definer for f, that S(f) has to be true. For how is it going to be implicit in someone's behavior with S(f) that it is acting as an implicit definer? Presumably, by S(f)'s being used in a certain way—most plausibly, by its being held to be true come what may. But the point is that there is all the difference in the world between saying that a certain sentence must be held true, if it is to mean this that or the other, and saying that it *is* true.[5] But it's actually being true is what premise 2 of the ID Template requires.

What these problems suggest, therefore, if implicit definition is to be a genuine source of a priori entitlement, is that there must be a different way in which implicit definitions can generate entitlement other than by supplying premises from which the truth of various propositions may somehow be derived.

Call this premise-and-derivation model, on which we have been concentrating so far, the *inferential* conception of how meaning generates entitlement. On the contrasting *constitutive* model, the thinker doesn't start with some premise about some sentence S's meaning from which he deduces that S is true. Rather, the mere fact that the thinker grasps S's meaning entails that the thinker is justified in holding S to be true. Or, if we focus on inferences rather than sentences: the mere fact that the thinker grasps inference rule R's meaning entails that the thinker is justified in inferring according to R. How would this work?[6]

Look first at the case that is likely to be of most central interest, the case of an inference rule's being meaning-constituting. How might it turn out that, as a mere consequence of R's being meaning-constituting for a thinker T, T is justified in inferring according to R?

Suppose R is Modus Ponens (MPP) and suppose also—and plausibly—that being willing to infer according to MPP is constitutive of possession of the concept *if*. How could that fact explain how we might be entitled to reason according to MPP?

One initially helpful thought is this. Suppose it's true that my taking p and 'if p, then q' as a warrant for believing q is constitutive of my being able to have *if* thoughts in the first place. Then doesn't it follow

---

5. This point was first made in Boghossian 1994.
6. In "Analyticity Regained?" Harman correctly emphasizes the importance of the distinction between inferential and "direct" ways in which meaning might justify a proposition. However, neither his distinction nor his way of explaining direct a priori justification line up exactly with the notions that I outline here.

that I could not have been epistemically blameworthy in taking p and 'if p, then q' as a reason for believing q even in the absence of any reason for taking those premises to be a reason for believing that conclusion? If inferring from those premises to that conclusion is required, if I am to have the ingredient propositions, then it looks as though so inferring cannot be held against me, even if the inference is, as I shall put it, *blind*—unsupported by any positive warrant.

Problems for the Meaning-Entitlement Connection[7]

This explanation, however, is flawed. If we spell out the principle underlying it, it would be this:

(*Meaning-Entitlement Connection*, or *MEC*): Any inferential transitions built into the possession conditions for a concept are *eo ipso* entitling.

And the trouble is that, at least as stated, there seem to be clear-cut counterexamples to the MEC: it doesn't in general seem true that if my taking A as a reason for believing B is constitutive of my believing B, that this *automatically* absolves me of any charge of epistemic blameworthiness. For there seem to be clear cases where the acceptance of some inference is written into the possession of a given concept but where it is also clear that the inference isn't one to which the thinker is entitled.

One famous illustrative case is Arthur Prior's connective 'tonk' (Prior 1960, 38–9). To possess this concept, Prior stipulated, a thinker must be willing to infer according to the following introduction and elimination rules:

(Tonk) $\dfrac{A}{A\ tonk\ B}$ $\dfrac{A\ tonk\ B}{B}$

---

7. The next two sections draw on material from my "Blind Reasoning" (Boghossian 2003).

Obviously, no one could be entitled to infer any B from any A; but that's exactly what is implied by the MEC.

A similar conclusion can be drawn from the case of racist or abusive concepts, for example the concept *boche* discussed by Dummett (1973, 454). According to Dummett, a thinker possesses the concept *boche* just in case he is willing to infer according to the following introduction and elimination rules:

(Boche) $\dfrac{x\ is\ German}{x\ is\ boche}$ $\dfrac{x\ is\ boche}{x\ is\ cruel.}$

Yet no one is entitled—let alone simply as the result of the introduction of a concept into the language—to the view that all Germans are cruel.

How should we think about such cases?

Robert Brandom has this to say about 'boche'-like concepts:

> The use of any concept or expression involves commitment to an inference from its grounds to its consequences of application. Critical thinkers, or merely fastidious ones, must examine their idioms to be sure that they are prepared to endorse and so defend the appropriateness of the material inferential commitments implicit in the concepts they employ. ... The proper question to ask in evaluating the introduction and evolution of a concept is not whether the inference embodied is one that is already endorsed, so that no new content is really involved, but rather whether the inference is one that *ought* to be endorsed. The problem with 'boche' is not that once we explicitly confront the material inferential commitment that gives the term its content it turns out to be novel, but that it can then be seen to be indefensible and inappropriate—a commitment we cannot become entitled to. (Brandom 2000, 70–2)

Unfortunately, Brandom's observations cannot help defend the MEC against the threatening counterexamples, for it's no answer to the challenge they pose to observe that whatever entitlement concept possession gives rise to it can be defeated by further considerations. No one should expect more than a defeasible entitlement, even from concept possession; and what's implausible in the case of 'tonk' and 'boche' is that there is any entitlement there at all, defeasible or not.

If we are to save the MEC, we must do one or both of two things:

either restrict it to certain concepts from which entitlement really does flow, or restrict what we count as a genuine concept. The latter strategy is suggested by the work of Christopher Peacocke who has long urged that we should require that the meaning-constituting rules of a genuine concept be truth-preserving.[8]

If we adopt this requirement, we can say that what's wrong with both 'tonk' and 'boche' is precisely that there is no concept that those terms express, for there is no reference for 'tonk' and 'boche' that's capable of making all of their constitutive rules truth-preserving.

While this might seem to yield the right result for 'tonk' it doesn't yield the right result for 'boche': it's hard to believe that racists who employ boche-like concepts fail to express complete thoughts. And even if we were to put this complaint to one side, it seems clear that truth-preservation alone will not suffice for dealing with our problem about the MEC.

Consider the concept *flurg* individuated by the following introduction and elimination rules:

(Flurg) $\dfrac{x \text{ is an elliptical equation}}{x \text{ is flurg}}$ $\dfrac{x \text{ is flurg}}{x \text{ can be correlated with a modular form}}$

It turns out to be a result that Wiles had to prove on the way to proving Fermat's Last Theorem that every elliptical equation can be correlated with a modular form (the Taniyama-Shimura conjecture). Once again, therefore, we have no independent reason to think that these introduction and elimination rules are not necessarily truth-preserving. But it's hard to see that one is a priori entitled, merely on the basis of introducing the term "flurg," to the Taniyama-Shimura conjecture. So there is still a problem for the claim that entitlement flows from meaning-constitution, given only the requirement that a concept's introduction and elimination rules be truth-preserving.

---

8. See Peacocke 1993. I myself took this line in my (2001), so the present paper represents a change of heart on this point.

Defective Concepts and Blameless Inference

I propose a different diagnosis of what has gone wrong with concepts such as *flurg* and *boche*, one that doesn't depend on denying that they constitute genuine thinkable contents. That diagnosis will permit us to demarcate a class of concepts that are intuitively epistemically *defective,* with the result that inference in accord with their constitutive rules is not entitling.

Start with the example of flurg. The theorist who has conceived the need to introduce a term for the concept *flurg* has come to hold the following *theory*:

> There is a property, distinct from both that of being an elliptical equation and distinct from that of being correlatable with a modular form, which is such that: everything that is an elliptical equation has it, and anything that has it can be correlated with a modular form. Let me call this property "flurg."

Such a theorist already believes in elliptical equations and modular forms, we may suppose. He has come to hold an additional belief about the world, namely, that it contains a further property that behaves in the specified way.

Now, the way we have formulated the inferential rules for "flurg" essentially amounts to insisting that, in order to have the concept *flurg* you must be prepared to *believe* this little *flurg* theory. Given that you already believe in elliptical equations and modular forms, the only way for you to acquire the concept *flurg,* on this account of its inferential rules, requires you to *believe* that there is such a property as flurg and that some equations have it. One cannot so much as have the concept *flurg* without being prepared to believe that the corresponding property is instantiated.

And although it seems that one *can* define and then think in terms of such a concept, it does seem to be an epistemically questionable thing to do. Even if the flurg theorist were *certain* that there is such a property, he should want the concept he expresses by that term to leave it open whether there is. He should allow for the conceptual possibility that he is mistaken; and he should certainly allow others to intelligibly disagree with him about its instantiation. The concept itself should not be designed in such a way that only those who believe a certain creed are allowed to possess it.

Ordinary scientific terms in good standing—"neutrino" for example—are held to have just this feature, of intelligibly allowing for disagreement about their extensions. Thus, we don't think of the rules which correspond to our possession of the concept *neutrino* as consisting in the propositions that would actually be believed by a proponent of neutrino theory, but rather as corresponding only to what someone would be willing to believe who was *conditionalizing* on the truth of neutrino theory.

If, following Russell, Ramsey, Carnap and Lewis, we represent neutrino theory

T(neutrino)

as the conjunction of the two propositions

(S) $\exists F T(F)$

and

(M) $\exists F T(F) \rightarrow T(neutrino)$,

then the point is that we think of possession of the concept *neutrino* as requiring someone to affirm only M and not S as well.[9]

Now, someone could certainly introduce a concept that did not have the conditionalized structure that I've claimed is actually true of *neutrino*, but which consists rather in the inferences that are characteristic of neutrino theory unconditionalized. Call this *neutrino*$_+$. Such a person would insist that it is a condition on having *his* concept of neutrino that one be willing to endorse the characteristic claims and inferences of neutrino theory, and not merely the conditionalized claim captured in (M). But, for the reasons previously articulated, there would be something epistemically *defective* about this concept, even if its constitutive

---

[9]. This paragraph follows Paul Horwich's discussion of the conditional nature of semantic stipulation (Horwich 2000). I ignore various complexities that a thorough discussion of the representation of scientific theories would require and, in particular, the need to account for *uniqueness*. These further complexities would only have strengthened the case for the central claim that I will want to make later on, namely, that a considerable logical apparatus is presupposed in the possession of any conditionalized concept.

rules turned out to be truth-preserving.

Flurg and *neutrino₊*, then, suffer from the same problem: they are unconditional versions of a concept, when only its conditionalized version would be epistemically acceptable. I don't think we should put this by saying that they are not real concepts. Concepts are relatively cheap. But they are *defective* concepts. They are structured in such a way that perfectly reasonable questions about their extensions are foreclosed.

In so far as it is possible to do so, then, a concept should be governed by conditionalized rules, rules that conditionalize on the existence of an appropriate semantic value that would make its rules truth-preserving. What's wrong with *boche*, then, is that its rules are

$$\frac{Gx}{Bx} \qquad \frac{Bx}{Cx}$$

which amounts to implicitly affirming

$T(boche) = Gx \rightarrow Bx$ and $Bx \rightarrow Cx$

when all we are entitled to affirm is:

T(Condboche) If there is a property F such that T(F), then T(boche).

Under what conditions is only a conditionalized version of a concept acceptable? Here I want to make two claims, one sober, one bold.

(Bold) Whenever both a conditional and an unconditional version of a given concept are available, it is the conditional version that ought to be used. Given the availability of both versions, the unconditional version counts as epistemically defective.

(Sober) In the case of some concepts, only the unconditionalized version will be available.

We have just been examining the argument for Bold: You don't ever want the *possession conditions* for a concept to foreclose on the possible falsity of some particular set of claims about the world, if you can possibly avoid it. You want the possessor of the concept to be able coherently to ask whether there is anything that falls under it, and you want people to be able to disagree about whether there is. If in a certain range of cases, however, it is logically impossible to hold the governing theory at arm's length then, in those cases, obviously, it can hardly be a requirement that one do so. But in all those cases where it is possible, it ought to be done.

What about Sober? I think it is clear, given what it means to conditionalize on the truth of an arbitrary theory, that not every meaningful term in a language can be thought of as expressing a concept that conditionalizes on the existence of an appropriate semantic value for it. In particular, a certain number of logical concepts will be presupposed in any conditionalization and those that are so presupposed will not themselves have conditionalized versions.

Timothy Williamson has objected to this line of reasoning as follows:

> Although $\exists$ and $\rightarrow$ occur in the Carnap sentence $\exists FT(F)$, in place of that sentence Boghossian could have used the rule that allows one to infer $T(Neutrino)$ directly from any premise of the form $T(A)$. That rule is formulated without reference to the logical operators in the object-language, but is interderivable with the Carnap sentence once one has the standard rules for $\exists$ and $\rightarrow$. ... Logical operators may of course occur in the theory T itself, although Boghossian does not appeal to that point. In any case, it seems insufficiently general for his argument, since for some less highly theoretical concepts than *neutrino*, the analogue of the theory T for conditionalization may consist of some simple sentences free of logical operators (Williamson 2003, 287).

Of course, I did not mean to suggest that one could simply read off the Carnap sentence that existential quantification and conditional would be presupposed by any conditionalization, though no doubt my presentation was overly elliptical. In the cases of most central interest, the affirmation of the Carnap sentence would be *implicit* in the thinker's behavior and could not be supposed to amount to an explicit belief from which one could simply read off the ingredient conceptual materials.

To see whether we could have nothing but conditionalized concepts, we have to ask whether it is possible for someone to implicitly affirm the Carnap sentence for, e.g., boche, without possessing any of the logical concepts with which we would explicitly conditionalized our concepts.

We have agreed that for someone to affirm T(boche) implicitly is for them to be willing to infer according to the following introduction and elimination rules:

$Gx/Bx \quad Bx/Cx$.

Now, the question is: What would it be for a thinker to implicitly conditionalize his affirmation of T(boche) on the existence of an appropriate semantic value for these rules? Williamson says that this could be adequately captured by picturing the conditionalizing thinker as operating according to the following rule:

$T(A)$
———
$T(boche)$

But what this seems to me to say is something very different from what is needed. A thinker operating according to Williamson's rule is like someone who already has the concept boche but is now simply relabeling it with the word 'boche.' Whereas what I want to capture is the idea of someone who is only prepared to infer according to the boche rules because they antecedently believe that

There is a property F, such that $Gx \rightarrow Fx$ and $Fx \rightarrow Cx$

And I don't see how their reasoning could depend on that without their having, at a minimum, the conceptual materials that make up the antecedent of the Carnap sentence, including the quantificational apparatus and the conditionals that make up the statement of the theory.

If all of this is right, it follows that conditional counterparts for one's primitive logical constants will not be available and hence that one could hardly be blamed for employing their unconditionalized versions. In particular, you couldn't conditionalize on the existence of an appropriate truth function for the conditional, for you would need it in order to conditionalize on anything. In such a case, there is no alternative but to accept "conditional theory"—Modus Ponens and Conditional Proof, in effect—if you are to so much as have the conditional concept. It thus couldn't be epistemically irresponsible of you to just go ahead and infer according to MPP without conditionalizing on the existence of an appropriate truth function for it—that is simply not a coherent option in this case.

If we go back to the MEC, it seems clear how that principle needs to be modified:

(MEC*) Any rules that are written into the possession conditions for a *non-defective* concept are a fortiori entitling.

And with this principle in hand, we have the answer to our question: How could a thinker be entitled to reason according to MPP just in virtue of grasping the meaning of that rule? The answer is that he can be so entitled because MPP is a possession condition for the conditional, and the conditional is a non-defective concept.

Gilbert Harman has asserted that the only non-inferential route from grasp of meaning to entitlement must run through Conventionalism and, therefore, through the dubious doctrine of metaphysical analyticity (Harman 1996, 393–4). However, if the Constitutive Model I have offered is correct, his assertion is false, for the Constitutive Model is in no way committed to Conventionalism or to metaphysical analyticity.

Conclusion

The most fundamental relation between grasp of meaning and entitlement occurs when a thinker is entitled to reason in accord with a certain rule R simply by virtue of the fact that R is constitutive of a non-defective concept of his.

This Constitutive model could be extended to account for the thinker's entitlement to have certain beliefs, provided that those beliefs were similarly constitutive of the possession of a non-defective concept. I think that something like this story will explain how we get to be entitled to believe in the principle of non-contradiction and in the link between truth and meaning that featured in the templates described above.

With these two pieces in place, it becomes possible to invoke the Implicit Definition and Synonymy Templates to explain the a priori knowability of other, less fundamental, a priori truths.[10]

---

10. I am grateful to Stephen Schiffer for comments on an earlier version of this paper.

REFERENCES

Boghossian, Paul A. 1994: "Inferential Role Semantics and the Analytic/Synthetic Distinction", *Philosophical Studies* 73, 109–122.
— 1996: "Analyticity Reconsidered", *Noûs* 30, 360–391.
— 1997: "Analyticity," in: B. Hale and C. Wright (Eds.), *A Companion to the Philosophy of Language*, Oxford, 331–368.
— 2001: "How are Objective Epistemic Reasons Possible?", *Philosophical Studies* 106, 1–40.
— 2003: "Blind Reasoning", *Proceedings of the Aristotelian Society*, Suppl. Volume 77, 225–248.
Bonjour, Lawrence 1998: *In Defense of Pure Reason*, Cambridge.
Brandom, Robert 2000: *The Articulation of Reasons*, Cambridge, Mass.
Burge, Tyler 1993: "Content Preservation", *The Philosophical Review* 102, 457–488.
Dummett, Michael 1973: *Frege's Philosophy of Language*, New York.
Harman, Gilbert 1996: "Analyticity Regained", *Noûs* 303, 392–400
Horwich, Paul 2000: "Stipulation, Meaning and Apriority," in P. Boghossian and C. Peacocke (Eds.), *New Essays on the A Priori*, Oxford, 150–169.
Margolis, Eric and Stephen Laurence 2001: "Boghossian on Analyticity", *Analysis* 61, 293–302.
Peacocke, Christopher 1993: "Proof and Truth," in: J. Haldane and C. Wright (Eds.), *Reality, Representation and Projection*, Oxford/New York, 165–190.
Prior, Arthur 1960: "The Runabout Inference Ticket," *Analysis* 21, 38–39.
Quine, W. V. O. 1935: "Truth by Convention," in his *The Ways of Paradox and Other Essays*, 2nd edition, Cambridge, Mass.1976, 77–106.
Williamson, Timothy 2003: "Understanding and Inference," in *Proceedings of the Aristotelian Society*, Suppl. Volume 77, 249–293.

ANALYTICITY AND IMPLICIT DEFINITION

Kathrin GLÜER
Uppsala University

Summary

Paul Boghossian advocates a version of the analytic theory of a priori knowledge. His defense of an "epistemic" notion of analyticity is based on an implicit definition account of the meaning of the logical constants. Boghossian underestimates the power of the classical Quinean criticisms, however; the challenge to substantiate the distinction between empirical and non-empirical sentences, as forcefully presented in *Two Dogmas*, still stands, and the regress from *Truth by Convention* still needs to be avoided. Here, Quine also showed that there are no implicit definers for the logical constants. Moreover, even if they existed, their epistemic analyticity would, on Boghossian's own account, be doubtful.

1. Introduction

The concepts of analyticity and the a priori are certainly experiencing a renaissance these days. One of the most interesting suggestions defending both analyticity and the a priori has been made by Paul Boghossian. In his papers on analyticity, he advocates a version of what he calls the "analytic theory of a priori knowledge". This theory, dear to the logical positivists, can be separated, Boghossian claims, from another theory they also held, known as the "linguistic doctrine of necessity". Crucial to this is a distinction between two different notions of analyticity: the distinction between *metaphysical analyticity* and *epistemic analyticity*. Quine, Boghossian argues, was right about metaphysical analyticity; it cannot be defended, and the same holds for the linguistic doctrine of necessity based upon it. Epistemic analyticity, however, can be defended, and so can an analytic theory of a priori knowledge taking it as its basis.

Boghossian's version of the analytic theory of a priori knowledge employs Carnap's idea of implicit definition. He holds that at least some linguistic expressions, the logical constants, get their meaning by implicit definition. Implicit definers, that is, sentences implicitly defining an expression, Boghossian argues, are analytic in the epistemic sense: Belief in their truth is justified by knowing their meaning. The knowledge thus gained, the argument continues, is a priori—nothing but knowledge of meaning is required for having such knowledge. However, according to Boghossian, and contrary to standard logical positivist doctrine, such knowledge is factual knowledge, knowledge about the world. Boghossian thus defends what might be called a *moderate rationalism*—with Carnap against Carnap. But above all, of course, against Quine.

And it is Quine whom I am going to defend. Now, to be a bit more precise, what Boghossian argues for is that Quine's criticisms of analyticity are ineffective as long as they do not *depend* on the thesis of indeterminacy (cf. 1996, 361). In what follows, however, I shall mainly focus on two of the Quinean arguments from the classical anti-analytic campaign, arguments to be found in *Truth by Convention* and *Two Dogmas*. They not only ante-date the indeterminacy thesis, but clearly would not seem to depend on it, either. For most of what follows, I can therefore safely ignore this complication; there will be some occasion to come back to it, though. What I am going to do is roughly this: After setting out Boghossian's account in more detail (sections 2 and 3), I shall investigate how immune this semantic explanation of a priori knowledge really is with respect to the classical Quinean criticisms. I shall concentrate on two of them: the argument from epistemic holism from *Two Dogmas* (section 4) and the regress charge from *Truth by Convention* (section 5). In the last part of my paper, however, I shall argue that an implicit definition account, even if it could be defended against Quine, would still not provide an explanation of a priori knowledge.

2. *Two concepts of analyticity*

It has become standard to point out that Quine, in *Two Dogmas*, employed more than one concept of analyticity and to complain that he did not sufficiently distinguish between these. Tyler Burge, for instance, distinguishes between the notion of truth by virtue of meaning alone, on the one hand, and the idea of reducibility, by substitution of synonyms for synonyms, to the truths of logic, on the other (cf. Burge 1992, 7 ff.). Boghossian calls the latter kind of analyticity "Frege analyticity". Truth by virtue of meaning alone, in turn, can be read in two ways, namely as truth independently of matters of fact and as truth independently of experience. Now, all of these notions might in fact coincide according to standard logical positivist doctrine. From a more neutral point of view, however, their interrelations are far from clear. On Quine's own understanding of the truths of logic, as suggested in the later sections of *Two Dogmas*, truth by virtue of meaning and "Frege analyticity" would, for instance, come apart.

I mainly remind you of all this in order to contrast these distinctions with another distinction, namely that between a "metaphysical" and an "epistemic" notion of analyticity as suggested by Boghossian. He, too, charges Quine with not sufficiently distinguishing between these notions, but distinguishing between metaphysical and epistemic analyticity is not just bringing yet another two notions of analyticity into play. Rather, this distinction seems to cut across the others; at least the idea of truth in virtue of meaning clearly might come in a metaphysical as well as in an epistemic version.

What exactly, then, is the difference between metaphysical and epistemic analyticity? Boghossian takes analyticity in both senses to be a *semantic* notion and starts from the formula that analytic statements are *true in virtue of their meaning alone*. A statement is analytic in the *metaphysical* sense, he explains, if it "owes its truth value completely to its meaning, and not at all to the facts" (1996, 363). It is analytic in the *epistemic* sense "provided that grasp of its meaning alone suffices for justified belief in its truth" (ibid.).

Regarding the very idea of metaphysical analyticity, however, Boghossian wonders:

> What could it possibly mean to say that the truth of a statement is fixed exclusively by its meaning and not by the facts? Isn't it in general true—indeed, isn't it in general a truism—that for any statement **S**,
> **S** is true iff for some **p**, **S** means that **p** and **p**?
> How could the *mere* fact that **S** means that **p** make it the case that **S** is true? Doesn't it also have to be the case that **p**? (1996, 364).

The proponent of metaphysical analyticity need not deny this "meaning-truth truism" (1996, 364), that is, he need not deny that for any true statement there is a corresponding fact. Accepting the truism, however, will drive him into some sort of *creationism*, Boghossian thinks; "he will want to say (...) that, in some appropriate sense, our meaning **p** by S *makes it the case that p*" (1996, 364 f.). But that Boghossian regards as sheer mysticism. Consider the sentence

(S)   Either snow is white or it isn't.

It should be obvious that it was the case that either snow was white or it wasn't *before* (S) came to mean that (cf. 1996, 365).[1]

Notice, however, that there is a much simpler non-epistemic way of understanding the idea that a statement is true in virtue of its meaning alone: We might think of such statements as true statements whose meaning suffices to *determine* their truth value. The existence of such statements is perfectly compatible with any reading of the meaning-truth truism. For any true statement *S*, there can be a corresponding fact, no matter how this fact is created, no matter whether it is *metaphysically dependent* on our meaning *p* by *S* in any sense. The idea simply is that, for some statements, this is a *necessary* fact, a fact that, so to speak, obtains in every possible world. Therefore, the facts (or the world with respect to which the sentence is evaluated) cannot possibly make a *difference* to the truth value of such a statement. Given its meaning, its truth value is determined.[2] It seems to me that to claim the existence of such statements is to make an interesting metaphysical claim and that

---

1. There is a difference, however, between holding that our meaning *p* by *S* makes it the case that *p* and holding that our meaning *p* by *S* makes it the case that *S is true*. For one might very well think that its being the case that *p* is completely independent from our meaning *p* by *S* while at the same time holding that the primary truth-value bearers are *interpreted sentences*. Consequently, there would be no *truths* unless there are interpreted sentences, but the same would not necessarily hold for *facts*.

Boghossian, however, seems to think that avoiding creationism about facts commits us to a notion of *what a sentence expresses* as the primary truth-value bearer (cf. 1996, 365; 380). Given the observation just made, that would at least require further argument; moreover, such a view does not go very well together with his wanting to work with a picture that is "as hospitable as possible to Quine's basic outlook" (1996, 361) and, therefore, agreeing to consider the *objects of belief* to be interpreted sentences. For, surely, the objects of belief should be the same as the primary truth-value bearers, shouldn't they?

2. Such a determination relation between the meaning of an analytic statement and its truth value is of course presupposed by Boghossian's own (epistemic) conception of analyticity. According to him, an analyticity "can only be false by meaning something other than what it means" (1996, 387). That is, after all, *why* knowing its meaning suffices for justified belief in its truth (cf. ibid.).

Boghossian's rejection of any metaphysical notion of analyticity thus might turn out to be a tiny bit hasty.

Moreover, it seems worth noting that this idea fits remarkably well with early logical positivist doctrine. The logical positivists would have called a sentence like (S) a "tautology" (Carnap 1930/1, 142) and declared it devoid of empirical content exactly because no possible state of affairs would *make a difference* to its truth. Thus Carnap explains:

> If a compound sentence is communicated to us, e.g., 'It is raining here and now or it is snowing,' we learn something about reality. This is so because the sentence excludes certain of the relevant states-of-affairs and leaves the remaining ones open. In our example, there are four possibilities: 1. It is raining and snowing, 2. It is raining and not snowing, 3. It is not raining but it is snowing, 4. It is not raining and not snowing. The sentence excludes the fourth possibility and leaves the first three open. If, on the other hand, we are told a tautology, *no possibility is excluded but they all remain open* (Carnap 1930/1, 143, emph. mine).

According to Boghossian, the combination of these ideas with the attempted reduction of the notion of necessity to the conventions of language led the positivists to their version of creationism, i.e. linguistic conventionalism: "they attempted to show that all necessities could be understood to consist in linguistic necessities, in the shadows cast by conventional decisions concerning the meanings of words. Conventional linguistic meaning, by itself, was supposed to generate necessary truth; a fortiori, conventional linguistic meaning, by itself, was supposed to generate truth" (1996, 365). I am uncertain as to the historical accuracy of these claims, but this is not the place to discuss this. Notice, however, that conventionalism about truth does *not* follow from conventionalism about necessary truth; what is generated by linguistic meaning, according to conventionalism, might be the *necessity* of a statement, not its *truth*. Truth might be given independently, that is, and necessity added.

Be that as it may, Boghossian holds that a statement's truth always depends both on its meaning and on the facts.[3] The facts concerned might of course be very general facts about the world, as for instance

---

3. And insofar as this means nothing more than that he holds on to a non-creationist reading of the meaning-truth truism, there is of course no substantive conflict with the points just made.

the fact that everything is self-identical, but that does not make their statement any less factual. Boghossian thus holds a factualist view of analytic statements; according to him, they "are capable of genuine truth and falsity" (1996, 379), that is, they do have truth conditions and they do make claims about the world. But that, or so he claims, does not mean that they could not be known a priori, quite the contrary. For epistemologically speaking, analytic statements are statements where knowing the meaning alone is sufficient for justifiedly assigning truth values. Their *truth* is not independent of facts, but their *justification* is. Epistemically analytic statements, one might say, may not be *true* by virtue of meaning alone, but they are *justified by virtue of meaning alone*.

On the basis of an account of what it is to know the meaning of a statement, Boghossian then sets out to substantiate the claim that "the notion of analyticity can help explain how we might have a priori knowledge" (1996, 362). And he is very clear about that what he is after is a priori knowledge in a very *strong* sense. To have such knowledge, the following conditions must be fulfilled. First, the justification for the statements in question must be of an a priori nature in this strong sense. That means that holding such statements true must not only be "justified (...) without appeal to empirical evidence", but also "that the justification in question is not defeasible by any future empirical evidence" (1996, 362). Second, the justification must of course be strong enough for knowledge. And third, the statements in question have to be in fact true; if all these conditions are fulfilled, holding a statement true amounts to a priori knowledge in the strong sense Boghossian is defending.

3. *Implicit definition, analyticity and the a priori*

The question, then, of course is how any sentence could be epistemically analytic. Boghossian: "Clearly, the answer to his question has to be *semantical*: something about the sentence's meaning, or about the way that meaning is fixed, must explain how its truth is knowable in this special way" (1996, 366). It is here that implicit definition comes into the picture. Boghossian's strategy is to start with the truths of logic and show for them how an implicit definition account of their meaning would make them epistemically analytic and knowable a priori.

Regarding the meaning of the logical constants, Boghossian claims, there is no alternative to some kind of conceptual role semantics (cf. 1996, 383). And this should take the form of what he calls *implicit definition*:

> (I) It is by arbitrarily stipulating that certain sentences of logic are to be true, or that certain inferences are to be valid, that we attach a meaning to the logical constants. More specifically, a particular constant means that logical object, if any, which makes valid a specified set of sentences and/or inferences involving it (1996, 376).

Boghossian calls this an "implicit definition account of grasp" (ibid.), so principle (I) presumably is not only to account for how meanings are determined but also for what it is to "grasp" them. We could preliminarily formulate this idea as follows: it is by holding certain sentences true—I shall not bother with always mentioning the inferential alternative—that a speaker manages to attach a certain meaning to his logical constants and this, too, is what it is for him to "grasp" these meanings.[4]

How does an implicit definition work? Suppose we want to define the term F. An implicit definition proceeds by stipulating a sentence (or a set of sentences) S containing F to be true. Let's call such a sentence (or set of sentences) $S(F)$ an "implicit definer". Except F, all expressions in the implicit definer are already interpreted. The idea then is that given the interpretation of the other terms, the truth of the implicit definer suffices to determine the meaning of F. In the case of the logical constants, however, what seems to determine their meanings is that sentences of a certain form are true, regardless of the specific meaning of any other expression they contain. It therefore seems *prima facie* plausible to suggest that their implicit definitions would proceed via stipulation of their introduction and, maybe[5], elimination rules.

---

4. Boghossian does not argue for the claim that there is no alternative to some kind of conceptual role semantics for the logical constants. What he seems to have in mind is that patterns of holding sentences true/inferences valid are the only *evidence* for interpreting expressions as logical constants; that, however, we could agree to while holding that the semantics of choice for the logical constants is truth-functional.

5. It is standardly held that elimination rules can be justified by introduction rules. Therefore, for purposes of implicit definition, introduction rules would seem sufficient—they "fix" or determine the meaning in question. Of course, if someone *used* an expression according to, for instance, the introduction rule for conjunction but not in accordance with its elimina-

There are some more or less classical problems connected with implicit definitions. The question is: when is an attempt at implicit definition successful, that is, when does it succeed in attaching a meaning to the term that is to be defined? The two best known problems here are those of *existence* and *uniqueness* of the meanings to be determined. We might fail in the attempt at implicit definition in at least two ways: either no meaning gets determined or more than one. In neither case has the term in question been defined. A clear case of failure through non-existence is Prior's famous tonk-operator which is supposed to be implicitly defined by the introduction rule for *or* and the elimination rule for *and*, thus allowing for derivation of absolutely everything from anything. It is in order to allow for implicit definitions failing in this way that Boghossian formulates (I) the way he does: "a particular constant means that logical object, *if any*, which makes valid a specified set of sentences and/or inferences involving it" (1996, 376, emph. mine). Boghossian does not seem to worry about uniqueness, however, and neither shall we. What is important here is that, according to Boghossian, implicit definition determines meaning only if there is an interpretation of the implicit definer that makes it true. Otherwise, no meaning is conferred by an attempt at implicit definition.

Now, Boghossian is not interested in how certain expressions actually were introduced into existing languages. This is not a historical model of what happened, for instance, when 'and' was introduced into English. Most probably, there was nothing that could be called an act of implicit definition. Rather, implicit definition provides a model for how certain expressions *could* be introduced and given a meaning. Implicit definers thus are sentences by means of which an expression F (that actually already has a certain meaning) *could* be given that very meaning by means of implicit definition. At the same time and more importantly, however, implicit definition is to be a model for what it is to *have* certain meanings, that is, it is to actually provide a semantics for F. To understand this, we have to remember that according to Boghossian, implicit definition is to be a model for a conceptual role semantics for the logical constants. And elsewhere he explains: "If expressions

---

tion rule, we would not have much idea how to interpret these utterances. What this points to, I think, is a certain tension between the idea of meaning *"fixation"* or *determination* by implicit definition and the conditions for *ascribing* certain meanings to expressions on the basis of how speakers use them.

mean what they do by virtue of the inferences they participate in, then some inferences are *constitutive* of an expressions's meaning what it does, and others aren't" (1994, 110). Implicit definition does provide a semantics for the logical constants if implicit definers are taken to be *constitutive of their meaning*. For F to have a determinate meaning there has to be a determinate set of sentences constitutive of its meaning. Now, if such a set $S(F)$ constitutes F's meaning, then grasping F's meaning consists in holding $S(F)$ true;[6] holding its implicit definer to be false *ipso facto* means attaching a different meaning to F. And, as we saw above, in order for F to have any meaning at all, its implicit definer not only needs to be held true, it also has to be in fact true.

Now it looks as if the connection between implicit definition and a priori knowledge were fairly straightforward. If implicit definition is the right account of an expression's meaning, the following kind of justification might be given for its implicit definer:

1. If F means what it does, then its implicit definer $S(F)$ has to be true, for F means whatever in fact makes $S(F)$ true.
2. F means what it does.

Therefore,

3. $S(F)$ is true (cf. 1996, 376; 386).

Holding $S(F)$ true, it seems, can be justified from premises 1 and 2 above, and knowing them, in turn, does not seem to require anything but knowledge of meaning. Moreover, if F has a meaning, $S(F)$ is in fact true. Thus knowledge of meaning would suffice for knowledge of truth, and such knowledge would be a priori.

This is a wonderfully simple argument. Remember, however, that it rests on a number of highly theoretical assumptions. For instance, on the

---

6. Cf. 1996, 376: "The important upshot of these considerations was to make plausible the idea that grasp of the indefinables of geometry *consists precisely in the adoption of one set of truths involving them*, as opposed to another. Applied to the case of logic, it generates the semantical thesis that I shall call *Implicit definition*" (first emph. mine). Providing an account of what it is to grasp the logical constants thus would seem one of Boghossian's most important reasons for adopting the implicit definition account of their meaning. Cf. also 1996, 383, where Boghossian explicitly speaks of an implicit definer S as a sentence "that I *must* hold true if S is to mean what is does" (emph. mine).

assumption that a conceptual role semantics is the semantics of choice for the logical constants. And on the assumption that a conceptual role semantics necessarily operates with meaning constitutive inferences. These assumptions are surely controvertible. What I shall do next, however, is investigate whether the classical Quinean criticisms really are ineffective against this semantic account of the a priori. More precisely, I would like to look at the argument from holism from *Two Dogmas* and the regress charge from *Truth by Convention*. In the course of these considerations, I shall have occasion to at least touch upon the second of the above assumptions, though.

4. *Holism*

The first of the Quinean arguments I would like to look at is what could be called the argument from holism. Maybe it is exaggerating a bit to call it an argument, but in the last sections of *Two Dogmas* we find a very suggestive metaphor for both the inter-relations between our beliefs and the relations between our beliefs and experience or the world. The metaphor is, of course, that of a "fabric" or a "web" impinging on experience only at its fringes. And it seems that if a Quinean "web-of-belief" model is correct, then nothing is a priori. It is the whole web, or at least large parts of it, that face experience together, and, or so Quine suggests, there are no reasons in principle to exclude any particular sentence or set of sentences therein from possible defeat by empirical evidence. Or, to put this the other way round, there are no principles by which to distinguish sentences with empirical content from sentences without. Especially, there are no principles to distinguish highly obvious empirical sentences from non-empirical ones. Though empirical content does come in degrees on such a model, there is no reason to say that there are any sentences completely without.

I would like to argue for two things in this section: First, if we think, as most people do these days, that epistemological holism is very plausible for observational contexts, a certain tension arises. For it will be very difficult to prevent such holism from spreading. Thus, the distinction most important to Boghossian's account, that between meaning constitutive and other sentences becomes threatened. As long as it cannot be substantiated, however, the Quinean challenge stands unanswered. Second, however, I would like to ask how compelling the development of the idea of implicit definition into a general theory of meaning determination really is.

Boghossian does not discuss epistemological holism in the analyticity papers. He does endorse some form of it in other papers, though. There, he uses an argument from what he calls "the holistic character of belief fixation" (1991, 78, see also 1989, 539 f.) against information-theoretic semantics. "Under normal circumstances", Boghossian explains, "belief fixation is mediated by background theory—what contents a thinker is prepared to judge depends upon what other contents he is prepared to judge. And this dependence is again typically, arbitrarily robust: just about any stimulus can cause just about any belief, given a suitably mediating set of background assumptions" (1991, 78). Applied to observation contexts, holism of belief fixation means the following: Take an observational belief that p, for instance, the belief that there is a cow in front of you. There is no situation in which this belief could not be caused, given a set of sufficiently deviant background beliefs. Thus, there is equally no situation in which it could not be prevented from being formed by sufficiently deviant background beliefs.

In these contexts, Boghossian takes care to note that this is psychological holism, not the disputed doctrine of semantic holism. It seems pretty obvious, though, that the holism of belief fixation nevertheless creates a certain tension with the view that there are meaning constitutive inferences or sentences. Or at least it would, if such holism were endorsed in an unrestricted form. Consider, for instance, the belief that the creature in front of you is a cow. Assume, too, that in order for this to be a cow-belief, you also have to believe that the creature in front of you is an animal. An unrestricted belief holism would amount to the claim that there are situations in which you can believe that the creature in front of you is a cow without forming the belief that it is an animal—provided you hold a sufficiently deviant background theory. But this clashes with the assumption that the cow-animal connection is meaning constitutive. More generally, if in just about any situation, including other beliefs, a belief that p can be formed, and, conversely, nothing, including other beliefs, necessarily prevents a belief that p from being formed, then there are no particular inferences or sentences such that a speaker has to hold them true in order to have a belief that p. Thus, an unrestricted holism of belief fixation would not seem to go together with the existence of meaning constitutive sentences or inferences.

Now, Boghossian nowhere subscribes to an unrestricted holism of belief. What should be clear, though, is that he needs to restrict his holism by providing a distinction between empirical and non-empirical sentences. Without such a distinction, that between meaning constitutive sentences and others is lost as well. And one might think that, though they do not coincide, distinguishing meaning constitutive sentences from others could be a first step towards a viable distinction between the empirical and the non-empirical.[7] Be that as is it may, to say that belief holism needs to be restricted in order to accommodate meaning constitutive sentences is just to repeat the Quinean challenge: How are non-empirical sentences to be distinguished from others? What is the substantive content of such a restriction upon belief holism? Boghossian admits that this is a very good question, and also that he does not really have a good answer to it (cf. 1996, 383). Fair enough. But in the absence of a good reply, we should, also in all fairness, consider the Quinean challenge as unanswered.

Boghossian does not agree. As noted above, he only aims at meeting the Quinean challenge insofar as it does not depend on the indeterminacy thesis (cf. 1996, 361). But, or so he tries to convince us, "anyone who rejects radical indeterminacy of meaning must believe that a distinction between the meaning constituting and non-meaning-constituting can be drawn" (1996, 383). Why? Boghossian's argument runs like this: A conceptual role semantics is the only plausible semantics for the logical constants. According to a conceptual role semantics, an expression has a determinate meaning only if there is a determinate set of meaning-constitutive sentences or inferences. If Quine is right and, in Boghossian's words, "there is no fact of the matter as to which of the various inferences involving a constant are meaning-constituting" (ibid.), then the constants do not have determinate meanings. "And that, again, is just the dreaded indeterminacy of meaning on which the critique of analyticity was supposed not to depend" (ibid.).

---

7. This idea is, in fact, suggested by the overall architecture of Boghossian's rationalistic project: Starting with the implicit definers for the logical constants, he tries to work his way upwards to account for the a priori nature of all logical truth and, by means of the notion of Frege-analyticity, all conceptual truth (cf. 1996, 366 ff.). The way he presents the project here, implicit definition seems to be supposed not only to take care of all logical truth, but also the epistemic analyticity of sentences like 'Whatever is red all over is not blue'. It is, however, not spelled out how the account is supposed to extend beyond implicit definers for the logical constants.

Quite clearly, what Boghossian seems to have in mind when he says that the critique of analyticity is supposed not to 'depend on indeterminacy', is not just that it is not supposed to use *Quine's* thesis of the indeterminacy of translation[8] as a *premise*. Rather, *no* kind of 'indeterminacy of meaning' is supposed to *either be its premise or its conclusion*. Now, in the above argument 'indeterminacy of meaning' follows only given certain assumptions Boghossian subscribes to: That the semantics of choice for the logical constants is a conceptual role semantics and that such a semantics requires a distinction between meaning constitutive and other sentences or inferences. Both assumptions, as remarked above, are controvertible; in fact, I believe that both of them are false. Not being able to argue this in any detail in this paper, I shall confine myself to the following brief comments, however.

Grant, for the sake of argument, a conceptual role semantics. Does this require a distinction between meaning-constitutive and other sentences or inferences? The reason Boghossian thinks it does, presumably, is "the old hat" (Block 1993, 1) familiar from the recent wars on semantic holism:[9] Our basic semantic idea is that what a speaker means by an expression is determined by the inferences it participates in. This determination cannot be holistic, the argument goes, for if it were no two speakers could ever disagree about anything. Ergo, it is only certain inferences that determine meaning, not all of them; those that do are the meaning-constitutive ones. This argument relies on hidden premises about the nature of the determination relation supposed to hold between inferences and meaning, however. It goes through only on the assumption that this relation is a *one-one relation*, but can be blocked by allowing holistic determination to be *many-one*.[10] If inferences can determine meaning holistically, however, a conceptual role semantics does not necessarily commit us to meaning-constitutive inferences.[11] Even if we grant Boghossian a conceptual role semantics for the logical constants, it therefore does not immediately follow that "anyone who rejects radical indeterminacy of meaning [in Boghossian's sense]

---

8. As argued for in Chapter 2 of *Word and Object* (1960). According to *Word and Object*, the meaning of the logical constants does *not* fall within the realm of the indeterminate. Nor does Quine adopt a conceptual role semantics for them.

9. As documented, in part, in Fodor/Lepore 1992; 1993; cf. also Boghossian 1993.

10. This point is argued in detail in Pagin 1997.

11. In Glüer 2002, I argue that this, in fact, is an advantage a holistic semantics has over non-holistic ones exactly because it relieves us of the Quinean challenge discussed above.

must believe that a distinction between the meaning constituting and non-meaning-constituting can be drawn" (1996, 383). Pending further argument, it is fair, after all, to consider the Quinean challenge unanswered.

So far, I have argued that there is a certain tension between belief holism and the doctrine of implicit definition. This tension arises because of the latter's apparent commitment to meaning-constitutive sentences. In the remainder of this section, I would like to raise even more trouble for this development of the idea of implicit definition into a general theory of meaning determination. The question I would like to raise could be put like this: How plausible is it to hold that an implicit definer is a meaning-constitutive sentence?

Looking at it diachronically, from the perspective of expressions to be introduced into the language, so to speak, this is far from obvious. Quine certainly thought that expressions could be *introduced* by implicit definition. He called that "legislative postulation" (cf. 1954, 117 ff.). But being a postulation, he argued, is "a trait of events and not of sentences" (1954, 119) and concluded: "Legislative postulation contributes truths which become integral to the corpus of truths; the artificiality of their origin does not linger as a localized quality, but suffuses the corpus" (1954, 120). Theoretical terms in scientific theories would seem to provide a case in point. These might certainly be seen as being introduced by implicit definition, but afterwards, their implicit definers face experience along with the rest of the theory's sentences. That is, such sentences, once completely interpreted, can actually turn out to be empirically *false*. But then, they are clearly not implicit definers anymore. Once interpreted, it thus seems, the implicit definer loses both its claim to having to *be* true and its claim to having to be *held* true (in order for it to have a certain meaning). Once interpreted, it is just a sentence as any other. The possibility of actually introducing expressions by means of implicit definition therefore does not seem to force meaning constitutive sentences upon us.

What about looking at it from the perspective of an expression F that already is part of the language and has meaning? Are there sentences that have to be held true in order for F to mean what it does? Take the case of the logical constants. What does a speaker have to hold true in order for F to mean one of them? Inferences of the form specified by that constant's introduction and elimination rules, presumably. But what exactly does that mean? The most plausible requirement would seem to be that the speaker has to hold sentences true in accordance with these rules. For instance, he has to hold 'A and B' true when he holds A true and he holds B true. But saying that the set of sentences or inferences thus specified is constitutive for a certain meaning is to say that *any* of the indefinitely many inferences sharing the specified form is meaning constitutive. To mean one of the logical constants by an expression F thus would require absolutely impeccable reasoning with F. *Any* mistake automatically would prevent F from meaning this constant. Given the kind of creatures we are, this cannot be right, I am afraid; our logical (in)capacities would prevent most of us from ever expressing anything remotely resembling a logical constant.

But wasn't it Quine who taught us that the strongest possible evidence of bad interpretation is seeming to hold a basic logical truth false? Certainly (cf. Quine 1960, 57 ff.). If a speaker seems to deny basic logical truths, we should definitely check our interpretation. But is that the same as saying that in order to mean a specific constant every inference of elimination or introduction form needs to be gotten right? I doubt it. Consider a fairly normal speaker. We think he means conjunction by 'and'. What would count as good evidence for this interpretation's being bad? What would it be to interpret him as denying basic logical truths? Our speaker might not have sentences formulating those truths in his repertoire, and even if confronted with them, he might not be able to assign the right truth value. That by itself would *not* be a reason to doubt that he means conjunction by 'and', however. What he does mean by 'and' would rather be a matter of his holding true sentences according to the right inference patterns. But even here, getting the occasional one wrong would not necessarily be a reason for doubting that he means conjunction. Of course, these are matters of degree, but it seems fairly clear that our speaker would have to make quite a lot of mistakes of a rather inexplicable and destructive nature before we would have good evidence for bad interpretation.

Moreover, it is well known that the reasoning powers even of college students often in fact seem to be amazingly bad. Tests like the so-called selection task show that things as fundamental as reasoning with 'if-then' according to *modus ponens* frequently seem to go wrong (as reported, e.g., in Stich 1990, 4 f.). But then, conceiving of such basic inferences as constitutive of the meaning of the logical constants would commit us to saying that in practice, hardly anyone ever manages to express them. That does not seem right, however; despite these reasoning failures, it in practice most of the time does seem plausible to interpret normal usage of 'if-then' as a conditional fulfilling *modus ponens*.

This is of course not to claim that 'if-then', as used in natural language, expresses the material conditional. It does seem plausible to think that it expresses a conditional fulfilling *modus ponens*, however, and, therefore, that its meaning is not determined in accordance with the model of implicit definition. Mistakes regarding inferences of introduction or elimination form are possible without change of meaning. And there is no reason to think that this would not generalize to other implicit definers or, for instance, the speaker who does use 'if-then' to express the material conditional. *His* usage certainly would be tellingly different from everyday usage of 'if-then', but it need not be impeccably so.

An account working with meaning constitutive inferences thus seems too inflexible to deal with actual speakers in the most plausible way. It assigns *too much weight* to certain types of mistakes, making them, in effect, categorically impossible. Even though simple logical mistakes do seem to be the best evidence for bad interpretation, even the best evidence seems more plausibly construed as less than conclusive. To interpret actual practice in a plausible way, it therefore seems preferable to work with a model according to which (occasional) basic logical mistakes are possible.

One might feel like replying that a speaker can 'follow a rule' like an introduction or elimination rule without getting every single application right. In a way, that is just my point. For the defender of meaning-constitutive sentences, however, it means that we are back to square one. For the distinction between meaning-constitutive and other sentences or inferences was supposed to deal with exactly this problem: how to be able to countenance differences of application (mistakes) while ascribing the same meaning. Allowing mistakes of introduction or elimination merely postpones the problem; the question now becomes: which of the applications of an introduction or elimination rule are constitutive for its being 'followed' and which aren't?

To sum this discussion up: The challenge from epistemological holism and the web of belief model is to come up with a viable principled distinction between meaning-constitutive and other sentences. In the absence of such a distinction, the Quinean challenge must be considered as unanswered. Moreover, the distinction seems neither forced upon us by the possibility of introducing expressions by implicit definitions nor does it seem to be required by considering logical mistake the strongest evidence for bad interpretation. On the contrary, accounts dispensing with meaning-constitutive sentences seem to be able to make better sense of actual speakers. The case against the web-of-belief model and for meaning-constitutive sentences thus can, at best, be considered as still open.

5. *Conventionalism*

I would now like to leave this issue and look at another aspect of Boghossian's model, its conventionalism. Independently of any results reached so far, our question is whether this conventionalism can be defended against Quine's attack on a very similar conventionalism in *Truth by Convention* (1935).

According to Boghossian, the logical constants get their meanings by "our conventionally stipulating that certain sentences (or inferences) involving them are to be true" (1996, 380 f.). All this amounts to, is a *conventionalism about meaning*. For remember, interpreted implicit definers are factual sentences, according to Boghossian. What they express are language independent factual truths constitutive of a certain meaning. What is conventional is only *which expression* comes to have that meaning. Nevertheless, this model seems to offer an *explanation* for why we think of certain sentences as a priori: These are sentences that get their interpretations by being conventionally stipulated true. And as we saw before, being a definer on this model is not a passing trait; a sentence continues to have it as long as it continues to have the same meaning. To be held true by convention thus might well seem to be a distinguishing trait of meaning-constitutive sentences.

It is exactly such a conventionalism about the meanings of the logical constants that is under attack in *Truth by Convention*. There, Quine argues that the conventionalist is faced with a dilemma: His view either leads into an infinite regress, or, if modified so as to avoid the regress, loses all its explanatory power, all its power, that is, to make any real distinction.

Let's quickly look at the first horn of this dilemma, the infinite regress. According to Boghossian, the meaning for 'and' is fixed by our stipulating that the following inferences are to be valid:

A and B	A and B	A, B
A	B	A and B (1996, 381).

To be more precise, however, these are not inferences but inference-schemata. What needs to be stipulated is that *all* inferences having one of these forms are valid. Since there is an infinite number of such inferences, they cannot be stipulated true one by one. A general stipulation is needed. Any such general stipulation, however, needs to make use of a sentence containing already interpreted logical expressions—hence, regress.

It is widely thought that this Quinean argument, even though clearly valid against any sort of explicit conventionalism, can be easily circumvented by "going implicit". That is, the argument is taken to bite only, if the conventions in question have to be *explicitly stated* in order to be adopted. "Implicit conventions", however, do not have to be stated; they can be in force for and observed in behavior even though no one ever actually formulated them. By means of understanding the conventionalism about the meanings of the logical constants as one employing implicit conventions, then, it might seem that it can be saved from Quine's regress charge. And this seems to be exactly what Boghossian suggests to do, too. He writes: "surely, it isn't compulsory to think of someone's following a rule **R** with respect to an expression **e** as consisting in his *explicitly stating* that rule in so many words in the way that Quine's argument presupposes. On the contrary, it seems far more plausible to construe **x**'s following rule **R** with respect to **e** as consisting in some sort of fact about **x**'s *behavior* with **e**" (1996, 381).

We must not forget, however, that Quine anticipates the conventionalist's "going implicit". He readily admits that implicit conventionalism would fit actual language acquisition and use much better than explicit conventionalism. However, "going implicit" is not as easy as it might seem. For what exactly does it mean that something is an implicit convention? Or that behavior is following an implicit convention? What would, to speak with Boghossian, the "sort of fact about **x**'s behavior with **e**" exactly be that makes it convention-governed behavior? Of course, implicit definers would be sentences very firmly accepted. But, again, that is a characteristic they share with a lot of sentences that we would not want to classify as held true by convention, especially highly obvious empirical sentences. These are held true with equal regularity. It's the classical problem for the implicit conventionalist: How to distinguish convention-governed from merely regular behavior. And this is, of course, the second horn of Quine's dilemma: Unless the conventionalist can come up with a relevant behavioral difference, he risks explanatory emptiness. The notion of a linguistic convention reduces to an "idle label" if there is no difference between conventionally holding true and other forms of firm acceptance (cf. Quine 1935, 106).[12] "Going implicit" thus is more difficult than it might *prima facie* appear. It cannot be done by merely vaguely indicating "some sort of fact about (...) behavior" with an expression that would make it convention-governed; that just leaves us exactly where *Truth by Convention* got us, that is, in need of knowing the kind of fact that would do it.[13]

Moreover, this is only part of the story of *Truth by Convention*. That there is more is often overlooked, but this forgotten part of *Truth by Convention* is no less crucial to our investigation than the first. For it seems to show that quite independently of its conventionalism, an implicit definition account of the meanings of the logical constants is impossible; the conventions in question would not only have to be implicit, they would also have to be directed at something that does not exist.

Let me explain. The doctrine of implicit definition says: "It is by arbitrarily stipulating that *certain sentences* of logic are to be true (...) that we attach a meaning to the logical constants" (Boghossian 1996, 376, emph. mine). What gets stipulated to be true, according to implicit definition, are *sentences*. That is, no matter whether these definitions are adopted explicitly or implicitly, there need to be sentences that we could at least *ex post* identify as such that stipulating them to be true would result in the meaning assignment. However, as Quine argued, *there are no such sentences*. For they would have to be general, that is,

---

12. In Glüer 2002a, I go through a number of influential proposals for distinguishing implicit norms, rules, or conventions and try to show that they all, ultimately, are stuck between the horns of Quine's dilemma. I also give some reasons why, as long as we are after meaning or content determining norms, rules, or conventions, the dilemma might actually be inescapable.

13. Hinting at dispositions, as Boghossian does (without seeming to endorse his own hint, however; cf. 1996, 381 f.), surely does not help much — for regarding our dispositions to hold them true, there does not seem to be any difference between meaning constitutive and other firmly accepted sentences.

they would have to contain already interpreted expressions of the very kind they are to implicitly define.[14]

That this point is easily overlooked may be due to the fact that Quine presents it as one more aggravation for the conventionalist: He has to go for conventions that, at the point of adoption, cannot even be formulated. Otherwise, even implicit conventions do not help with the regress. Quine: "When we first agree to understand 'Cambridge' as referring to Cambridge in England, failing a suffix to the contrary, and then discourse accordingly, the role of linguistic conventions is intelligible; but when a convention is *incapable of being communicated until after its adoption*, its role is not so clear" (1935, 106, emph. mine). However, for an implicit definition account of the meaning of the logical constants, the point seems simply fatal. Sentences such that stipulating them to be true would result in giving the logical constants their meanings do not exist—neither before nor after the adoption of any convention, be it explicit or implicit, and regardless of our dispositions to use the expressions in question. Of course, in some sense the constants do get their meaning by their use. But *secunda facie* it does *not* seem plausible to use implicit definition to account for how that works.

To sum this discussion up: Again, the Quinean challenge to substantiate the crucial difference between meaning constitutive and other sentences, here in the guise of a distinction between those held true by convention and others, is left unanswered. Moreover, even if the distinction could be substantiated, that would not seem to help. For the forgotten part of the argument from *Truth by Convention* seems to generally rule out an implicit definition account of the meaning of the logical constants.

6. *The return of the facts*

So far, I have made use of classical Quinean arguments to convince you that his case against analytic apriorities should not be underestimated and, in fact, seems far from lost. I would like to conclude

---

14. And analogously, of course, for stipulating inferences valid: Whether implicitly or explicitly, we need to stipulate an indefinite number of them to be valid. According to the model of implicit definition, this is done via a *specification* of the inferences. The stipulation, that is, requires a linguistic expression representing the inferences in question. And this, again, would need to be general, i.e. to contain expressions of the very kind to be defined.

by raising yet another worry. For there seems to be a question as to whether, even granted everything else, implicit definers would really be analyticities—even if we understand analyticity in the epistemic sense recommended by Boghossian. And that would, of course, destroy the prospects of giving an analytic explanation of the a priori by means of implicit definition.

Recall Boghossian's epistemology for implicit definers:

1. If F means what it does, then its implicit definer $S(F)$ has to be true, for F means whatever in fact makes $S(F)$ true.
2. F means what it does.

Therefore,

3. $S(F)$ is true (cf. 1996, 376; 386).

Recall also, that $S(F)$, according to Boghossian, is a factual sentence. Knowing that $S(F)$ is true thus amounts to knowing a fact about the world. At the same time, $S(F)$ is supposed to be epistemically analytic, justified in virtue of its meaning alone: All we need to know in order to be justified in our belief in $S(F)$'s truth is its meaning. That is, even though $S(F)$ itself is a factual sentence, its justification is *not* to depend on or involve matters of fact.

But how could that be so given the model of implicit definition employed by Boghossian? Look at premises 1 and 2 together. That F means what it does depends on there in fact being something that makes $S(F)$ true, according to premise 1. Only if there is such a fact does F have any meaning. Being justified in believing premise 2, therefore, requires being justified in believing that there is something that makes $S(F)$ true. Moreover, it requires being justified in believing *that S(F)*.

To put this in terms of propositions, let P be the proposition that $S(F)$ expresses. On Boghossian's account, it seems to me, being justified in believing that $S(F)$ means P *presupposes* being justified in believing P. Of course, it then *follows* from being justified in believing that $S(F)$ means P, that I am justified in believing P. However, believing P cannot be *justified* this way; for knowledge of the meaning of the sentence already requires such justification and, therefore, cannot provide it.

This would mean two things. First, implicit definition does not *explain* a priori knowledge. If there is a priori knowledge of the proposition expressed by an implicit definer, its justification has to take some independent way.[15] And second, implicit definers are *not epistemically analytic*. Knowing their meaning does not provide justification by virtue of meaning alone, for knowledge of meaning itself turns out to already require knowledge of facts about the world. It does not seem, therefore, as if the distinction between metaphysical and epistemic analyticity could be sustained—at least on the Boghossian model, the facts do return, and with a vengeance.

Conclusion

I have considered two classical Quinean ways of attacking the version of the analytic theory of the a priori that Boghossian is trying to salvage. On both counts, the attacks still seem very powerful. Epistemological or belief holism is not easily moderated by means of any principled distinction between empirical and non-empirical sentences, thus endangering the a priori in general. More particularly, there seems to be good reason to prefer accounts of meaning that do not require a distinction between meaning constitutive sentences or inferences and others. Conventional implicit definition accounts of meaning, even more particularly, have additional liabilities. Conventionalism, especially when it has to go implicit, needs to be saved from being an idle label. And in the crucial case of the logical constants, implicit definers do not even exist. Last, but not least, I have argued that even independently of the Quinean attacks implicit definers are, after all, not (epistemically) analytic. The prospects of implicit definition to provide an analytic explanation of a priori knowledge are, I am afraid, rather bleak.[*]

---

15. Bonjour makes a similar point; cf. Bonjour 1998, 50 f.

[*] For helpful comments on earlier versions of this paper I would like to thank Paul Boghossian, Sten Lindström, Peter Pagin, Åsa Wikforss and audiences in Berlin, Konstanz, Umeå and at a Birkbeck College (University of London) study weekend at Cumberland Lodge.

REFERENCES

Block, Ned 1993: "Holism, Hyper-analyticity and Hyper-compositionality", *Mind and Language* 8, 125.

Boghossian, Paul 1989: "The Rule-Following Considerations", *Mind* 98, 507–549.

— 1991: "Naturalizing Content", in: B. Loewer and G. Rey (Eds.), *Meaning in Mind. Fodor and his Critics*, Oxford and Cambridge, Mass., 65–86.

— 1993: "Does an Inferential Role Semantics Rest Upon a Mistake?", *Mind and Language* 8, 27–40.

— 1994: "Inferential Role Semantics and the Analytic/Synthetic Distinction", *Philosophical Studies* 73, 109–122.

— 1996: "Analyticity Reconsidered", *Noûs* 30, 360–391.

— 1997: "Analyticity", in: B. Hale and C. Wright (Eds.), *A Companion to the Philosophy of Language*, Oxford, 331–368.

— 2000: "Knowledge of Logic", in: P. Boghossian and C. Peacocke (Eds.), *New Essays on the A Priori*, Oxford, 229–254.

Bonjour, Laurence 1998: *In Defense of Pure Reason*, Cambridge.

Burge, Tyler 1992: "Philosophy of Language and Mind 1950–1990", *The Philosophical Review* 101, 3–51.

Carnap, Rudolf 1930/1: "Die alte und die neue Logik", *Erkenntnis* 1, 12–26, quoted from the translation by I. Levi: "The Old and the New Logic", in: A. Ayer (Ed.), *Logical Positivism*, New York 1959, 133–146.

Fodor, Jerry and Ernest Lepore 1992: *Holism. A Shopper's Guide*, Oxford.

Fodor, Jerry and Ernest Lepore (Eds.) 1993: *Holism. A Consumer Update*, Amsterdam.

Glüer, Kathrin 2002: "Alter Hut kleidet gut. Zur Verteidigung des semantischen Holismus", in: G. W. Bertram and J. Liptow (Eds.), *Holismus in der Philosophie*, Weilerswist, 114–128.

— 2002a: "Implizites und Explizites Regelfolgen", in: U. Baltzer and G. Schönrich (Eds.), *Institutionen und Regelfolgen*, Paderborn, 157–176.

Harman, Gilbert 1996: "Analyticity Regained?", *Noûs* 30, 92–400.

Pagin, Peter 1997: "Is Compositionality Compatible with Holism?", *Mind and Language* 12, 11–33.

Quine, Willard Van Orman 1935: "Truth by Convention", in his *The Ways of Paradox and other Essays*, sec. ed., Cambridge, Mass. 1976, 77–106.

— 1951: "Two Dogmas of Empiricism", in his *From a Logical Point of View*, sec. ed., Cambridge, Mass. 1980, 20–46.

— 1954: "Carnap and Logical Truth", in his *The Ways of Paradox and other Essays*, sec. ed., Cambridge, Mass. 1976, 107–132.

— 1960: *Word and Object*, Cambridge, Mass.

Stich, Stephen 1990: *The Fragmentation of Reason*, Cambridge, Mass. and London.

IMPLICIT THOUGHTS:
QUINE, FREGE AND KANT ON ANALYTIC PROPOSITIONS

Verena MAYER
Ludwig-Maximilians-Universität München

Summary
Quine criticised the semantic notion of analyticity that is often attributed to Frege and Kant for presupposing an essentialist theory of meaning. In what follows I trace back the notion from Quine via Carnap to Frege and Kant, and eventually examine Kant's distinction between analytic and synthetic judgements in more detail. It turns out that the so called Frege-Kant-notion of analyticity can not be attributed to Kant. In contrast, Kant had a distinctly pragmatic notion of analytic judgements. According to him analytic propositions elucidate certain presuppositions of our conceptual scheme, thereby serving the anti-metaphysical project of transcendental philosophy.

1. *Quine's background assumptions*

According to Quine there are two dogmas of empiricism: first that a clear distinction between analytic and synthetic propositions can be made, second that all statements can be reduced to empirical ones. The second dogma is dependent on the first, since the confirmation conditions for a statement are part of the statement's analytic implications, if verificationism should be true (Fodor/Lepore 1992, 37). Therefore, if the a/s-distinction fails, reductionist empiricism has to be abandoned as well.

While reductionism was a prominent and provocative thesis of neo-empiricism, the a/s-distinction seems to have been a rather traditional assumption that for some time was not put into doubt. An early article by Morton White (White 1952)[1], however, shows that there was some discussion of the concept of analyticity even before Quine's *Two Dogmas*

---

1. The paper is a revised version of one read 1949.

was published in 1951. Quine's main arguments, as explicated also by White, were officially directed against the notion of analytic statement (the first dogma of empiricism), but were meant to destroy meanings as merely postulated entities. The argument goes as follows: Analytic statements are statements that are derived from logical truths (identity statements) by substitution of synonyms. Thus, the identity statement "All bachelors are bachelors" becomes the analytic statement "All bachelors are unmarried men" by substituting the term "bachelor" with the complex synonymous term "unmarried men". The origin of analyticity thus is synonymy, synonymous terms being explained as "having the same meaning". In this sense the notion of analyticity is grounded in the notion of meaning.

It seems, however, that the notion of analyticity was meant to be used the other way round, i.e. as an explication of the concept of meaning. Thus Carnap, at whom Quine's attack was directed, explains in his preface to the first edition of *Meaning and Necessity* that the main target of his book is a semantic analysis of meaning, and that "the method here proposed takes an expression, not as naming [a concrete or abstract entity], but as possessing an intension and an extension" (Carnap 1956, ii). Intension is then defined in terms of L-truth, while L-truth must be given by the semantic rules of the system in question. The formal definition of L-truth makes use of the notion of possible worlds or state-descriptions, postulating that the L-true or analytic sentences of S are those true in all state-descriptions of S. But state-descriptions, in turn, presuppose semantic rules, which are of two kinds: the first kind, explicitly formulated by Carnap, states relations between certain constants and their designation. Thus, for a very restricted object language S_i there is a rule that says: "'Hx'—'x is human'", where the hyphen is to be read as "means the same as" (ibid., 4). In *Meaning and Necessity* the second kind of semantic rules, which Carnap later calls "meaning postulates", is merely given as an aside, when Carnap says: "The English words here used are supposed to be understood in such a way that 'human being' and 'rational animal' mean the same." (ibid.) Analyticity is thus in fact based on a prior notion of meaning, and Carnap's attempt to explicate meanings in terms of abstract entities (with help of state descriptions and possible worlds) failed. Since meanings are not defined through or reduced to other concepts, they are simply presupposed.

As Quine later said in his reply to Alston it was not so much the hypostasis of meanings itself that was the target of his critique, but the fact that "prior assumption of an unexplained domain of objects called meanings is no way to explain synonymy or anything else" (Quine 1998, 73). If meanings could be explained, for instance, as abstractions from classes of sentences, no objection would prevail; however, such classes would presuppose the notion of meaning again. The problem led to Quine's later behavioural construction of reference, as well as to many attempts of other scholars of saving some kind of meaning. The strict connection between analyticity and meaning, however, that Carnap had established and that formed the background of Quine's critical attacks, was seldom questioned.

The received view followed Carnap and Quine in that the connection between meaning and analyticity was not only a systematic, but also a historical fact. While it was well known that neither Leibniz nor Kant formulated their notion of necessary or analytic judgements in terms of meaning, it was understood that the translation of their concept of analyticity into semantic terminology was unproblematic. In what follows I will trace back the development to the source of analyticity in Kant's works. It will turn out that the modern notion is incompatible with the original view. If analyticity is understood as depending on a prior notion of meaning, then Kant's analytic judgements are not analytic, and if Kant's notion of analyticity is taken as relevant to modern analysis, no fundamental problem with a presupposed notion of meaning emerges. My proposal will be to drop not the notion of meaning, as Quine did, but the notion of analyticity in the sense Carnap has introduced.

2. *Quine's reconstruction of analyticity*

Quine starts his analysis in *Two Dogmas* with a reference to Kant who had coined the terms "analytic" and "synthetic". Quine's mentioning Kant is only a pretext to the following transition to Aristotelian essentialism which is, following Quine, the true origin of the concepts of meaning and analyticity. While Aristotle spoke of objects having essential and accidental properties, the "doctrine of meaning" attributes meanings (or intensions) and referents (or extensions) to words. As Quine observes, the two doctrines involve important logical differences: For Aristotle it makes sense to attribute to a certain man (as an object) the essential property of being rational, and at the same time the accidental property of being biped; from the standpoint of the theory of meaning, however, it makes no sense to attribute essential and accidental properties to the referent of the concept man. Two-leggedness may be involved in the meaning of "biped" while rationality is not, so that the same person were and were not rational essentially and accidentally at the same time. This alone shows that the transition from essentialism to meanings is not as smooth as philosophical common sense believes. Quine, however, skips the question with the famous metaphorical remark that "meaning is what essence becomes when it is divorced from the object of reference and wedded to the word" (Quine 1961, 22).

As for Kant's notion of analyticity, Quine seems to think that it already belongs to the post-essentialist meaning-theoretic stage. With reference to Kant Quine mentions the following two informal conceptions of analyticity:

Q1 A statement is analytic if it attributes to its subject no more than is already conceptually contained in the subject.
Q2 A statement is analytic if its denial is self-contradictory.

Quine attributes the first explicitly to Kant, and treats the source of the second as uncertain. It is widely accepted, however, that both definitions are in agreement with Kant. For the moment I want to take both formulations as if they were Kant's and only restate Quine's critique.

Q1 is a formulation that is sometimes explained in terms of semantic content, such that a statement is analytic if the semantic content of the predicate term is the same as the content of the subject term. Following Quine, Q1 is to be rejected because it uses the concept of containment at a merely metaphorical level. Moreover, it seems to hold for sentences of subject-predicate form only and seems unable to cover e.g. analytic conditionals.

The formulation Q2 has to do with justification. This version of analyticity is to be rejected because the notion of self-contradiction, following Quine, is as much in need of clarification as analyticity itself. According to Morton White the problem was seen to be connected with the presupposition of Q1: we do not know what self-contradiction in sentences of subject-predicate form should possibly mean. Thus, a proposition like "All men are rational animals" is presumably analytic, syntactically, however, its denial shows nothing like "A and not-A", which is the formal notion of contradiction. So in a sense the notion of self-contradiction here is metaphorical as well.[2]

Quine reconstructs the seemingly vague and metaphorical classical definitions of analyticity in terms of meanings, as Carnap had done before:

Q3   A statement is analytic if it is true by virtue of meaning and independently of fact.

While a formulation like Q3 is not found in Kant's works, Quine nevertheless believes that it agrees with Kant's intentions. He rejects the definition because of its purported implicit reliance on Aristotelian essence. As a sincere essentialist Kant should have characterized analyticity in a non-semantic way as follows:

Q4   A statement is analytic if it attributes to its subject essential properties only.[3]

This at least is the position which Quine implicitly attributes to Kant, though in the short paragraph on Kant it is never explicitly formulated.

According to Quine, modern definitions of analyticity struggle in vain to avoid this essentialist background of the notion. Even if they stress, as Carnap does, that meanings aren't entities of any sort, they have to explicate the notion of analyticity in a way that doesn't itself already presuppose some other semantic notion that in turn presupposes analyticity in the sense of Q3. The already mentioned general form of any such strategy of avoidance, as Quine puts it, may be formulated as follows:

Q5   A statement is analytic if it is either a logical truth or can be turned into a logical truth by suitable substitution of some of its parts.

Here it is presupposed that the notion of a logical truth is innocent with regard to hidden metaphysical entities like meanings. Now, "suitable

---

2. White 1952, 324. The riddle is of course solved if it is taken into account that for Kant (as in traditional logic in general) subject-predicate-statements always have to be reconstructed as partial identities of the form "S is (a) P" (see below 4.1).

3. This would make no difference, since (following Quine) meanings already *are* essences, so that Q4 is equivalent with Q3.

substitutions" in logical truths may be based on synonymy, meaning postulates, definitions and the like in the following way:

Q6 A statement is analytic if it is either a logical truth or can be turned into a logical truth by putting synonyms for synonyms (meanings for meanings and so on).

As was already indicated the strategy fails since there is no way to define synonymy or related notions without making use of Q3-analyticity and other semantic substitution instances again. Analytic sentences thus are either trivial logical truths or they imply a hidden reference to Aristotelian essence.

3. *An intermediate step: Frege's notion of analyticity*

3.1 *Frege and Kant*

Instances of formulation Q5 or Q6 are sometimes referred to as the Frege-Kant notion of analyticity. Since the Frege-Kant notion today counts as the standard conception of analyticity (the one Quine argued against), we will first have a look at Frege's view of the matter. In his *Foundations of Arithmetics*, Frege discusses the Kantian distinction between analytic and synthetic judgements, while reformulating it in a way that is adjusted to logicism. On the one hand, Frege rejects the version Q1 (the formula of "containment") because, as he says, it concerns the "content" of the judgement, not its justification, the latter being for Frege the real target of the a/s-distinction. On the other hand, he characterizes analytic judgements as those that can be (in getting justified) traced back to general logical truths and definitions only, thereby implicitly relying on something like the second definition of analyticity Q2 (the formula of "contradiction"):

> The problem becomes, in fact, that of finding the proof of the proposition, and of following it up right back to the primitive truths. If, in carrying out this process, we come only on the general logical laws and on definitions, then the truth is an analytic one, bearing in mind that we must take account also of all the propositions upon which the admissibility of any of the definitions depends. If, however, it is impossible to give the proof without making

use of truths which are not of a general logical nature, but belong to the sphere of some special science, then the proposition is a synthetic one.[4]

According to this, analyticity can be condensed in the following thesis, which Frege in fact mentions in a letter to Marty:

F   A statement is analytic if it can be proved with help of general logical laws from definitions only.[5]

From Frege's logicist program it is clear how F was meant to be used: The statements of arithmetic are analytic because they follow from some definitions (e.g. the definition of number) by the laws of logic only. Here is the main difference between Kant and Frege, since for Kant statements of arithmetic are synthetic a priori. The source of the difference is, as will be shown, not so much a difference in the view of mathematics but in the notion of analyticity. While the point can only be seen in detail after the exploration of Kant's beliefs on the subject, some general aspects already emerge from the Quinean reconstruction of Kant in Q1 and Q2. First, Frege simply speaks of "truths which are of a general logical nature" instead of the law of contradiction (as Q2 does in correspondence to some remarks of Kant). Kant had thought that logic could be founded on the law of contradiction, while Frege, in contrast, in his *Begriffsschrift* had developed a far more complex notion of logic that incorporated several fundamental logical laws. Second, Frege had replaced the traditional analysis of propositions into subject, copula and predicate by a functional analysis. Thus, analytic and synthetic judgements could no longer be described in terms of the subject-predicate-scheme. Therefore, in contradistinction to Kant, Frege could rely on a rich system for the generation of non-trivial analytic statements.

The main reason behind Frege's reformulation of analyticity thus was his interest in the necessity of mathematical truth which he did not believe to be guaranteed by the Kantian synthetic a priori. His distrust was mainly due to the fact that the notion of a priori made reference to some kind of intuition. To be synthetic a priori in the Kantian sense, arithmetical propositions had to be schematic constructions using the pure intuition of time, while for Frege no intuition was needed in arith-

---

4. Frege 1986, §3 (English translation: J. L. Austin, Oxford 1950).
5. Letter to Marty 29.8.1882, in Frege 1976, 163.

metics at all. Thus he proved in the *Begriffsschrift* that the notion of a successor, which is necessary for the construction of numbers, is a purely logical concept that in no way presupposes a time-linear process of adding units. The necessity of arithmetic propositions could be guaranteed only by a formal procedure of deduction and proof.

3.2 *Frege and Quine*

Thus Frege's interest in the foundation of mathematics is responsible for his restricted notion of analyticity in terms of a formal proof. From the formulation F as well as from Frege's writings in general it seems clear that he would never have accepted the possibility of analytic sentences in natural language. Since concepts of natural language have no sharp boundaries and are notoriously vague and ambiguous they can not be defined, and therefore nothing can be proved there in a strict and formal sense.[6] What is at issue in the debate around *Two Dogmas*, however, is not formal analyticity in the Fregean sense, but a more general notion of analyticity that would cover natural language as well. This is already clear from Quine's discussion in the section on definitions of *Two Dogmas*. Here Quine rejects definition as a suitable substitution instance in Q, since it always has to rely on prior synonymy relations except when it is a sheer abbreviation for formal purposes. The latter case, which Quine accepts as "a really transparent case of synonymy created by definition" (op. cit., 25 f.), he obviously thinks to be fruitless and out of the intended scope of the notion of analyticity. Thus, for Quine analytic statements were not meant to be restricted to formal purposes as in Frege's logicist program but should comprise natural (meta-)language. Analyticity for Quine is essentially connected with synonymy precisely because even formal semantic systems have to rely on meta-language synonymy relations.

Thus, in *Two Dogmas* Quine accepted "good" nominal definitions and rejected "bad" explications of concepts. Yet the distinction between the two is blurred in Frege's definition of numbers as well as in the neo-empiricist notion of "rational reconstruction". Following Quine, Frege's analytic propositions of arithmetic would be transparent in terms of using a nominal definition, while being inscrutable in terms

---

6. Note that even the standard example "All bachelors are unmarried men" would not be analytic in the Fregean sense.

of explicating a natural concept. Already Strawson and Grice had noted this air of incoherence in *Two Dogmas*, since it remains unclear why the sheer act of explicitly defining something should create a fundamental difference within the realm of meanings, and turn metaphysical essences into innocent entities (Grice/Strawson 1956, 152 f.).

4. *Kant's notion of analyticity*

The history of Kant's notion of analytic judgements is full of distortion and misunderstanding. While Frege reduced the traditional notion of analyticity to logical deduction from definitions, logical empiricism deprived it of another major distinction. As is well known, in his critical philosophy Kant separated two kinds of aspects that the modern conception seems to blur: the analytic/synthetic-distinction on the one hand, the a priori/a posteriori-distinction on the other. Since analytic judgements are always a priori, this gives three possible types: synthetic a posteriori, synthetic a priori and analytic (a priori) judgements. The difference between the synthetic a priori and the synthetic a posteriori was crucial to Kant, since the main purpose of the *Critique of Pure Reason* was to show how synthetic a priori judgements, whose existence Kant never questioned, are possible.

In contrast to this, for Quine synthetic statements always are "grounded in fact", i.e. empirical statements, while the possibility of statements that are synthetic and a priori is dropped.[7] The job of Kant's synthetic a priori now seems to be divided between the two remaining kinds of statements, the analytic (a priori) and the synthetic a posteriori. Perhaps this additional burden is the source of some of the problems Quine has detected. This, however, can only be seen clearly by going back to the original Kantian typology.

4.1 *Analytic and synthetic judgements*

According to Kant's *Critique of Pure Reason* all judgements are either analytic or synthetic. Analyticity is characterized sometimes in terms of containment, and sometimes in terms of the law of identity or contradic-

---

7. Frege, in contrast, accepted synthetic a priori judgements in geometry; therefore he retained the Kantian two-dimensional distinction.

tion. The first of these aspects is expressed in the following passage:

> In all judgments in which the relation of a subject to the predicate is thought (...), this relation is possible in two different ways. Either the predicate B belongs to the subject A, as something which is (covertly) contained in this concept; or B lies outside the concept A, although it does indeed stand in connection with it. In the one case I entitle the judgment analytic, in the other synthetic.[8]

It was sometimes suspected that the next citation, which follows immediately after the previous one, gives another systematic description of analyticity which is not overall compatible with the first:[9]

> Analytical judments (affirmative) are therefore those in which the connection of the predicate with the subject is thought through identity; those in which this connection is thought without identity should be entitled synthetic. (ibid.)

The connection between the two passages is explained easily. Kant thought of the containment relation as partial identity (i.e. inclusion) of concepts, which corresponds to the traditional view of the basic structure of sentences in terms of relations of concepts. Thus the sentence "All bodies are extended" was analysed according to the structure "S[P1, P2 ...] is P1", where the subject term S[ ] was thought to be a complex concept containing partial concepts [P1, P2 ...]. The copula "is", then, stands for the relation of partial identity between the complex, and a partial concept, which is a "character" (Merkmal) of the subject concept.[10] Thus the statement "All bodies are extended" by analysis shows the structure "body[extension, ...] is extension", and in this sense "is thought through identity", i.e. in terms of a partial identity between subject and predicate. In this sense the predicate "belongs to" the subject or is "contained" in it. When Kant sometimes characterizes analyticity in terms of the law of contradiction, nothing new is introduced: The denial of an analytic judgement yields a contradiction exactly because the subject term already contains the predicate. Thus "Not all bodies are

---

8. *Kritik der reinen Vernunft*, hereafter KrV, A 6/B 10. This is presumably the source of Quine's Q1-formula.
9. Cf. Marc-Wogau 1951.
10. See for example *Logik Jäsche*, AA IX. 102. For slightly different formalizations see also Beck 1965, 74 ff., and de Jong 1995, 616 f.

extended" would read as "body [extension, ...] is not extension".[11]

Nevertheless, this conception of analyticity in terms of content is qualified by another often cited text in the first Critique that contains a third characterization of analytic judgements in terms of explication. Kant says:

> The former [i.e. analytic judgements, V.M.], as adding nothing through the predicate to the concept of the subject, but merely breaking it up into those constituent concepts that have all along been thought in it, although confusedly, can also be entitled explicative. The latter, on the other hand, add to the concept of the subject a predicate which has not been in any wise thought in it, and which no analysis could possibly extract from it; and they may therefore be entitled amplicative. (A 6 / B 10)

In contrast to the second description of analyticity, the third adds something new: The function of analytic judgements is not only to break up the subject term into its constituent parts, but also to make clear what was "confusedly thought" in it. It is important to note that Kant in this third formulation (as in many other places) connects analyticity with our thinking or cogitation and thereby disconnects it from judgements. Analyticity is now no longer an objective logical structure attributable to sentences. Nearly all of Kant's explanations of the analytic express this qualified point of view. Thus the predicate is "covertly" contained in the subject, i.e. unconscious to our thinking; the containment is thought through identity; the constituents of the subject concept are thought in a confused manner and so on. This aspect of thinking the containment relation is entirely dropped in the modern "reconstructions" Q1–Q6 that Quine mentions. The main reason might have been that confusion or clarification of thought seems to be a mere psychological aspect of analyticity that has nothing to do with the logicist program or with formal semantics. However, as it will turn out, it was the most important and central aspect of the notion for Kant.

This can be seen clearly from Kant's pre-Critique essay „An Enquiry into the Distinctness of the Principles of Natural Theology and Mor-

---

11. „Alle analytische Urtheile beruhen gänzlich auf dem Satze des Widerspruchs und sind ihrer Natur nach Erkenntnisse *a priori*, die Begriffe, die ihnen zur Materie dienen, mögen empirisch sein, oder nicht. Denn weil das Prädicat eines bejahenden analytischen Urtheils schon vorher im Begriffe des Subjects gedacht wird, so kann es von ihm ohne Widerspruch nicht verneint werden ..." *Prolegomena*, AA IV, 267 f.

als" (1764)[12] where the distinction between analytic and synthetic judgements is introduced for the first time, yet already in terms of a fundamental difference between philosophical and mathematical truths. Following the *Enquiry* there are two ways of reaching knowledge: first through arbitrary connection of concepts, which yields knowledge "per Synthesin", second through analysis of concepts, "per Analysin". Mathematics always starts with synthetic definitions, for example by fixing a term like "trapezium" for a certain geometrical figure. The concept is not given in advance but established through the definition. Philosophy, in contrast, starts with everyday concepts which are already given but in a confused and indefinite way. Analytic judgements are those that, after a process of analysis, state the implications hidden in the use of such concepts. Analytic and synthetic judgements therefore get their names from the method whose result they are.[13]

Kant insists that it is the most important task of philosophy (Weltweisheit) to dissolve confused beliefs[14], while it is always a fault to try to use the "mathematical method", i.e. synthesis, in philosophy. Leibniz, for instance, after using a synthetic definition to establish his concept of a monad—which he invented—tried to draw metaphysical conclusions from it. Another famous example for the synthetic method in philosophy is Spinoza's *Ethica more geometrico demonstrata*. Metaphysics in this "bad" sense is always tempted to borrow its method from mathematics instead of analysing what is known "with certainty" without trying to end in definitions, i.e. synthetically.

Thus at the bottom of the Kantian analytic/synthetic-distinction lies a sharp contrast between nominal ("synthetic") definition and the philosophical process of conceptual analysis. The strict use of the term "analytic" in the sense of "being the result of a process of analysis" is also seen in later texts, where Kant speaks about identical judgements.[15] Since analytic sentences are partial identity statements, Kant could have called the two kinds of judgements "identical" and "non-identical" judgements. This, however, would not have expressed the cognitive aspect of the dis-

---

12. "Untersuchung über die Deutlichkeit der Grundsätze der natürlichen Theologie und der Moral", AA II, 273–301.
13. Cf. Beth 1968, Allison 1975 and 1985, Peijnenburg 1994.
14. "[...] verworrene Erkenntnisse aufzulösen", ibid., 289.
15. "Welches sind die wirklichen Fortschritte, die die Metaphysik seit Leibnitzens und Wolff's Zeiten gemacht hat?" (1804), AA XX.

tinction that was important to him. The identity of concepts is not worth to be mentioned, since nothing is analysed.[16] However, the same would hold for tautologies and logical truths in general, and thus the Quinean definition Q5 would not generate analytic sentences.

Thus it seems that the analytical character of analytic statements has to be taken literally. There is no way to reduce analytic statements in Kant's sense to logical truths, as it was proposed by Carnap and Quine, and taken for granted since then. Kant's elucidative notion of analyticity can be expressed in the following thesis:

K   A statement is analytic if it can be justified by a process of analysis of the subject term.

To analyse a concept we have to "consider the idea in its relations to other ideas", to find thereby its characters and partial concepts, and to compare those concepts to see their implicational relations with each other—a process quite similar to the method analytic philosophy makes use of in distinguishing logical implications and other aspects of the usage of a term.[17] In his *Enquiry* Kant describes the procedure of synthesis in terms of construction while the process of analysis consists in the clarification of a concept. Thus, if there already is a certain concept that consists of characters it can be analysed into, we can "make the concept distinct" (einen Begriff deutlich machen) by exhibiting the relevant parts. On the other hand, if we make up or construct a concept out of

---

16. In 1804 Kant writes: „Wenn man solche (i.e. analytic) Urtheile identische nennen wollte, so würde man nur Verwirrung anrichten; denn dergleichen Urtheile tragen nichts zur Deutlichkeit des Begriffs bei, wozu doch alles Urtheilen abzwecken muß, und heißen daher leer; z.B. ein jeder Körper ist ein körperliches (mit einem andern Wort, materielles) Wesen. Analytische Urtheile gründen sich zwar auf der Identität, und können darin aufgelöset werden, aber sie sind nicht identisch, denn sie bedürfen der Zergliederung und dienen dadurch zur Erklärung des Begriffs; da hingegen durch identische, idem per idem, also gar nicht erklärt werden würde." (AA XX, 322) This reference to the distinction between analytic and identical propositions is presumably also due to the critique of Eberhard (see below) who tried to show that analytic judgements are nothing else but Leibniz' identical judgements.

17. „Es ist hier der Begriff von einem Dinge schon gegeben, aber verworren und nicht genugsam bestimmt. Ich muß ihn zergliedern, die abgesonderte Merkmale zusammen mit dem gegebenen Begriffe in allerlei Fällen vergleichen und diesen abstrakten Gedanken ausführlich und bestimmt machen. ... Ich muß diese Idee in allerlei Beziehungen betrachten, um Merkmale derselben durch Zergliederung zu entdecken, verschiedene abstrahirte Merkmale verknüpfen, ob sie einen zureichenden Begriff geben, und unter einander zusammenhalten, ob nicht zum Theil eins die andre in sich schließe." AA II, 277

different characters by definition, we "make a distinct concept" (einen deutlichen Begriff machen). The result of making a concept distinct is an analytical judgement, while the result of making a distinct concept is a synthetic truth. Wherever definition is involved, the resulting judgement is synthetic, not analytic, since by defining something a distinct concept is constructed.

It now seems to be clear why the modern notion of analyticity is not compatible with Kant's. In Kantian terms the modern concept is a mixture of analytic and synthetic elements, which, by the way, is similar to what Kant criticized as bad metaphysics. Instead of being content with the result of conceptual analysis, which gives a clarification of thought and may yield a starting point of philosophical deliberation, philosophers try to fix such knowledge in definitions which lead to far-reaching unjustifiable conclusions. Kant's early critique of metaphysics therefore shows a certain similarity to Quine's critique, only that the latter is directed against analytic propositions while the former goes against the synthetic method in philosophy. Now it seems that the modern notion of analyticity has its roots not so much in Kant's idea of analyticity but in his notion of synthetic judgement.

4.2 *A priori and a posteriori*

In his *Enquiry* Kant only talks about synthetic judgements—which are essential to mathematics—and about analytic judgements as the results of philosophical analysis. The distinction is not meant to be exhaustive or to comprise all possible kinds of propositions. Thus, statements of ordinary language would be neither synthetic nor analytic, the distinction being restricted to certain "scientific" methods. In his critical philosophy, Kant's approach to analytic and synthetic propositions essentially remains the same. Nevertheless, by adding the distinction between a priori and aposteriori knowledge a new aspect comes into play that modifies the notion of synthetic judgements in a certain sense. Now synthetic propositions are no longer defined as the product of formal definition and deduction only. Rather, the more general feature of the synthesis of concepts in a new concept is exploited such that some kind of, so to speak, empirical (a posteriori) definition is possible as well. At the same time the necessary character of mathematics is accounted for by connecting the process of concept construction (which formerly seemed to be somehow arbitrary) with pure intuition.

The development of Kant's view of mathematics is illuminating here. In the *Enquiry* the method of mathematics was construction by way of signs or characters which serve as substitutes of the concepts they refer to. Mathematics considers "the general under the characters in concreto", which means that the mathematician not only operates with concrete signs as representatives of general concepts but recognizes the result of such operations directly from the signs, thus seeing, as Leibniz once put it, the truth *au coup d'oeuil*. In contrast, philosophy considers the general through the signs "in abstracto"[18], which the philosopher does not take into consideration; he merely abstracts from them, "looks through" them directly at the general concepts he is dealing with. Arithmetical judgements thus are operations with concrete characters, while philosophical deliberation is, so to speak, an operation with general concepts.

In the first Critique this approach is explicated in more detail. What could it mean exactly to see "the general under the characters in concreto"? Now Kant describes the process as a construction of the concept in terms of an exhibition a priori of the intuition which corresponds to the concept (B 713). This intuition must be concrete, as the *Enquiry* proposed, and simultaneously general, since arbitrary properties of the sign can not play a constructive role. Thus, what is needed is a "non-empirical intuition" which shows a single object, and yet is a universal representation, that is valid for all possible intuitions which fall under the same concept. While Kant in the first Critique generally refers to the geometric example of the triangle, the description is meant to cover also the judgements of arithmetic. The constructive process in arithmetic Kant mentions shortly in the chapter on the schematism of pure reason. The operation with characters from the *Enquiry* now is described as successive addition of units in time (B 182). Here Kant adds the idea of pure intuition in contrast to empirical intuition, an explication which has deterred Frege from adopting the Kantian view.

In the field of mathematics Kant's notion of a priori means reference to pure intuition. Nevertheless, analytic judgements are a priori as well, which might have tempted readers of the first Critique to think that analytic propositions also rely on pure intuitions of some kind. Thus

---

18. „Die Mathematik betrachtet in ihren Auflösungen, Beweisen und Folgerungen das Allgemeine unter den Zeichen *in concreto*, die Weltweisheit das Allgemeine durch die Zeichen *in abstracto*." (AA II, 278) See also KrV B 742.

in analogy to the mathematical case philosophers would "see" general concepts "through" signs of natural language, which would, in turn, suggest an essentialist theory of concepts. As is well known, however, this is not what Kant intended. He himself often defines a priori knowledge as knowledge independent of experience, thus leaving open the possibility of totally different kinds of such an independence. In fact, the analytic a priori differs fundamentally from the synthetic one. If we think of the a priori/a posteriori distinction in terms of justification, the synthetic a priori is justified with reference to pure intuition, while the analytic a priori is justified with respect to what is "implicitly thought with" a certain concept. But what does the latter kind of justification consist in? Up to now, the Kantian move to the analytic method might still be viewed as a mere sidestep on the way to essentialism. Do we not think B always together with the concept A because B is a necessary part of the meaning-entity A? Thus, the relation between concepts and meanings has to be analysed in more detail.

4.3 *Meaning and the Clarification of Concepts*

In *Two Dogmas* Quine complained that he did not know whether the statement "Everything green is extended" is analytic. Yet he denied that his indecision over this example betrays an incomplete grasp of the "meanings" of "green" and "extended". Quine seems to have the following point in mind: Analytic sentences purport to give meanings in an essentialist sense (for short: E-meanings); yet it is possible to understand a sentence without knowing if it is analytic or not, i.e. without knowing its E-meaning. Consequently, we do not need to know E-meanings for understanding language. For Kant this whole reasoning would seem to be quite acceptable, albeit from a "conceptualist" instead of a semantic point of view. As we have seen, for Kant the signs of natural language serve only as representatives of our concepts with the function to reproduce them occasionally.[19] Thus he talks of concepts instead of meanings, concepts, not linguistic expressions, being the primary object of analytic deliberations.[20]

---

19. In this connection, Kant says that in discursive thought the sign accompanies the concept to make later reproduction of the concept possible. Cf. *Anthropologie in pragmatischer Absicht*, AA VII, 191. See also *Logik Philippi*, „Vom Gebrauch der Worte", AA XXIV.1, 484 f.

20. As a consequence of this representationalist view of language, it is always possible to

Concepts consist of the two aspects "form" and "matter", which correspond roughly to what Frege later called "Sinn" and "Bedeutung", and what Carnap called intension and extension.[21] For to understand a term it seems sufficient to know its matter or the "object" which is referred to. Thus to understand what "green" means (to be able to use the term, to have the concept), it is necessary to know objects that belong to the extension of the concept. Nevertheless, it is not necessary to know if everything green is extended. Therefore, it is possible to understand a term without being conscious of its partial concepts and its logical implications that are explicated in analytic propositions. There is no need to know what is implied in a certain concept, as long as we do not draw conclusions or argue from conceptual premises alone. The feeling that we know perfectly well what "extended" and "green" means is thus quite justified with respect to our understanding of the "matter" of the term.

If we start to reflect on the implications or even the truth of the sentence, however, we turn to philosophical analysis and therefore to the "form" of a concept, which is its logical structure, consisting of subordinated and coordinated characters. Coordinated characters are the partial concepts of a concept—thus, for instance, extension is a coordinated concept of the concept body—while subordinated characters are those that are derived from a partial concept or subordinated under it—thus gold is a subordinated concept of the concept metal. These distinctions are important for a proper understanding of the three possible types of concepts: empirical concepts, mathematical concepts and concepts of reason.

In empirical concepts we can find indefinitely many coordinated "Merkmale", while the subordinated characters are limited insofar as there must be some indivisible simple concepts. Nevertheless, since we never can be sure to know all coordinated partial concepts, there is in principle uncertainty about the subordinated ones as well. There-

---

give different concepts different names. There are no real synonyms, since it makes no sense to attach different names to the same concept, while on the other hand difference of names always hints at differences in the concepts. Quine's discussion of synonymy therefore would have been pointless to Kant.

21. Kant's notion of a concept has been subject to thorough analysis before, see e.g. de Jong 1995. Allison 1985 places the theory of concepts within Kant's general account of judgement and intuition. Therefore, I will restrict myself to those aspects of the discussion that are of relevance for the modern notion of analyticity.

fore, no definition of empirical concepts is possible; they can only be described or explicated. Any attempt to lay out all the characters of the concept "bachelor" would be idle and a logical failure. Mathematical concepts, in contrast, are "self-made". Thus, since all possible characters or partial concepts are known from the start, analytic propositions with mathematical subject terms would be useless. Concepts of reason (e.g. the concept of cause) can be justified transcendentally as forms of possible experience, which in principle gives them a sharp boundary and makes them ideal candidates for philosophical analysis. Only here, in the realm of philosophical analysis, the a/s-distinction can be of use. In mathematics analysis is useless, while in empirical matters it is always preliminary and uncertain. Only philosophy, in dealing with the forms of possible experience, can profit from the exhibition of conceptual knowledge. For sure, philosophy then only explicates what is already implicit in our knowledge, yet such an analytic explication reveals much more than the simple linguistic "meaning" of our words. However, what precisely is analytic explication?

Kant describes the method of analysis with reference to the traditional idea of knowledge "clare et distincte". Here, his position is not always clear and distinct in itself. Following the *Logik Jäsche*, a concept is clear, if it is conscious to the epistemic subject, while in the *Logik Blomberg* even a conscious representation may be "dark".[22] The idea seems to be that a "really" conscious concept is already explicated or was subject to some reflection. The meaning of subject terms is always a concept, be it clear or dark, yet it is not so much clearness but distinctness that is at issue in connection with analytic propositions. Clear concepts can be distinct or indistinct (deutlich oder undeutlich). A distinct clear concept is already analysed into its characters, while an indistinct concept lacks such an analysis. Thus, the meaning of a term might be a clear indistinct concept. For example, most people have the concept of beauty, i.e. know its meaning, yet they do not know its constitutive characters.[23] If we add to this talk of distinctness the previous distinction

---

22. „Bin ich mir der Vorstellung bewußt: so ist sie klar; bin ich mir derselben nicht bewußt, dunkel." *Logik Jäsche*, AA IX, 33.
23. „Ein jeder hat von der Schönheit einen klaren Begriff. Allein es kommen in diesem Begriffe verschiedene Merkmale vor, unter andern, daß das Schöne etwas sein müsse, das 1) in die Sinne fällt und das 2) allgemein gefällt. Können wir uns nun das Mannigfaltige dieser und andrer Merkmale des Schönen nicht auseinandersetzen, so ist unser Begriff davon doch immer noch undeutlich." Ibid., 34.

between form and matter, it follows that of a clear indistinct concept we would know its matter but not its form.

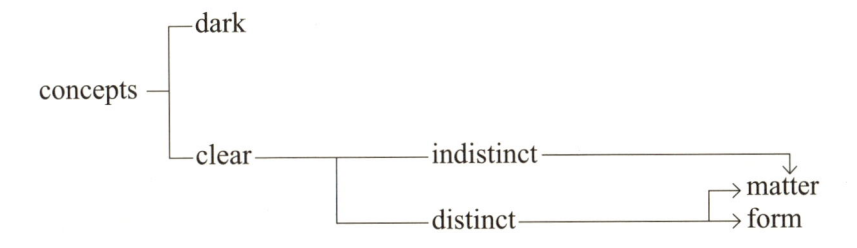

```
concepts ─┬─ dark
          └─ clear ──┬── indistinct ─────────────┐
                     │                           ↓
                     │                          → matter
                     └── distinct ──────────────→ form
```

Concepts are developed by constitutive processes of comparison, reflection, and abstraction. By comparison of intuitions we gain a range of similar objects, by reflection we find a comprising category, by abstraction we detach everything that is irrelevant to the similarity in question. During this process we may come to simple concepts, which are necessarily indistinct, since they can not be analysed into constituents. Analytic propositions containing simple subject terms are therefore impossible. Nevertheless, most of our concepts are complex, consisting of characters and subordinated partial concepts that have to be explicated through analysis. How should this be done?

The rules of philosophical research Kant laid down in his *Enquiry* seem to give a regulative starting principle here. Following the *Enquiry*, analysis should begin with what is "immediately known with certainty" as being implied in the concept in question. This sounds like a rather fuzzy criterion, but is meant to be a serious restriction on possible analytic sentences. The question whether "Everything green is extended" is analytic is thereby blocked since, as Quine confirmed, nothing is known "immediately" here. Judgements of immediate certainty would be e.g. "Everything green has a colour", or "Everything which is green all over is not red", the former attributing to the subject its genus proximum, the second attributing the differentia specifica that distinguishes the subject from other members of the same genus.[24] In the *Enquiry*, however, Kant does not mention logical relations between concepts, but recommends to start analysis with what is given by language use (Redegebrauch) without relying on definitions or explanations of the term involved. Thus from the concept of a body he thinks it could immediately be known that

---

24. For the relation of distinctness to traditional definition theory see de Jong 1995.

it is divisible, without presupposing any definition, or without knowing what a body "really" is. Likewise, that the concept of desire presupposes a desired object, belongs to the concept's analytic implications that are open to the first intuitive reflection. Note that it is not necessary here to refer to a special faculty of intuition other than a certain "Sprachgefühl". However, Kant's later remarks on analyticity in his logic lectures do not rely on such kind of linguistic intuition, but already start with attempts to find logical differences and analytic implications of a concept by means of comparison and reflection.

While this seems to be Kant's idea how analysis may start (i.e. with certain and simple linguistic intuition on the one hand, and with specifying logical differences on the other hand), there is a second and more indirect step that leads to analytic propositions in the proper and philosophically interesting sense. Here the concept, as well as its immediately known features, has to be "developed" with the purpose of explicating ambiguities, thereby making it possible to distinguish what might be called family resemblance concepts. For instance, developing the term "consciousness" shows that the term is used ambiguously for what we remember and what we experience immediately. Kant is never quite explicit as to how this development should proceed, but he seems to imply a reconstruction of the natural process of conceptualisation. Since all concepts are abstractions from intuitions, the process of analysis itself has to proceed "in abstraction", using examples, imagination and thought experiment, thus finding "signs" for the concept in question that are at once general and concrete. During this process of concept development it might turn out that some of the immediate certainties presupposed are in fact analysable into other more detailed concepts, or that seemingly unified concepts in fact comprise inconsistent subsets of characters and partial concepts. Thus philosophical analysis may not only clarify our thinking but eventually initiate a revision of our conceptual scheme.

4.4 *Concepts and essence*

While Kant's lectures on logic justify a pragmatic reconstruction of Kant's notion of analyticity, Quine's presumption of essentialism is fuelled by other texts, where the notion of essence seems to play a certain role. In his critical works Kant was reluctant to use the word "essence" (Wesen), whereas in his *Lecture on Metaphysics* (Pölitz) and in the discussion with Eberhard he seemed more willing to accept the term for his own purposes.[25] At the same time, however, he denied an essentialist reading of the a/s-distinction. Kant is eager to distinguish the logical essence of a concept from the real essence of a thing. The logical essence of a concept (and indirectly of the thing falling under the concept) is the set (Inbegriff) of its coordinated characters. The characters are, as explicated above, what is implicitly contained in the concept, i.e. the set of those concepts we always connect with it (even without being conscious of them) in our use of the respective terms. The real essence of a thing, in contrast, is what the thing "in reality" is. While real essence comprises much more than logical essence, our knowledge of it is constantly extended by (empirical) synthetic propositions. Thus attraction of bodies belongs to the real essence of corporeal things, and is not part of the logical essence of the concept of a body. Real essences are a question of synthesis, i.e. must be stated by propositions that add characters not necessarily logically connected in the concept. In contrast, logical essence is made up by the analysis of a concept[26] which again explicates its characters.

It seems that logical essence, as described in analytic propositions, consists only of "necessary" characters, i.e. those that are always "thought together with" the concept, in contrast to characters that are accidental even if somehow important, fruitful, or useful.[27] Thus, the logical essence of a concept is the complex of necessary characters it is to be identified with. That we think in a way that gives us certain char-

---

25. The Kant-Eberhard Controversy was analysed and commented in detail by Henry Allison 1975. Again I will only mention some central points that are crucial for Quine's critique.

26. "Ein logisches Wesen setzen wir durch die Analysis des Begriffes." *Vorlesung über die Metaphysik (Pölitz)* AA XVIII, 552.

27. As Schulze explained, logical essence comprises only those characters of a concept that are sufficient to distinguish it from other concepts. (cf. Allison 1975, 175). Kant (or perhaps rather Jäsche) notoriously misrepresents his point in talking of "necessary characters of the represented thing" instead of the necessary characters of the concept under which the thing falls, while in the same context he insists on the difference between essence of thing and essence of concept. Thus he says: "Nothwendige Merkmale sind endlich diejenigen, die jederzeit bei der vorgestellten Sache müssen anzutreffen sein. Dergleichen Merkmale heißen auch wesentliche und sind den außerwesentlichen und zufälligen entgegengesetzt, die von dem Begriffe des Dinges getrennt werden können." (*Logik Jäsche* AA IX, 60.) Nevertheless, it is clear from the argument that by "Sache" Kant in fact means the concept of the thing that falls under it.

acters in combination does not mean that by analytic propositions we know the real essences of things. The point of the distinction between real and logical essence in fact seems to be that the logical essence is not real in a metaphysical sense, but has to do with the organisation and structure of our thought.

This distinction between real and logical essentialism is constantly blurred in the discussion on the a/s-distinction. When Quine asks if "everything green is extended" is analytic, we naturally would try to find out if the green things we happen to know are necessarily extended. This, however, would mean to look after the real essence of things, which for Kant was a matter of empirical investigation. Instead, following Kant, we should ask if the concept of "being green" has the logical structure of always being thought together with the concept of extension. Kant formulates the question of the logical essence of concepts in different ways. Thus he invites us to look "what we think when we hear a (certain) word"[28], or to search for the "first inner foundation of everything contained in the concept".[29] Nevertheless, in this context Kant frequently uses seemingly "metaphysical" notions like necessity or apodicity. Thus the question if Kant is an essentialist boils down to the question if logical essence is a metaphysical notion that implies something like innate ideas or ideal entities with necessary properties and attributes.

Given Kant's anti-metaphysical program it would seem strange if such a kind of essentialism could be attributed to him. Why then does he explicitly say that analytic judgements are necessarily or a priori true and therefore apodictic? The problem and the answer can be seen most clearly from Kant's discussion of the critique that Eberhard, a Wolffian philosopher, formulated in the years 1788–1790.[30] Eberhard contended that traditional metaphysics, as laid down in the system of Wolff, already has given an answer to the main question of the first Critque „How are synthetic a priori propositions possible?". To show this, Eberhard criticises Kant's a/s-distinction as being implicit in Leibniz' theory of

---

28. "... was wir uns bey dem Worte von einem Dinge dencken ... ", *Logik Blomberg* AA XXIV.1, 117.

29. "... der erste innere Grund alles dessen, was im Begriffe enthalten ist" *Vorlesungen über die Metaphysik (Pölitz)* AA XXVII, 552 f.

30. "Über eine Entdeckung, nach der alle neue Kritik der reinen Vernunft durch eine ältere entbehrlich gemacht werden soll", AA VIII, 187–251. For illuminating presentations of the controversy see Allison 1975 and de Jong 1995, 632 ff.

predication. It is a somewhat ironical sideswipe of history that the dogmatist Eberhard anticipated Quine's analysis Q5 in writing:

> In all universal affirmative judgments the predicate is either one with the subject or it is not; and if it is one with it, either entirely or partially. [...] Now this identity may be undeveloped, as in the proposition: all triangles are triangles; all bodies are bodies; or it may be developed through a definition, as in the proposition: all triangles are three-sided figures; all bodies are extended things which have motive and inertial force.[31]

Thus, in analytic judgements the predicate is either identical with "the essence of the subject itself" or with one of its "essential parts". What Kant seemed to have overlooked according to Eberhard was a special type of judgement that asserts an "attribute" of the subject; attributes being concepts that are not characters of the subject but concepts of which the subject is the sufficient reason. They express a necessary connection between subject and predicate, and are therefore a priori. Nevertheless, since the predicate is not an immediate part of the subject, they correspond to Kant's synthetic propositions, hence are what Kant called "synthetic a priori".

Eberhard thus gives an essentialist reading of the Kantian distinction that would quite readily be confirmed by Quine. In his polemical answer to Eberhard Kant rejects the alleged identity of this interpretation with his own transcendental perspective, yet he accepts Eberhard's notion of an attribute as a "necessary consequence" of the subject term with respect to a priori propositions. Such propositions (either synthetic or analytic) state that the predicate is part of or a consequence of the logical essence of the subject, and thereby indeed belongs to the logical essence itself (op. cit., 229). To accept this, however, does not mean to identify the synthetic a priori with necessary attribution. In contrast, the question remains, how the "a priority" of the statement is fixed: either by the law of contradiction, which makes the sentence analytic a priori, or by pure intuition, which makes it synthetic a priori. Thus again, what is crucial for the distinction between analytic and synthetic sentences is not a metaphysical relation between subject and predicate but the way by which the relation can be detected: either by conceptual analysis or by intuition. As a consequence, Kant distinguishes again two kinds of the a priori: logical apriority, which is the basis of analytic a

---

31. Cited in Allison 1975, 37.

priori judgements, and transcendental apriority that yields synthetic a priori judgments.

Kant illustrates the difference with the familiar example of the concept of a body: In the sentence "All bodies are divisible" the predicate "divisible" is an attribute, since it is a consequence of the concept of extension, which is in turn an essential coordinate characteristic of the concept body. Yet the question, if "divisible" is an analytic or a synthetic attribute, therefore, whether the proposition "All bodies are divisible" is analytic or synthetic (a priori), is still open. Now, following Kant, the truth of the proposition can be proven from the law of contradiction, since the proposition "body A is indivisible" is a contradictio in adjecto. Therefore, the sentence is analytic a priori. In contrast, the sentence "All bodies are inert" is synthetic a priori, since inertness never can be proven to be a consequence of one of the concept's essential characters by the law of contradiction. To prove its being part of the logical essence of the concept body, intuition is required. Thus, talk of attributes alone can not tell how synthetic a priori propositions are possible; an independent explanation in terms of pure intuition is required.[32]

4.5 *Necessary Relations*

In the first Critique Kant connects the a priori with necessity by definition when he says that if we have a proposition "which in being thought is thought as necessary, it is an a priori judgment" (KrV B 4). Necessity is therefore a criterion of a priori knowledge, but this alone does not tell us what necessity consists in. In the logical sense of the term, to be necessary for Kant means to belong to the logical essence of a concept. For if something is part of the logical essence of a concept, it can not be negated without contradiction. This explanation corresponds to the formal definition of necessity Kant gives in his *Lecture on Metaphysics*: Necessary is that of which the contrary is impossible.[33] The formal notion of necessity makes analytic statements always necessarily true, since they are by definition true in virtue of the law of contradiction. Formal necessity and analyticity therefore coincide. Nevertheless, in his critical works Kant is interested mainly in the metaphysical notion

---

32. For a clear statement of the argument see also Kant's preparatory works to the reply to Eberhard, in AA XX, 366 f.
33. *Vorlesungen über die Metaphysik*, AA XXVIII, 556.

of necessity which he calls "real" necessity, i.e. in the question if some things necessarily exist, or if there are propositions (in addition to the analytic ones) that are necessarily true. Within the field of real necessity Kant distinguishes between two types: hypothetical necessity on the one hand (necessity secundum quid a priori), and absolute necessity on the other (simpliciter a priori). To know something in the first sense means to know its truth a priori from concepts which in turn are based in experience (as is the case e.g. with the categories of duration and cause). To know something in the second sense, i.e. absolute necessity, is impossible, since the existence of something can never be known independent of experience. Thus only logical and hypothetical necessity are left. While the former corresponds to the analytic a priori, the latter corresponds to the synthetic a priori. Therefore, formal or logical necessity is at issue with respect to the notion of analyticity, while the question of reality, and metaphysics in general, is out of play.

The conception of logical necessity now seems to lie at the heart of the whole Quinean debate. Why is it that certain concepts have certain characters or attributes necessarily and others arbitrarily? Since we already know that logical necessity is not grounded in the reality of things, the answer can not be, as Quine contended, that some objects have some properties essentially and others accidentally. This would correspond to Eberhard's misunderstanding of Kant's a/s-distinction. On the contrary, concepts have necessary characters and attributes only insofar as those sub-concepts can not be denied of them without contradiction. The three notions of analyticity, necessity and apriority thus boil down to applicability of the law of contradiction. The question remains, why there should be contradiction if not because there are essential properties. Yet the answer is much less exciting then the whole metaphysical terminology suggests.

The most detailed description of what it means to be true in virtue of the law of contradiction, i.e. true with logical necessity, we find in the *Logik Blomberg*. Here Kant describes the logical essence of a concept as "what I think when speaking certain words and connecting them with certain concepts".[34] For instance, with the word "matter" he associates extension, impenetrability, inertness and inanimateness which form the logical essence of the concept matter. However, since the logical essence is to be distinguished from real essence, the concept itself tells us noth-

---

34. *Logik Blomberg*, op.cit. 116.

ing about the reality of matter. Logical essence therefore does not give objectivity but only subjectivity, as Kant constantly suggests in referring to "what we always think". Another person might associate more or less characters with the concept in question. At the same time, our empirical concepts are changeable since experience enlarges our knowledge constantly. Therefore, the logical essence of empirical terms changes as well, for in the course of time our knowledge of a thing will comprise more and more characters. Thus the logical essence of the concept water for Kant already contains the feature that water is 14 times lighter than mercury, since, being educated in physics, this characteristic (he says) was always implied when he made use of the term.

The most perspicuous expression of the matter, however, is not given by Kant himself, but by his disciple Schulze, who defended Kant in the second volume of the *Philosophisches Magazin* against the attacks from the Eberhard School, especially against Maaß' critique of the a/s-distinction. Maaß had criticised the Kantian division as being vague, because one could not tell of any given sentence if it be analytic or synthetic: "one person could think this, another that" under the subject concept. Schulze agreed with this without qualification. He even adds the following example:

> Now, suppose that I find, in a judgement which two philosophers express in the same words, that one of them connects the subject with a rich concept in which the predicate is already contained, while the other, on the other hand, connects it with a concept in which the predicate in question is not contained. I would then be entirely correct in saying that the judgement of the first one is analytic, and of the second one synthetic.[35]

It is thus clear that Kant's repeated definition of analyticity as "what we always think" when using a certain concept, is meant to be taken literally. Predication of a character of a concept, albeit necessary in the logical sense, is neither necessarily true in the real sense of the word nor immune to revision. Analyticity is therefore dependent on the temporary conceptual organisation of our belief system. If we use a concept C in such a way that we always implicitly think it together with the coordinated concept S, denial of S in connection with C is a contradiction, from which it follows that the resulting sentence is analytic. Nevertheless, if the connection between subject and predicate does not only

---

35. Appendix B in Allison 1975, op.cit. 175.

rely on our floating conceptual scheme but can be justified otherwise, e.g. as being founded on pure intuition or the presuppositions of every possible experience, we may formulate synthetic a priori judgements. If the possibility to do the latter is denied, the distinction between analytic and synthetic propositions does not break down, only the task of philosophy shifts from looking for absolute necessity to logical necessity in the Kantian sense. The revisability of the a/s-distinction thus does not lead to slippery-slope-paradoxes, as is often contended in the discussion of semantic holism.[36]

It turns out that the alleged essentialism in the traditional notion of analytic propositions rests on a misunderstanding of the a/s-distinction in Kant. The distinction itself is innocent with respect to any essentialist presuppositions, while the objective necessity of some analytic sentences is due to Kant's system of transcendental idealism, not to the notion of analyticity itself.

5. Conclusion

In his first Critique Kant insisted that his distinction between analytic and synthetic judgements was original and "has never previously been considered". (KrV B 19). His controversy with Eberhard showed clearly why: It was because the analytic-synthetic distinction reduced the typology of propositions in terms of metaphysical content to a distinction within the belief system of the epistemological subject. Therefore, the different versions of analyticity Quine had reconstructed are appropriate with respect to Leibniz and Eberhard, but not with respect to Kant. While Q1 and Q2 only give misleading readings of Kant, the semantic version Q3 corresponds to the Kantian notion only in a restricted sense. It is true that "meanings" to Kant are concepts associated with words; moreover, such concepts can have implications that are not always accessible to our immediate consciousness but are in need of analysis. Nevertheless, those meanings are not metaphysical essences, immune to empirical input and change, and knowable without "looking at the facts". For sure, to know what "bachelor" means we should not only look at real bachelors but analyse the concept. Something about bachelors we will know immediately, something only after thorough

---

36. See Mayer 1997, Ch. I.

analysis, and many details we will not know from pure analysis of concepts but from empirical analysis only. Nevertheless, such details, once detected, may enter in the concept thereby amplifying its scope and making it distinct. Since analytic sentences are not true "in virtue of meanings and independently of facts" but in virtue of conceptual relations within our web of beliefs, the essentialist reading Q4 can not count as an explication of Kant's notion of analyticity either.

For Kant words are only external representatives of concepts, while concepts are logically distinct; therefore, there are no real synonyms. At the same time, identical judgements, i.e. tautologies, can not count as analytic propositions. Thus, a substitution instance of Q5 that is based on synonymy (meaning postulates, semantic rules, and the like) is not analytic. In a certain sense, a sentence like "All bachelors are unmarried men" could be called an analytical definition; however, the epithet "analytical" would exactly block use of the sentence as a means for substitutional deduction. Moreover, since empirical concepts are "infinite" with respect to analysis, no exactly synonymous expression can ever evolve. It should be clear that substitutions of something weaker than synonyms would not work, since merely implicated notions do not even yield true sentences. The (allegedly) analytic statement "All bachelors are unmarried" can not be transposed into "All men are unmarried", although the concept bachelor implies ("contains") the concept man. Thus Q5 and Q6 do not render the Kantian notion of analyticity either.

Analytic propositions in the sense of Kant do not spell out the literal meaning of their subject terms, but are rather similar to Wittgenstein's grammatical sentences in that they elucidate or describe the use of a concept. In the *Enquiry* Kant calls analytic sentences unprovable ("unerweislich"), giving them the role of "material axioms" which are not given simply through "Sprachgefühl" or understanding of meaning. On the contrary, as has been shown, it is possible to use and understand a term correctly without being able to analyse it into its constitutive characters.

Analytic philosophy, while officially at odds with the classical a/s-distinction, in fact fulfils the Kantian program quite literally. Of course, most modern philosophers do not believe in the existence of "concepts of reason" abstracted from the "forms of our judgments", and the idea of space and time as pure forms of intuitions was dropped as well. Thus, they do not believe in the special content of certain synthetic a priori judgements Kant tried to justify by transcendental philosophy. However, they adopted the method of analysis of our concepts with the help of comparison, generalization and abstraction, by thought experiment, logical deduction and rational argument. Thus, the greater part of analytic discussions can be summarized under the Kantian title of "making a concept distinct", while yet another part does what Kant called "making a distinct concept". In this second sense, the sample sentences of Language L mentioned by Carnap in *Meaning and Necessity* are synthetic a priori instead of analytic, and the whole Quinean critique could be seen as being directed against a Fregean disguised notion of synthetic a priori.

From the standpoint of semantic holism, it seems advisable to drop the Kantian conception of synthetic a priori propositions, since it only makes sense where concepts with a fixed logical essence, i.e. concepts of reason, are presupposed. Simultaneously, however, the Carnap/Quine notion of analyticity should be disposed of as presupposing meanings in an essentialist sense. This, however, does not mean to stop the analysis of language or concepts, or to blur the analytic/synthetic distinction. Against the methods of bad metaphysics Kant had developed a pragmatic notion of analytic judgements; this concept of analyticity we should try to restore.

REFERENCES

Allison, Henry E. 1975: *The Kant-Eberhard Controversy*, Baltimore and London.

Allison, Henry E. 1985: "The Originality of Kant's Distinction between Analytic and Synthetic Judgements", in: R. Kennington (Ed.), *The Philosophy of Immanuel Kant, Washington*, 15–38.

Beck, Lewis W. 1965: *Studies in the Philosophy of Kant*, New York.

Beth, Evert W. 1968: *The Foundations of Mathematics*, Amsterdam.

Beth, Evert W. 1956/57: "Über Locke's 'Allgemeines Dreieck'", *Kant-Studien* 48, 361–380.

Carnap, Rudolf 1956: *Meaning and Necessity. A Study in Semantics and Modal Logic*, Chicago.

Fodor, Jerry and Ernest Lepore 1992: *Holism. A Shoppers Guide*, Oxford/Cambridge, Mass.

Frege, Gottlob 1986: *Die Grundlagen der Arithmetik. Eine logisch mathematische Untersuchung über den Begriff der Zahl*, Christian Thiel (Ed.), Hamburg.

Frege, Gottlob 1969: *Nachgelassene Schriften*, Hamburg.

Frege, Gottlob 1976: *Wissenschaftlicher Briefwechsel*, Hamburg.

Garver, Newton 1969: "Analyticity and Grammar", in: *Kant Studies Today*, ed. L.W. Beck, Illinois, 246–248.

Grice, Herbert Paul and Peter F. Strawson 1956: "In Defense of a Dogma", *Philosophical Review*, 141–158.

Jong, Willem R. de 1995: "Kant's Analytic Judgements and the Traditional Theory of Concepts", *Journal of the History of Philosophy* 33, 613–641.

Kant, Immanuel AA: *Kants Werke. Akademie-Textausgabe*, Berlin 1902 f.

Marc-Wogau, Konrad 1951: "Kants Lehre vom analytischen Urteil", *Theoria* 17, 140–157.

Mayer, Verena 1997: *Semantischer Holismus. Eine Einführung*, Berlin.

Quine, Willard Van Orman 1961: "Two Dogmas of Empiricism", in his *From a Logical Point of View*, Cambridge/Mass. 1953 (second, rev. edition), 20–46; first edited in *The Philosophical Review* 60 (1951).

Quine, Willard Van Orman 1998: "Reply to William P. Alston", in: L. E. Hahn and P. A. Schilpp (Eds.), *The Philosophy of W.V.O. Quine*, La Salle, Ill., 73–75.

Peijnenburg, Jeanne 1994: "Formal Proof or Linguistic Process? Beth and Hintikka on Kant's Use of 'Analytic'", *Kant-Studien* 85, 160–178.

Walker, Ralph C. S. 1978: *Kant*, London.

White, Morton 1952: "The Analytic and the Synthetic: An Untenable Dualism", in: L. Linsky (Ed.), *Semantics and the Philosophy of Language*, Urbana, 272–286.

ANALYTIC TRUTHS—
STILL HARMLESS AFTER ALL THESE YEARS?

Christian NIMTZ
Universität Bielefeld

Summary

Hilary Putnam once proposed a semantic approach to, as well as a deflationist resolution of, the problem of analyticity. I take up and defend both ideas. First of all, I defend Putnam's semantic construal of the issue against Quine's reductive understanding. Secondly, I devise a semantics that successfully explains the genesis of the relevant analytic truths and that shows them to be harmless. Finally, I rebut the aspirations of the neo-descriptivist semantics, prominently propounded by David Chalmers and Frank Jackson, that is widely presumed to spearhead the re-establishment of substantial analyticities. I conclude that analytic truths—at least those discussed—are indeed harmless.

1. *"Two Dogmas" and Beyond*

Fifty years ago, Quine's rejection of the analytic-synthetic distinction sparked one of the most passionate disputes in analytic philosophy. However, hardly any contribution to this dispute can match the refreshing originality of Putnam's *The Analytic and the Synthetic*. Published some ten years after *Two Dogmas of Empiricism*, Putnam's paper propounds what amounts to a deflationist attitude towards the issue of analyticity. Arguing that the problem of analyticity is to be understood as one *within* rather than *about* semantics, Putnam claims that Quine is evidently wrong. Some truths are analytic, and some are not. Still, Putnam wholeheartedly endorses the thrust of Quine's case. Putnam believes that a semantic approach lends itself quite naturally to a deflationist resolution of the problem of analyticity. He maintains that once we have provided an adequate semantics, suited to explain the genesis of analytic truths and apt to evaluate their importance, we will see that analytic truths are *harmless*. That is to say, they are trivial and hence ill-suited to play any exceptional epistemological or methodological role. Putnam consequently agrees with Quine on the deep issue: the distinction between analytic and synthetic truths is not a suitable ground to rest one's philosophical position on. The logical positivists assumed otherwise. This is what in the end discredited their stance.

In this paper, I will sort of uphold both of Putnam's contentions. First of all, I explore and defend Putnam's semantic approach to the problem of analyticity. Secondly, I consider Putnam's own attempt to defend his deflationist conclusions. I argue that it fails because Putnam employs a flawed semantics. Thirdly, I provide an adequate semantics and contend that it explains how analytic truths do come about. Finally, I argue that many of the truths effected are indeed harmless, thus sustaining Putnam's deflationist ambitions. This will be the hardest part. For a semantics similar to the one I endorse has recently been the prime vehicle for those who think that substantial analytic truths are the means as well as the aim of philosophy. I rebut these aspirations, prominently propounded by David Chalmers and Frank Jackson. I will conclude that Putnam is right. There are analytic truths, but they are harmless.

However, putting it thus overstates my case. I will neither be concerned with mathematical and logical truths. Nor will I brood over purported analyticities involving concepts such as 'knowledge' or 'freedom'—or, for that matter, 'shadow' or 'table'. Following Putnam, I will concentrate on terms such as 'crow' and 'energy'. Maybe there are informative analyticities involving 'knowledge', and maybe the whole of mathematics is analytic. I doubt this, but I will not sustain this scepticism here. What I will argue is that there are no substantial analytic truths concerning energy, crows, and the like.

2. *Putnam's Approach to the Problem of Analyticity*

Putnam's approach to the issue of analyticity is shaped by two convictions. For one, he is convinced that Quine's rejection of the analytic-synthetic distinction is flawed. Even though he agrees with Quine that it is wrong to think that any sentence is either analytic or synthetic (Putnam 1962, 38 f.), he rebuffs Quine's idea that there are no (non-tautological) analytic truths:

That Quine is wrong I have no doubt. This is not a matter of philosophical argument: it seems to me that there is as gross a distinction between "All bachelors are unmarried" and "There is a book on this table" as between any two things in the world, or, at any rate, between any two linguistic expressions in the world. (Putnam 1962, 36)

We cannot give "All bachelors are unmarried" up unless we were to adopt a new "linguistic convention" (Putnam 1962, 39) for the term 'bachelor' (Putnam 1962, 53, 50). Moreover, "All bachelors are unmarried" is such that "grasp of its meaning *alone* suffices for justified belief in its truth" (Boghossian 1997, 334).[1] From this Putnam concludes that there patently are analytic truths. Consequently, Putnam does not even attempt to discharge the arguments Quine offered in his *Two Dogmas*.[2] He thinks that there is no need to do so.

This bears witness to the fundamentally different perspectives Quine and Putnam take on the issue of analyticity. Quine's argument is clearly intended to be *about* semantics. Quine's rejection of the analytic-synthetic distinction is meant to challenge the very tradition in semantics he should later deride as 'introspective' (Quine 1987, 9) and 'mentalistic' (Quine 1975, 86). In his *Two Dogmas*, Quine puts the core ideas of traditional semantics to the test and finds them wanting; his later argument for the indeterminacy of translation proceeds along similar lines (Quine 1960, ch. 2). Putnam, on the other hand, takes the problem of analyticity to be a problem *within* semantics. He consequently believes that an appeal to our most refined intuitive judgements and to our best semantic theories is a perfectly legitimate means to tackle it.

Even though he holds that there are analytic truths, Putnam still thinks that there is a problem of analyticity. This is his other conviction:

[W]e are in a position of knowing that there is an analytic-synthetic distinction but of not being able to make it very clear just what the nature of this distinction is. (Putnam 1962, 35)

---

1. His conventionalist leanings (cf. Putnam 1962, 39, 68 f.) might make Putnam succumb to the stronger view that "a statement is analytic provided that, in some appropriate sense, it owes its truth-value completely to its meaning, and not at all to 'the facts'"(Boghossian 1997, 334). Since nothing in his argument hinges on this, I will assume that Putnam makes do with the weaker 'epistemological' idea.—For an overview on definitions of 'analyticity', cf. Bealer 1998.

2. For a thorough and critical discussion of Quine's arguments cf. Glock 2003, ch. 3, Boghossian 1997 and, still, Grice/Strawson 1956.

We know that there are analytic truths. But we do not know how they come about, and which role they can play. According to Putnam, this is the problem of analyticity. He believes that all we need to solve it is an adequate semantic theory. The challenge that arises from Quine's critique thus is to provide an adequate semantics that yields the explanation sought, and allows for the evaluation wanted. Given such a semantics, "we should be able to indicate the nature and rationale of the analytic-synthetic distinction" (Putnam 1962, 35). According to Putnam, successfully accomplishing this robust semantic project would in turn dissolve the problem of analyticity. For once we have devised the semantics sought, we will see that analytic truths are harmless.

I take this to be a perfectly warranted approach to the issue of analyticity. Putnam is right: we do not need to meet Quinean strictures to convincingly justify the claim that there are analytic sentences. We evidently are able to consistently classify sentences from an open class with respect to their fundamental semantic properties (Grice/Strawson 1956, 142 f.; Searle 1969, ch. 1.2; Glock 2003, ch. 3). We all do agree that, say, "Bachelors are unmarried" falls into one category, and "Snow is beautiful" into another. This robust ability gives us sufficient reason to maintain that some truths are analytic, and some are not.

Quine is not impressed. He will not admit that there is a distinction to be drawn unless we define 'analytic' in extensional terms (Quine 1951), or explain 'analytic' relying exclusively on a behaviouristic naturalism (Quine 1960, ch. 1–2). The former cannot be done, and the latter will not work. But this does not undercut the argument given. It rather warrants the charge that Quine assumes incoherent standards of explication (Glock 2003, ch. 3), that he relies on a parochially narrow understanding of 'naturalism' (Nimtz 2002, 156–165), and that he forgets about his own naturalistic standards for the acceptance of theoretical terms (Sober 2000). Hence, Putnam is right. The task is not to determine whether there are analytic truths. The task is to explain how they come about.

One might still want to hold that a satisfactory explanation of analyticity must reveal how analyticity is constituted by non-semantic properties.[3] It for sure would be nice to have such an explanation. However, if our account happens to be enlightening as well as projectible, and if it employs only the well-tested notions of established semantics, it does

---

3. This idea shapes Quine's approach to reference, cf. Nimtz (2002), esp. ch. 3 and 4.

what we want: it explains how analytic truths do come about. The fact that it falls short of providing a reductive explanation does not undercut its explanatory import (Grice/Strawson 1956, 148–151). Again, if all we want is to understand how analytic truths do come about, there is no need to prop up our explanation with a naturalistic reconstruction of semantic categories. That is to say, the task is to *semantically* explain how analytic truths come about.

I will thus take up Putnam's approach to the problem of analyticity. Taking it for granted that there are analytic truths, I will seek a semantics that provides an explanation of their genesis and an evaluation of their importance. The latter is very much at the heart of the debate about analyticity. Hardly anyone ponders this issue out of an interest for semantic taxonomy. Most who do rather want to know whether certain sentences can play an exceptional epistemological and methodological role simply in virtue of their semantic properties. This is the deep issue behind the problem of analyticity. Quine's rejection of the analytic-synthetic distinction was specifically intended to maintain that there are no such sentences. We have already seen that this rejection is flawed. However, this fact merely reflects Quine's infelicitous perspective on things. The deep issue is not whether there are analytic truths. The deep issue rather is whether the analytic truths there are can play the role alluded to, and hence whether "there are (…) analyticities that cannot be discovered by the lexicographer or the linguist but only by the philosopher" (Putnam 1962, 36 f.). Putnam maintains that there are none of those. This is precisely what his deflationist resolution consists in.

This identification of the deep issue allows us to resolve a puzzle put forth by Boghossian (Boghossian 1997, 331 f.). Most philosophers reject Quine's idea that translation is indeterminate. They hold that there are facts about meaning as well as sameness of meaning. They nevertheless voice agreement with Quine's claim that there is no analytic-synthetic distinction. This might appear incoherent. However, I do not think it is. The professed agreement with Quine on the analytic-synthetic distinction is to be understood as an agreement on the deep issue. What most philosophers do reject is the idea that there are sentences suited to play an exceptional epistemological or methodological role simply in virtue of their semantic properties—and *this* view does not oblige them to deny that some truths are analytic, and some are not.

3. Putnam's "The Analytic and the Synthetic"

Poised to carry out his deflationist agenda, Putnam devises a semantics he expects to yield an explanation of analyticity and to allow for an evaluation of the importance of analytic truths. The semantics Putnam offers is a version of descriptivism. It pivots on the ideas that meaning determines reference, that meaning is given by a body of knowledge, and that the respective body is typically constituted by an inferential network. Putnam embraces the following principles (Putnam 1962, 50–54):

(1) Typical ordinary general terms such as 'crow' are cluster terms. Their meaning is constituted by a cluster of properties governing the application of the term.
(2) Typical general terms that figure in advanced scientific theories such as 'energy' are law cluster concepts. Their meaning is constituted by a cluster of laws governing the application of the concepts.

Putnam uses the latter principle to argue that ordinary scientific statements are very unlikely to be analytic. Statements that contain law cluster terms are, he claims, not immune to revision. For within the cluster that determines the meaning of the concept, "any one law can be abandoned without destroying the identity of the law cluster concept involved" (Putnam 1962, 52). Since the statements and laws of an advanced science will typically contain law cluster terms and since analytic statements are those "that a rational man must hold immune from revision" (Putnam 1962, 50), Putnam infers that statements such as "$f = ma$" or "$e = \frac{1}{2} mv^2$" are not analytic. By parity of reason, we may conclude that analyticity does not affect large parts of ordinary discourse either. Many ordinary general terms are cluster-terms. Since the statements that make up these clusters are not immune to revision either, it follows that sentences containing these terms, too, will not be analytic.

The principles mentioned are meant to explain how analytic truths do not arise. Putnam's explanation as to how these truths do arise rests on another descriptivist idea:

(3) General terms such as 'bachelor' are one-criterion words. Their meaning is constituted by a cluster that contains just a single property governing the application of the term.[4]

The network that determines the meaning of a one-criterion-word F comprises just a single statement, predicating of F the single criterion for its application. That is to say, it predicates of F those necessary and sufficient conditions for something's being an F that are such that people can and do use them to determine whether something happens to be an F (Putnam 1962, 67). This is what is done, for example, in "All bachelors are unmarried men". Any such statement will consequently be analytic. Since it states *the only* criterion for the application of the term in question, we cannot give it up if we want to hold on to the term's established use. However, any such statement will be rather trivial indeed. It will be immediately recognised as true by every competent speaker, and since the only strict implication F is involved in is the statement we are concerned with, it will have hardly any "systematic import" (Putnam 1962, 39) at all.

Putnam's descriptivist semantics thus provides a straightforward explanation of analyticity: analytic truths arise by way of one-criterion words. More precisely, "the exceptionless principle that provides the criterion governing a one-criterion concept [is] analytic" (Putnam 1962, 68). (At least, this is how basic analytic truths arise. All implications of these truths are analytic as well). At the same time, Putnam's analysis implies that terms whose meanings are constituted by rich networks do not give rise to analytic truths—analyticity arises *exclusively* by way of one-criterion words. Since one-criterion words do not give rise to informative statements, it follows that all analytic truths are harmless. Putnam's account thus sustains his deflationist ambitions: analytic truths are trivial and hence ill-suited to play a prominent epistemological or methodological role.

His discussion inspires Putnam to give us a piece of methodological advice: just ignore the analytic-synthetic distinction. For if you do not, you will consistently be wrong (Putnam 1962, 36). The proper way to proceed is *as if* there was no such distinction at all. Quine thus is right on the deep issues pertaining to the analytic-synthetic distinction. It hence is hardly surprising that Quine has nothing but praise

---

4. Or very few properties. I will ignore this complication.

for Putnam's account (Quine 1986, 427). Quine moreover emphasises that his own analysis of analyticity in *The Roots of Reference* proceeds along Putnamian lines. He there maintains that a sentence is analytic "if everybody learns that it is true by learning its words" (Quine 1973, 79). This is precisely what is true of a sentence predicating a criterion of the one-criterion word it governs.

4. *The Quest for an Adequate Semantics*

Putnam's doctrine of one-criterion words offers a convincing semantic explanation for humdrum analyticities. Putnam's argument from law cluster-terms is less compelling. For one, Putnam combines two ideas that do not sit easily with one another. On the one hand, he holds that the meaning of a law-term F is determined by the cluster of laws L_1, ..., L_n the term figures in. On the other hand, Putnam maintains that we can give up any one law in F's cluster without changing the meaning of F. It is very hard to see how both claims can be true. If a law-term's F meaning is determined by $L_1, ..., L_n$, dropping, say, L_7 will plausibly lead to a change in intension and hence in the meaning of F. If it didn't, there might be good reasons to conclude that L_7 does not contribute to F's meaning after all and that it is at least misleading to say that F's meaning is determined by $L_1, ..., L_n$ rather than by $L_1, ..., L_n$ *minus* L_7 to begin with. What is more, Putnam's account evidently yields an analytic truth that is far from trivial. Given that F's meaning is determined by the laws $L_1, ..., L_n$, it follows that, necessarily, something is F if and only if it satisfies $L_1, ..., L_n$. Thus Putnam's account does not live up to its deflationist aspirations.

One might be tempted to conclude that there are substantial analytic truths, and that deflationism is flawed after all. I would like to propose a rather different diagnosis: Putnam simply relies on an inadequate semantics. His descriptivism provides a flawed account for terms such as 'crow' and 'energy'. Putnam's deflationist claims thus remain so far unscathed. We can still cling to the idea that once we have devised an adequate semantics suited to explain the genesis and allowing for an evaluation of analytic truths, we will see that these truths are harmless. All we now need is a convincing semantic theory. So let me briefly ponder the question what an adequate semantics for some natural language would have to be.

Ignoring questions of force (Dummett 1976, 73 ff., Davies 1981, ch. 1) as well as communication (Grice 1987) and concentrating on austere accounts of literal meaning, it is plausible to maintain that any adequate semantics for some natural language has at least to get the truth-conditions of the sentences and utterances of that language right (Nimtz 2002, 30–61). Assuming that truth-conditions can be equated with intensions and taking into account the fact that a sentence's truth-conditions allow of a compositional analysis in terms of the semantic values of its parts, any adequate semantics is moreover bound to specify the semantic values of words in such a way as to account for the intensions of sentences or utterances, respectively. In so doing, it has to respect further strictures arising from various characteristics of natural languages. Let me highlight three of those. First of all, the semantic values of indexicals such as 'I' and demonstratives such as 'that F' vary systematically with the contexts these expressions are employed in; a kindred variety of context-dependence might affect shape-predicates such as 'is triangular' and relational expressions such as 'is in Reykjavik'. Secondly, we are intuitively pretty sure that 'Amundsen' would not have designated Wisting, even if the latter had in fact been the first to arrive at the South Pole; and we are pretty sure that any utterance of "It's necessary that I am here" is false, even though any utterance of "I am here" must be true. Thirdly, natural languages are spoken by ordinary people like you and me who are neither particle physicists nor ornithologists. We nevertheless are competent users of terms such as 'electron' or 'robin'.

An adequate semantics thus has to assign semantic values in a way that accounts for the phenomenon of context-dependence, squares with our modal intuitions, and respects the fact that one can be a competent speaker even though one does not know all that much. Putnam's vintage 1960s descriptivism apparently fails on all three counts. As Putnam himself later was keen to point out, this variety of descriptivism does not respect our modal intuitions, and it burdens the competent speaker with a load of knowledge that she plausibly will not have (Putnam 1975, Kripke 1980). I will come back to both points in due course. Taken together with Kaplan's arguments designed to show that indexicals are not simply synonymous with descriptions (Kaplan 1977, 497), we have to conclude that Putnam's descriptivism is in fact a flawed semantics.

We consequently are in need of an adequate semantic theory. I am inclined to think that there is an obvious candidate to fill the slot. For want of a better name, I will call it 'sophisticated Kripkeanism'. This semantics is on the one hand emphatically Kripkean. It employs talk of 'possible worlds' to model truth-conditions and other intensions, and it vigorously embraces the general account to be found in Kripke, Putnam and Kaplan as to how intensions are determined. On the other hand, sophisticated Kripkeanism transcends the Kripkean layout. For it combines the ideas mentioned with a Kaplan-Stalnaker-style two-dimensional framework designed to accommodate context-dependence (Putnam 1975, Kaplan 1977, Kaplan 1989, Kripke 1980, Stalnaker 1978, Stalnaker 1999, Lewis 1981). I will deal with these points in reverse order.

Imagine Jørgensen pointing to a row of sleek black snowmobiles and uttering "I want one of those". Let us make the plausible assumption that she thereby says *that Jørgensen wants a 2003 Yamaha snowmobile*. She evidently does so partly because the sentence she utters means what it does, and partly because the context she utters the sentence in is as it is. If we want a lucid model of the dependencies involved, we have to make two distinctions. On the one hand, we have to distinguish the content of an expression as uttered in a context from the context-invariant content of the expression-type involved. Call the former content a *secondary* and the latter a *primary intension*. Primary intensions determine secondary intensions. That is to say, if taken together with a context c, the primary intension of an expression(-type) determines the secondary intension expressed by an utterance of that type as made in c.[5] Given that she happens to stand in front of 2003 Yamaha snowmobiles, the primary intension of "I want one of those" determines that Jørgensen expresses the secondary intension *that Jørgensen wants a 2003 Yamaha snowmobile*. If she had been in a different context, the secondary intension expressed would have been different. Whereas a sentence(-type) thus is taken to have a single and unchanging primary intension, it gets assigned one secondary intension for each context it is uttered in.

---

5. That's not quite right. Since the primary intension of an expression e yields a mere extension for a context c, you need additional rules determining how the intension of e as uttered in c depends on that expression's extension in c to fix the expression's secondary intension. These rules will plausibly drawn on well-entrenched pragmatic delineations such as the referential/attributive distinction. I will, however, ignore this complication and stick to the simplified account given.

On the other hand, we have to distinguish two roles played by possible worlds. Centred possible worlds—i.e. worlds with a region and a speaker highlighted—figure as contexts an utterance is made in, and non-centred possible worlds are employed to spell out what is expressed by such an utterance. Call centred worlds playing the former role *contexts*, and call worlds playing the latter role *indices*. Given the context of her utterance, Jørgensen expresses a secondary intension that is true at any index in which Jørgensen wants a 2003 Yamaha snowmobile. This allows us to devise model-theoretic representations for the two kinds of contents involved. A primary intension can be modelled as a function f_1: $w_c \to e$ from contexts to extensions, whereas a secondary intension must be represented by a function f_2: $w_i \to e$ from indices to extensions.[6]

The two-dimensional framework provides a versatile tool to accommodate context-dependence within a possible worlds semantics. But it remains an empty structure unless it is married to a substantial doctrine. This doctrine, *not* the two-dimensional structure it is embedded in, makes up the core of the semantics. As mentioned, the core of sophisticated Kripkeanism consists in the account to be found in Kripke, Putnam and Kaplan. It pivots on three ideas. First of all, there is Kripke's idea of *rigid designation* (Kripke 1980, lecture 1). Kripke argues that names such as 'Samuel Clemens' or kind terms such as 'gold' designate rigidly—they pick out one and the same individual or substance, respectively, in all possible worlds. The fact that some of our terms are rigid designators implies that some of our true identity statements are necessarily true. Given that the terms involved are rigid designators, it follows that "Samuel Clemens = Mark Twain" and "Gold = the element with the atomic number 79" are true in all possible worlds.

Secondly, there is Kaplan's idea of *direct reference* (Kaplan 1977, 497, ibid., 483). It is best understood thus: an expression is directly referential if all it contributes to the intension expressed is the item it picks out (Kaplan 1977, 497). Think of Jørgensen uttering, "I want one of those". The term 'I' she employed most certainly means something like 'the speaker'. But if Kaplan is right, this descriptive meaning does not contribute to what Jørgensen says. What figures in what she says rather is the person this descriptive content picks out in the context

---

6. These representations are not to be mistaken for the contents they model; meanings or contents *for sure* are not model-theoretic entities.—Cf. previous footnote.

she utters her sentence in. The content she expresses is *that Jørgensen wants a 2003 Yamaha snowmobile*. She does not assert *that the speaker wants a 2003 Yamaha snowmobile*.

The third idea is due to Putnam (Putnam 1975). Putnam argues that for a substantial number of predicates F, neither the knowledge a competent user of F is rightly expected to have nor those aspects of its use transparent to the linguistic community suffice to fix F's semantic value. Take the term 'tiger'. According to Putnam, it applies to something x if and only if x is of the same kind as—has the same genetic micro-structure as—the paradigmatic items we employ in introducing the term. This account generalises: for many predicates F it holds that what determines F's intension is an object-anchoring, i.e. a set of paradigmatic items and a suitable sameness-relation. Which entities are relevantly similar to the paradigmatic items will in many cases depend on non-obvious properties of the things involved—whether Shahir really is a tiger does not depend on his black stripes and yellowish fur, but rather on his genetic pawprint. It hence is hardly surprising that the semantic values of many predicates outrun our knowledge-cum-transparent-use. For we have to do empirical research uncovering the non-obvious properties in order to determine what they apply to.

5. *Deflationism Revamped*

Sophisticated Kripkeanism assigns semantic values—truth-conditions, intensions, extensions—in a way that accounts for context-dependence, that squares with our modal intuitions, and that respects the fact that one can be a competent speaker even though one does not know all that much. In fact, it has been tailor-made to do so. Hence, there is every reason to believe that sophisticated Kripkeanism in fact is an adequate semantics. Sophisticated Kripkeanism moreover yields an explanation as to how analytic truths arise, and it provides an evaluation of their importance that supports the main contention of deflationism. This is what I am going to argue now.

Sophisticated Kripkeanism comes with an assumption about semantic competence. It is taken for granted that a competent speaker must have grasped the primary intensions of the expressions she uses. She will thereby get to know many secondary intensions. For, in all cases where what is said does not vary with the context, primary and secondary intensions coincide, effecting precisely the same function from worlds to extensions. Anyone who has grasped the primary intension of, say, "Grandmothers are lovely" will know the secondary intension assigned to any utterance of this sentence. This does not hold for, say, "I want one of those". You will not grasp the secondary intension of such an utterance unless you are informed about the non-linguistic aspects of the context it is made in. Consequently, if a sentence is such that "grasp of its meaning *alone* suffices for justified belief in its truth" (Boghossian 1997, 334), this will inevitably be due to one's grasp of its primary intension. Any explanation as to how analytic truths come about can hence focus on primary intensions. Since analyticity as explained is an overtly epistemic category, we have to hook up the semantic apparatus outlined with a suitable epistemology—we have to explore *what it is to know or grasp a primary intension*. I fear that, on Kripkean premises, such an exploration does not yield a uniform account. It rather appears that we have to distinguish three different basic cases, each concerning a specific category of terms and pivoting on a specific way of grasping a primary intension.

First of all, spelling out the primary intensions of some of our terms comes down to specifying a context-insensitive or, as I will call them, *pure* description[7]. For instance, we can spell out the primary intension of 'grandmother' thus: 'grandmother' applies to something x in a context c iff x is a female parent of a parent. Anyone who grasps the primary intension of 'grandmother' must know this. Consequently, any competent speaker will know that "Grandmothers are female" is true simply in virtue of having grasped the term's primary intension. This case smoothly generalises. Anyone who understands an expression F whose primary intension is given by a pure description knows that the extension of that expression in a context c is whatever satisfies the description. Consequently, if *being G* is part of the primary intension of F as captured by a pure description, any competent speaker will know that "All F are G" is true. This yields our first partial explanation as to how analytic sentences arise:

(4) "All F are G" is analytic if *being G* is a vital part of the primary intension of F as captured by a pure description D.

---

7. Or, if you prefer: context-insensitive conditions of application for the term in question.

In fact, any speaker who understands an expression F whose primary intension is captured by a pure description containing *being G* will know that "All F are G" is a context-invariant necessity. "Grandmothers are female" is not only true in any context it is uttered in. Any utterance of this sentence will moreover express a secondary intension that is true at all indices, and a competent speaker must know this.

Let me add that it is immaterial how rich the description D might be. D could comprise just a single property. This is why "Bachelors are unmarried" comes out analytic. Our explanation thus accords with Putnam's analysis of one-criterion words. However, D could also comprise a whole theory. This is why we have to admit that "Crows are birds" comes out analytic if we, against better judgment, assume that the meaning of 'crow' is determined by a suitable inferential network. This suggests a diagnosis as to why Putnam's account is flawed. Putnam holds that the meaning of *both* 'bachelor' and 'crow' are determined by networks or theories. The only difference between those cases is that the one theory is simple, and the other complex. But it is not obvious that a mere difference in complexity can yield a difference in categorical semantic properties. What is needed might rather be a difference in kind.

As for the second case, spelling out the primary intensions of some of our terms comes down to specifying context-sensitive descriptions. For instance, we can spell out the primary intension of 'I' thus: 'I' applies to something x in a context c iff x is the speaker in context c. This is what a competent user of 'I' must know. Generalising, we can say that anyone who understands an expression whose primary intension is given by a context-sensitive description knows that the extension of that expression in a context c is whatever fills a certain context-specific role in c (Strawson 1950, Perry 1998). Any competent user of 'I' and 'here' knows that 'I' picks out whoever plays the speaker-role in c, and that 'here' picks out the position that fills the role 'being the location of this utterance' in c. This yields another partial explanation of analyticity:

(5) "F is G" is analytic if *being G* is part of context-specific role associated with F.

There are three points to be noted. First of all, role terms give rise to analyticities that are more complex than those captured by (5). The most prominent example is "I am here now". Secondly, indexicals and demonstratives are by no means the only role terms we employ. Think of 'the secretary general of the UN' or 'the home team'. These role terms yield analytic truths. Just consider "The home team plays at its own pitch".

Finally, the knowledge someone acquires by grasping the primary intension of a role term contrasts sharply with knowledge of the "Grandmothers are female"-variety. On the one hand, what is known to be true are utterances rather than sentence-types. Having grasped the primary intension of 'here', I know that any utterance of "Here is the location of this utterance" will be true. Yet I do not even assign a truth-value to this sentence-type. On the other hand, what one of these utterances expresses will typically be a contingent rather than a necessary truth. Since they usually refer directly and designate rigidly, role terms mostly contribute the items they pick out in the context they are uttered in to the secondary intension expressed, and these items will not vary with the respective indices. This yields room for contingency. For example, what Amundsen expressed by uttering "Now I am here!" on December 14th, 1911 at the South Pole was *that Amundsen is at the South Pole on December 14th 1911*. This is not necessarily true. There are worlds in which Amundsen made it to the Pole long after Scott got there on January 18th, 1912.

There is a third case we have to consider. For some of our terms, spelling out their primary intension comes down to specifying an object-anchoring. For instance, we can spell out the primary intension of 'tiger' along the lines already indicated: 'tiger' applies to something x in a context c iff x is of the same kind as the paradigmatic items we used to introduce the term 'tiger'. Ignoring deference and idealizing rather heavily, we may assume that a competent user of 'tiger' must somehow know this. Consequently, any competent speaker will somehow know that tigers are of the same kind as the paradigmatic items anchoring the intension of 'tiger' simply in virtue of having grasped the primary intension of 'tiger'. Moreover, even if we assume that any competent speaker must know a true instance of the scheme "Tigers are of the same kind as the Gs", where the description 'the Gs' picks out the respective paradigmatic items, we have to admit that the instances known to be true might vary wildly. Since the extension of 'tiger' is not affected by the way the paradigmatic items are identified, a speaker might employ any identifying description of these items she likes. Hence, you do not need to know that "Tigers are of the same kind as the whitish catlike animals owned by Siegfried and Roy" in order to be a competent speaker. But someone's grasp of the term's primary intension might rest precisely on this piece of information.

If we agree that a sentence can be analytic only if everyone who grasps its primary intension will know it to be true, terms whose primary intension are object-anchored do not yield any interesting analytic truths at all. The only analytic truths seems to be this:

(6) "*F*s are of the same kind as the paradigmatic items anchoring the intension of '*F*'" is analytic if *F*s primary intension is determined by an object-anchoring.

This is almost as trivial as "Oblique things are those 'oblique' applies to". There is a reason for this. The intension of 'tiger' is determined externally—it depends on the animals involved. *This in turn makes the semantic and epistemic properties of the relevant sentences come apart.* Given that our use of 'tiger' is anchored in animals with the DNA sequence *t*, "Tigers have DNA sequence *t*" is true in all contexts. Moreover, given that natural kind terms are rigid designators, any utterances of "Tigers have DNA sequence *t*" expresses a necessary truth. Yet you will not know any of this simply in virtue of having grasped the primary intension of 'tiger'. Your knowledge will be exhausted by (6) together with an instance of the scheme "Tigers are of the same kind as the *G*s". Therefore, unless you do empirical research and find out that the *G*s have DNA sequence *t*, you will not know that "Tigers have DNA sequence *t*" has a necessary primary as well as a necessary secondary intension—even though it does.

On sophisticated Kripkean premises, understanding a term consists in grasping its primary intension. This grasp may amount to associating it with a description, a context-sensitive role, or an anchoring, depending on the kind of term involved. In each case you will learn some truths simply by improving your semantic competence. This is why any competent speaker will know that bachelors are unmarried, or that the home team plays at its own pitch, or that tigers are of the same kind as those items anchoring the use of 'tiger'. It should be obvious that none of this forces us to admit that there are substantial analytic truths about, say, energy, electrons, crows, and polar bears. For the intensions of these terms are best understood to be of the object-anchored type. Grasp of their primary intension amounts to no more than knowing that they are so anchored, and this yields exclusively analytic truths that are trivial and hence ill-suited to play any prominent epistemological or methodological role. All analyticities concerning energy, electrons, crows, and polar bears hence are utterly harmless.

All this makes it plain to see why Putnam's 1960s descriptivism provides a flawed semantics for law terms. Putnam assumes that the meaning of, say, 'polar bear' is encapsulated in a rich description D which in turn is determined by our overall theory of polar bears. Since pure descriptions hold in all contexts and at all indices, this implies that, say, "Polar bears have a thick white coat" states a necessary truth. This manifestly violates our modal intuitions. Worse still, it implies that any competent speaker must know a lot about polar bears. In fact, she must know that polar bears satisfy D. Yet it is implausible that a competent speaker will have such extensive knowledge about the animals involved. This yields a second diagnosis as to why Putnam's account is flawed: he misclassified the respective terms. Expressions such as 'energy', 'crow', and 'polar bear' are object-anchored terms, whereas Putnam took them to be purely descriptive expressions. That is hardly surprising. For given that his semantics was all-out descriptivist, he did not have a choice.

6. *The Neo-Descriptivists' Challenge*

Sophisticated Kripkeanism is a state-of-the-art semantics that allows to explain and evaluate analytic truths. Since it holds that the primary intensions of 'energy', 'electron', 'crow', and 'polar bear' are determined by object-anchorings and that all resulting analyticities must be trivial, it moreover underscores Putnam's deflationism. However, sophisticated Kripkeanism is neither the only nor the most popular state-of-the-art semantics. Frank Jackson and David Chalmers have recently devised a well-received semantic theory that I call 'neo-descriptivism' (Chalmers 1996, ch. 2, Jackson 1998a, ch. 2, Chalmers forthcoming a, Chalmers & Jackson 2001). Neo-descriptivism is suited to explain and evaluate analytic truths, but it apparently undercuts rather than underscores the deflationist programme (Jackson 1998a). For neo-descriptivism implies that the truths someone gets to know by way of grasping the primary intensions of 'energy' or 'polar bear' are substantial rather than trivial. This poses a serious challenge to the deflationist attitude I promised to defend. In the remainder of this paper, I will strive to rebut it.

On the face of it, neo-descriptivism and sophisticated Kripkeanism are fairly similar semantic accounts. Both comprise a two-dimensional possible worlds framework, and both rely on a distinction between primary and secondary intensions. However, the two semantics are driven by rather different doctrines. Sophisticated Kripkeans adopt a two-dimensional framework to account for humdrum context-dependence. They think of contexts as just that—possible environments for utterances. Neo-descriptivists, on the other hand, employ the two-dimensional structure to model the epistemic or conceptual abilities they assume to underlie our understanding (Chalmers forthcoming a, 16). Neo-descriptivists assume that someone's conceptual abilities can be gauged from his willingness to assign extensions to terms in 'worlds considered as actual' or 'epistemic possibilities', that is 'specific way[s] the actual world might turn out to be, for all one can know a priori' (Chalmers & Jackson 2001, 324; cf. Chalmers 2002, § 3.1) They go on to identify what I have called 'contexts' with *possibilia* of this kind, and they consequently understand primary intensions to be purely conceptual contents that yield extensions for epistemic possibilities. Still, they agree that these primary intensions in turn yield rather ordinary secondary intensions.[8]

In the end, however, it is not the changed perspective on the framework that leads neo-descriptivists to hold that there are numerous substantial analyticities concerning kinds. The reason for this is rather that neo-descriptivists take 'electron', 'gold', and 'polar bear' to be *role terms*. They hold that understanding these terms amounts to grasping complex roles encapsulating epistemic or conceptual knowledge concerning the kinds in question (Jackson 1998a, ch. 2). For instance, neo-descriptivists believe that grasping the primary intension of 'gold' amounts to knowing that 'gold' applies to whatever fills the gold role in a world considered as actual. That is to say, it applies to the malleable, yellowish etc. metal we are acquainted with in the world under scrutiny. On the neo-descriptivist picture, then, "Gold is a malleable, yellowish metal" comes out analytic. So presumably does "Polar bears have thick white coats".

---

8. For a more detailed discussion of these differences—as well as some other arguments against neo-descriptivism—cf. Nimtz (2004).

Neo-descriptivists admit that Putnam was wrong to employ a simple descriptivist semantics for kind terms. They even agree that 'electron' and 'polar bear' designate rigidly and refer directly. Neo-descriptivism can thus account for the modal intuitions classical descriptivism foundered on. However, neo-descriptivists believe that for any law-term F, there is an associated F-role determining F's extension in any world considered as actual; and they hold that any competent speaker will know that "F is G" must be true whenever uttered, given that *being G* is part of the F-role. This lets them conclude that there are substantial analytic truths involving law terms.

To be sure, our language *could* work this way. But I will argue that it does not. More precisely, I will argue that neo-descriptivism is subject to the second flaw diagnosed in Putnam's descriptivism: it makes wildly implausible assumptions about what competent speakers do know. Neo-descriptivists might get the modal properties right. Their semantics correctly implies that no utterance of "Polar bears have thick white coats" will be necessarily true. But they do get the epistemic properties wrong. Their semantics still implies that you will know that polar bears have thick white coats simply in virtue of having grasped the meaning of 'polar bear'.

7. *The Argument from Ignorance*[9]

Neo-descriptivists maintain that anyone who understands a law term must have grasped the role associated with it. It follows that any competent speaker is bound to know quite a lot about the role the respective kinds are presumed to play. At first sight, this appears to be nothing to worry about. Most of us will know that gold is a malleable and very valuable metal, that it is in most cases yellowish, and that large quantities of it are stored in Fort Knox. Moreover, we expect the members of our community to possess such knowledge. This is precisely what neo-descriptivism predicts.

However, a closer look reveals that the neo-descriptivist epistemology runs into trouble. To begin with, we do not need to assume that

---

9. The general thrust of this argument is well-known. Cf. Devitt/Sterelny 1987, 46 ff. and Jackson 1998c, 208 ff. However, note that I am concerned with *primary* intensions rather than with common descriptions. This makes things rather different.

speakers have conceptual knowledge to account for our expectations. We quite naturally presuppose that the members of our community know certain facts about the world. For instance, we quite naturally presuppose that they know that Reykjavik is the capital of Iceland, or that Amundsen beat Scott to the South Pole. Hence, it is not at all puzzling that we expect them to know that gold is a mostly yellowish metal, even if they do not have to know this in order to be competent speakers. This explanation squares better with our actual behaviour than the one provided by neo-descriptivism. Just think of the way we treat the local ignoramus. We do not assume that his mastery of the English language is impaired because he neither knows that electrons have a charge nor that they have a spin. Still, if he tells us that electrons have 1/1800 the mass of hydrogen atoms, we will add this to our beliefs about electrons.

Secondly, neo-descriptivism's contention that understanding a kind term presupposes grasping a descriptive role conflicts with an observation emphasised by the proponents of externalist accounts: actual competent speakers do not know much about kinds. This might go unnoticed as long as we are concerned with water, gold, or tigers. But if we think about, say, magnesium or tapirs, this becomes obvious. To be sure, almost everybody will know something about the metal and the animal in question, e.g. that magnesium is used in flares or that tapirs are four-legged animals with trunks. Yet almost nobody will be able to come up with an account that is rich enough to determine credible roles for the terms. As neo-descriptivists maintain, such a role has to be purely qualitative. It hence is not allowed to contain pieces of non-qualitative identifying knowledge some of us might possess, e.g., "Gold is the stuff my wedding ring is made of". What is more, such an account would have to be rich enough to single out all and only the gold in all possible worlds considered as actual. But it is unlikely that any purely qualitative account an ordinary speaker can come up with would even single out the gold in our world.

Finally, neo-descriptivism's epistemology cannot deal with speakers who endorse eccentric theories about kinds. Imagine John to believe that gold is actually a radioactive mineral from outer space, a fact most people are ignorant of since our governments are desperate to cover it up. If John now asserts "The US keep their gold in Fort Knox for good reasons", neo-descriptivists have to deny that he just claimed that the US keep their gold in Fort Knox for good reasons. For the primary intension determined by his understanding and the primary intension determined by our account are very different indeed. They for sure do not pick out the same stuff in our world—on neo-descriptivist premises, our term 'gold' might very well pick out some of the gold that happens to be around, whereas John's term has an empty extension. However, it seems to be fairly obvious that we can and of course would disagree with John's bizarre theory. But that presupposes that our term 'gold' has at least roughly the same reference as John's term 'gold'. On neo-descriptivist premises, this cannot be the case.

8. *The Argument from Subjectivity*

Neo-descriptivists believe that these arguments do not affect their stance. For they acknowledge that different speakers might very well assign *different* roles to, and hence associate *different* primary intensions with, one and the same natural kind term (Chalmers & Jackson 2001, 327, Chalmers forthcoming a, 32, Chalmers forthcoming b, 30). They even hold that these intensions might be *very* different indeed: you, being a city-dweller who knows nothing of oceans, might use 'water' non-deferentially for the liquid that comes out of faucets, whereas I, being a beach-dweller who knows nothing of faucets, might use 'water' non-deferentially for the liquid in the oceans (Chalmers & Jackson 2001, 328). The variability of primary intensions does not, they argue, undercut successful communication, and it does not forestall disagreement, since both can be grounded in the common referent (Chalmers forthcoming b, 32).

This is hardly a convincing response, though. On the one hand, it does nothing to solve the problem of eccentric primary intensions. On neo-descriptivist premises, a term's primary intension is what determines the term's referent: 'gold' applies to whatever satisfies the role associated with it. But if that is so, there is no common referent that could ground disagreement between John and us, since there just is nothing that satisfies the eccentric role he propounds. On the other hand, acknowledging variability trades a serious problem for a very serious one. For, as neo-descriptivists admit, if primary intensions are subject-relative, so are *analytic truths* (cf. Chalmers & Jackson 2001, 327; Chalmers forthcoming b, 30)—some sentences might be analytic for me, but not for you. I admit that I find it very hard to make sense of this, which is why I have assumed above that a sentence is analytic only if everyone who grasps its primary intension will know it to be true. However, let us assume for a moment that a sentence might be analytic for you but not for me. Yet if that is so, what is it for a sentence *s* to be *analytic simpliciter*?

Firstly, one could hold that a sentence *s* is *analytic simpliciter* if it is analytic for some speaker in our community (Chalmers forthcoming a, 20). That, however, will yield far too many analyticities. For if *P* describes a procedure to successfully identify an instance of a natural kind *n*, there might be a speaker in our community for whom it is analytic that *n* satisfies *P*. For instance, there might be speakers who can, without recourse to experience, justify that alligators are dangerous or that water flows from faucets, since this is just how they non-deferentially use 'alligator' and 'water', respectively. Secondly, one could hold that a sentence *s* is analytic *simpliciter* if it is analytic "for any given subject and time in our community" (Chalmers & Jackson 2001, 320).[10] This evidently yields too few analytic truths. For if primary intensions are allowed to vary as outlined, it is almost certain that for many purportedly analytic sentence *s*, there will be a speaker in our community who will not know that *s* is true simply by grasping its primary intension. Thirdly, one could maintain that *s* is analytic *simpliciter* if and only it is analytic for a speaker 'given ideal rational reflection' (Chalmers forthcoming b, 30). But it is hard to see how improved rational powers can change anything. For instance, assume that I am the beach-dweller mentioned above. For me, the only analytic truth about water is that water is the liquid in the oceans. I cannot see how improved powers of rational reflection could possibly lead me to richer—and intuitively more accurate—conceptual truths about water. For this I do rather need to improve my knowledge.

The neo-descriptivist manoeuvre hence does not solve the problem of ignorance. I guess that this adds to the appeal of sophisticated Kripkeanism. Allowing variability leads neo-descriptivists to admit that communication concerning kinds is not grounded in what we believe about them, but rather in the shared referent—just as Kripke and Putnam maintain. Moreover, given the difficulties arising from variability, one

---

10. This is how Chalmers and Jackson spell out their thesis that there is an *a priori* entailment from microphysical(-cum-indexical-cum-phenomenal) truths to ordinary macrophysical truths.

might very well be tempted to adopt the simple solution propounded by Kripke and Putnam who hold that beliefs such as "Gold is that mostly yellowish, malleable, and valuable metal" do not enter into the meanings of kind terms *at all*. All they do is pick out the samples that determine these meanings.

9. *The Argument from Belief Revision*

Neo-descriptivists hold that to know the primary intension of a law-term is to know a role. On neo-descriptivist premises, we should therefore expect a competent speaker to have knowledge of two rather different kinds about polar bears or snow. On the one hand, she will have conceptual knowledge concerning the roles associated with 'polar bear' and 'snow'. On the other hand, she will have empirical knowledge about the local fillers of these roles. It hence should make a difference whether information a competent speaker receives concerns roles or local fillers. In the one case, she will have to revise a role, whilst in the other case, she will have to update her beliefs about some filler.

This is precisely what we find if we look at uncontested role terms. Learning that that man over there is snow-blind does not change the context-sensitive role I associate with 'that man over there'. It for sure does not restrict application of this complex demonstrative in worlds considered as actual to snow-blind persons. Very much the same holds for other role terms. Take 'the secretary general of the UN'. Let us assume that the role associated with this terms is determined by legal and procedural regulations of the United Nations. Hence, "The secretary general of the UN calls in the meetings of the General Assembly" will count as a conceptual truth, whereas "The secretary general of the UN wears stylish suits" will surely be about the respective filler. Competent speakers are sensitive to this difference. Learning the former might very well change the way someone applies 'secretary general of the UN' in worlds considered as actual. Learning the latter will not. Our knowledge attached to 'secretary general of the UN' hence is stratified. It consists of a conceptual layer and an empirical layer.

Nothing of this holds for our knowledge attached to law terms. Here information that neo-descriptivists must take to be about fillers might very well change the way we employ the respective term in worlds considered as actual. To cite the well-worn example, neo-descriptivists assume that "Water is the transparent, odourless, colourless etc. liquid of our acquaintance" states the role that is around here filled by H_2O. Hence, learning that water is a bipolar is to acquire knowledge concerning the filler rather than the role. But our willingness to apply 'water' in worlds considered as actual will be affected by this. We will be somewhat reluctant to say of some stuff in a world considered as actual that it is water if we know that it does not have a bipolar molecular structure. Very much the same holds for 'gold', 'polar bear', or 'electron'. Being told that the mass of an electron is about 1/1800 of that of a hydrogen atom might very well affect our application of 'electron' in worlds considered as actual. Our knowledge attached to law-terms thus does not appear to have a layered structure. All our knowledge concerning kinds rather seems to be on a par.

Neo-descriptivists devise epistemic possibilities to allow for scientific discoveries. They take it that our water-experts could have announced that water has the chemical structure XYZ rather than H_2O. Neo-descriptivists argue that this would not have affected our concept of water. For if we consider a world as actual that is just like ours, except for the fact that it contains the water-like substance XYZ where our world contains H_2O, we would be willing to apply 'water' to XYZ. This might be right. But this will not lead to a clear distinction between filler and role, and it will not give rise to conceptual knowledge. For it tremendously underestimates the power of our experts. Our experts could have announced almost anything. They could have announced that water really is non-transparent, or that gold is not a metal after all. This would have led us to change beliefs that, on the neo-descriptivist construal, concern the respective roles rather than the fillers. Again, we apparently have to conclude that all our knowledge concerning kinds seems to be on a par.

To be sure, it does not *feel* that way. We somehow sense that "Water is transparent" is more vital to us than, say, "Water is sparse in sub-Saharan Africa". There is a straightforward explanation for this. We do possess what I call 'local epistemic shortcuts' for water, gold, polar bears, and the like. That is to say, we possess simple reliable procedures to identify specimens of kinds in our in fact actual world: we carefully bite coins or look out for thick white coats. These procedures are useful, just like identifying grandmothers by their appearance is. But these procedures are not conceptual, and you do not need to acquire any such procedure in order to be a competent user of a natural kind term. Still, that some dependencies serve as local epistemic shortcuts can account for the felt asymmetry.

10. *Analytic Truths—Still Harmless After All These Years?*

It's time to take stock. In his *Two Dogmas of Empiricism*, Quine famously argued that we cannot produce an adequate justification for our contention that there are analytic truths. Putnam claims that Quine is obviously wrong. Some sentences evidently are analytic, and some are evidently not. Rejecting Quinean strictures on justification, he contends that the problem of analyticity is not a problem about, but rather a problem within semantics. I have argued that this is a perfectly warranted approach to the issue of analyticity. We do not need a reductive explanation to justify the obvious fact that some sentences are analytic. We are allowed to draw on our most refined intuitive judgements, and on our best semantic theories. Since our intuitions are projectible and univocal, it appears that Quine is indeed wrong: there are analytic truths. Just think of "Bachelors are unmarried".

The fact that Quine's rejection of (non-tautological) analyticities is seriously flawed does not resolve the issue of analyticity, though. In fact, establishing that there are analytic truths does not even touch upon the deep issue. Here Quine might still be right. It might still be the case that there are no truths that are destined to play a prominent epistemological or methodological role simply in virtue of their semantic properties. More precisely, there might be no such truths concerning energy, electrons, crows, polar bears, and the like. This is what Putnam believes. He holds that once we have devised an adequate semantics that yields an explanation as to how analytic truths arise, and that allows for an evaluation of their importance, we will see that they are harmless. I have argued that this is right. Even though Putnam's own attempt fails, once we have drawn on the resources of an adequate state-of-the-art semantics, we do indeed see that there are no non-trivial analytic truths about polar bears or electrons. It takes some argument to establish this. I did not only have to devise a rather complex explanation-cum-evaluation in order to secure it. I also had to rebut the aspirations of neo-descriptivism.

Analytic truths—at least the ones concerning law terms—thus indeed still are harmless. In fact, they are *necessarily* harmless: given that their primary intensions are determined by object-anchorings, no competent speaker *can* learn something substantial by getting to know their primary intensions. That is not true of the analytic truths that arise from descriptive or role terms. "Grandmothers are female" and "The home team plays at its own pitch" are, as it were, trivial by accident; there might very well be some substantial analytic truths of these kinds, arising from complex descriptions or intricate roles. Then again, there might not. For it could very well turn out that there are hardly any pure instances of descriptive or role terms. Yet I won't speculate on that matter.

BIBLIOGRAPHY

Alexander, George 2000: "On Washing the Fur without Wetting It: Quine, Carnap, and Analyticity", *Mind* 109, 1 24.

Bealer, George 1998: "Analyticity", in: Edward Craig (Ed.), *The Routledge Encyclopedia of Philosophy*, London.

Boghossian, Paul 1997: "Analyticity", in: Bob Hale and Crispin Wright (Eds.), *A Companion to the Philosophy of Language*, Oxford, 331–368.

Chalmers, David 1995: "The Components of Content", <www.consc.net/papers/content.html>, as of 25. 5. 2003.

Chalmers, David 1996: *The Conscious Mind. In Search of a Fundamental Theory*, New York/Oxford.

Chalmers, David forthcoming a: "The Foundations of Two-Dimensional Semantics", <www.consc.net/papers/foundations.html>, as of 25. 5. 2003.

Chalmers, David forthcoming b: "On Sense and Intension", <www.consc.net/papers/intension.html>, as of 25. 5. 2003.

Chalmers, David forthcoming c: "The Nature of Epistemic Space", <www.consc.net/ papers/espace.html>, as of 25. 5. 2003.

Chalmers, David and Frank Jackson 2001: "Conceptual Analysis and Reductive Explanation", *Philosophical Review* 110, 315–360.

Davies, Martin 1981: *Meaning, Quantification, Neccessity. Themes in Philosophical Logic*, London.

Devitt, Michael and Kim Sterelny 1987: *Language and Reality*, Oxford.

Dummett, Michael 1976: "What is a Theory of Meaning (II)?", in: Gareth Evans and John McDowell (Eds.), *Truth and Meaning*, Oxford, 67–137.

Edwards, Sean 1973: "Putnam on Analyticity", *Philosophical Studies* 24, 268–270.

Glock, Hanjo 2003: *Quine and Davidson on Language, Thought and Reality*, Cambridge.

Grice, Paul 1987: "Logic and Conversation", in his *Studies in the Ways of Words*, Cambridge, Mass. 1989, 22–57.

Grice, Paul and Peter Strawson 1956: "In Defence of a Dogma", in: J. Rosenberg (Ed.), *Readings in the Philosophy of Language*, Englewood Cliffs, NJ 1971, 81–94.

Jackson, Frank 1998a: *From Metaphysics to Ethics. A Defence of Conceptual Analysis*, Oxford.

Jackson, Frank 1998b: *Mind, Method and Conditionals. Selected Essays*, London/New York.

Jackson, Frank 1998c: "Reference and Description Revisited", *Philosophical Perspectives* 12, 201–218.

Kaplan, David 1977: "Demonstratives", in: J. Almog et. al. (Eds.), *Themes From Kaplan*, Oxford 1989, 481–563.

Kaplan, David 1989: "Afterthoughts", in: J. Almog et. al. (Eds.), *Themes From Kaplan*, Oxford 1989, 565–614.

Kripke, Saul 1980: *Naming and Necessity*, Oxford.

Lewis, David 1981: "Index, Context and Content", in: S. Kanger and S. Öhman (Eds.): *Philosophy and Grammar*, Dordrecht, 79–100.

Nimtz, Christian 2002: *Wörter, Dinge, Stellvertreter. Quine, Davidson und Putnam zur Unbestimmtheit der Referenz*, Paderborn.

Nimtz, Christian 2004: "Two-Dimensionalism and Natural Kind Terms", forthcoming in *Synthèse*.

Perry, John 1998: "Myself and I", in: M. Stamm (Ed.): *Philosophie in synthetischer Absicht*, Stuttgart, 83–103.

Putnam, Hilary 1975: "The Meaning of 'Meaning'", in his *Mind, Language, and Reality, Philosophical Papers, Vol. 2.*, Cambridge 1975, 215–271.

Putnam, Hilary 1962: "The Analytic and the Synthetic", in his *Mind, Language, and Reality, Philosophical Papers, Vol. 2.*, Cambridge 1975, 33–69.

Quine, Willard V.O. 1935: "Truth by Convention", in his *The Ways of the Paradox*, Cambridge, Mass. 1976, 77 106.

Quine, Willard V.O. 1951: "Two Dogmas of Empiricism", in his *From a Logical Point of View*, Cambridge, Mass. 1953, 20–46.

Quine, Willard V.O. 1960: *Word and Object*, Cambridge, Mass.

Quine, Willard V.O. 1963: "Carnap on Logical Truth", in his *The Ways of the Paradox*, Cambridge, Mass. 1976, 107–132.

Quine, Willard V.O. 1973: *The Roots of Reference*, La Salle.

Quine, Willard V.O. 1975: "Mind and Verbal Disposition", in: S. Guttenplan (Ed.): *Mind and Language*, Oxford, 83–95.

Quine, Willard V.O. 1986: "Reply to Hilary Putnam", in: L.E. Hahn and P.A. Schilpp (Eds.), *The Philosophy of W.V.O. Quine*, La Salle, Ill., 427–431.

Quine, Willard V.O. 1987: "Indeterminacy of Translation Again", *Journal of Philosophy* 84, 5–10.

Sober, Elliot 2000: "Quine's Two Dogmas", *Aristotelian Society Supplement* 74, 237–280.

Stalnaker, Robert 1978: "Assertion", *Syntax and Semantics* 9, 315–332.

Stalnaker, Robert 1999: "Introduction", in his *Context and Content*, Oxford, 1–28.

Strawson, Peter F. 1950: "On Referring", *Mind* 59, 320–344.

AN A POSTERIORI CONCEPTION OF ANALYTICITY?

Åsa Maria WIKFORSS
Stockholm University

Summary

At the time that Quine wrote "Two Dogmas" an attack on analyticity was considered a simultaneous attack on the very idea of necessary truth. This all changed with Kripke's revival of a non-epistemic, non-linguistic notion of necessity. My paper discusses the question whether we can take Kripke one step further and free *analyticity* from its epistemic ties, thereby reinstating a notion of analyticity that is immune to Quine's attack, and compatible with his epistemic holism. I discuss this question by examining Tyler Burge's claim that truths of meaning depend on features of the external environment and are a posteriori. I argue that although Burge's construal of analyticity circumvents Quine's objections, it is not well-motivated philosophically and has problematic implications. Kripke's strategy with respect to necessity, I conclude, is not easily transferable to analyticity.

1. Introduction

Quine's attack on analyticity in *Two Dogmas* was widely considered, both by Quine and by his contemporaries, to be a simultaneous attack on the very idea of necessary truth. There is, of course, a good reason for this: Quine's main target was Carnap, and Carnap had joined analyticity and necessity precisely by suggesting that the necessary, as well as the a priori, could be explained in terms of our linguistic conventions or rules. However, if there is one aspect of *Two Dogmas* that appears dated today, it is this assumption that skepticism about analyticity entails skepticism about necessity. This, of course, is due to Kripke and his well-known appeal to a non-linguistic, non-epistemic, notion of necessity (Kripke 1972). By reviving de re necessity, it seems, Kripke inoculated necessity from Quine's objections to the positivist notion of analyticity: Kripkean necessities are not true in virtue of meaning alone, and being a posteriori they do not seem to be at odds with Quine's holistic picture of belief revision and his skepticism about the a priori. Once Kripke freed necessity from its epistemic ties, therefore, it suddenly appeared possible to agree with everything Quine says about the positivist conception of analyticity, and yet hold on to the idea that there is an important distinction between contingent and necessary truths.

This raises an interesting question. If necessity can be freed from its epistemic ties, and the assumption that all necessary truths must be a priori is rejected, could not a similar move be made with respect to analyticity? Perhaps we can take Kripke a step further and free *analyticity* from its ties with the a priori, thereby reinstating a notion of analyticity that is immune to Quine's attack, and compatible with his holism. That there is logical space for such a position is quite clear. Kripke follows the positivists when it comes to analyticity, and stipulates that analytic truths are a priori: "I am presupposing that an analytic truth is one which depends on *meanings* in the strict sense and therefore is necessary as well as a priori" (Kripke 1972, 122). However, in and of itself the notion of analyticity does not seem to be an epistemic notion. Or, at any rate, there are notions of the analytic that are not intrinsically epistemic.[1] Thus, while it is clear that necessity is not an epistemic notion, and equally clear that the a priori is, the analytic is up for grabs. Historically the analytic has been connected with the a priori, of course, but it seems perfectly possible to argue that this connection is just an historical accident.

Moreover, even if analyticity should be given an epistemic construal, it does not follow that there is an intrinsic link between the analytic and the a priori. For instance, Paul Boghossian has argued that the most interesting notion of analyticity is an overtly epistemological notion: "a statement is 'true by virtue of its meaning' provided that grasp of its meaning alone suffices for justified belief in its truth" (Boghossian 1996, 363). However, Boghossian points out that this formulation is neutral as to the question whether such knowledge need be a priori, since it does not follow from this construal of analyticity that the meaning of our terms is knowable a priori. For instance, Boghossian says, most

---

1. Putnam, for instance, makes this point and argues that "Quine *confused* analyticity and a prioricity because of positivist assumptions" (Putnam 1983, 92). A similar point is made by Paul O'Grady, in "Analyticity and the A-priori" (unpublished MS).

externalist views have the implication that facts about sameness and difference of meaning are not a priori (Boghossian 1996, 367).

In this paper I shall examine the prospects of a posteriori analyticity by taking a closer look at how it is developed by one of the foremost contemporary externalists, Tyler Burge. Burge is of particular interest since he explicitly endorses Quine's rejection of the positivist conception of analyticity, as well as Quine's epistemic holism, while at the same time subscribing to the idea that there are truths of meaning that play a philosophically important role. The reason he does not take this to be incompatible with Quine's rejection of analyticity is precisely that truths of meaning, on Burge's construal, are dependent on facts about the external world and therefore a posteriori. Although my discussion will be largely critical, I think it is clear that if there is to be an account of a posteriori analyticity, it has to be developed along the lines suggested by Burge.[2]

I begin, in section 2, with an account of Burge's position on analyticity, and of the connection between this and his externalism. In section 3 I examine the motivations behind Burge's account of truths of meaning, and in section 4 I spell out the implications of making such truths a posteriori. Burge's account of analyticity relies on a problematic form of essentialism, I argue, and leads to difficulties in accounting for the cognitive role of meaning and concepts. I end by suggesting that this demonstrates a broader problem with the analytic a posteriori, and that, therefore, Kripke's strategy with respect to necessity is not easily transferable to analyticity.

2. Burge on Quine and Analyticity

2.1 The Positivist Conception of Analyticity

Throughout his writings, Burge expresses a great deal of sympathy with Quine's attack on the positivist notion of analyticity. Thus, Burge wholeheartedly endorses Quine's rejection of the idea that there are truths that are true 'purely' in virtue of meaning, independently of facts.

---

2. It should be noted at the outset that Burge himself does not really use the phrase 'a posteriori analyticity'. However, since he speaks of truths of meaning that can only be known a posteriori, it is clear that he is committed to the analytic a posteriori.

In 1986, for instance, Burge writes: "I take it that Quine's challenge to justify a disjoint distinction between 'truths of fact'... and mere 'truths purely by virtue of meaning'—has gone unmet"(Burge 1986, 700, fn 5). And again, in 1992: "There is no ground for claiming that certain sentences are vacuously true, with no dependence on the way the world is" (Burge 1992, 6). The conception of analyticity that Burge rejects here is what Boghossian has labeled "the metaphysical conception" (Boghossian 1996, 363). Burge and Boghossian both claim that the idea of something being true in virtue of meaning alone, independently of the way the world is, makes little sense. No support can be given, Burge argues, for a distinction between truths that depend for their truth on meaning alone, and "truths that depend for their truth on their meaning together with (perhaps necessary) features of their subject matter" (Burge 1992, 9).

However, Burge goes further than Boghossian in his endorsement of Quine. Burge also expresses sympathy for Quine's skepticism about the a priori, and subscribes to Quine's holistic picture of belief revision. Discussing the Quine-Duhem thesis that belief revision is holistic and that there is no set formula for saying which sentences within the theory might be revised, and which should be held on to, Burge continues:

> In fact, the practice of empirical science suggests that virtually any scientific claim, including one that serves as a definition, is subject to possible revision in the interest of accounting for new findings ... Subsequent discussion has made it seem hopeless to claim that in every one of these cases the old definition remains true (because it is a definition!) and a new theoretical notion (e.g. a new notion of atom or momentum) is introduced with the new definition. Rather, it is often the case that the old definitions are false ... (Burge 1993, 313).

Burge is therefore in substantial agreement with Quine: He rejects the idea that a statement can be true in virtue of meaning alone, and he grants that belief revision is holistic in character and that purported definitions can turn out to be false. However, Burge does not take any of this to imply that there is no philosophically interesting notion of analyticity. We must, Burge suggests, distinguish between two notions of analyticity, both attacked by Quine:

Analyticity 1 = Statement S is analytic if it is true in virtue of meaning alone.

Analyticity 2 = Statement S is analytic if it is derivable from logic together with definitions.

The first notion, again, is that of metaphysical analyticity, endorsed by the positivists, and is traditionally connected with the a priori. The second notion of analyticity, however, does not imply that the truth of an analytic statement depends on meaning alone, and, Burge says, "is completely neutral on the metaphysical and epistemological status of logical truth and definitions" (Burge 1992, 10). The two notions are often run together, Burge suggests, since it is assumed that definitions are vacuously true. But there is a tradition stemming from Aristotle that rejects this assumption. On this view, Burge says, definitions state essences and so are not vacuously true, nor are they knowable a priori. Consequently, once the positivist construal of definitions is rejected, it is possible to agree with everything Quine says about the metaphysical notion of analyticity without therefore rejecting analyticity altogether.

Indeed, not only does Burge suggest that Analyticity 2 can be salvaged from Quine's attack, he also suggests that it *thrives* on it. By getting rid of the idea that there are truths in virtue of meaning alone, and emphasizing the holistic character of belief revision, Burge suggests, Quine paves the way for a notion of analyticity freed from the positivist baggage. What Quine's discussion shows, by emphasizing that no statement is immune from revision, is not that there are no truths of meaning, but that truths of meaning are simultaneously truths of fact and need not be knowable a priori. Contra the positivist, truths of meaning are dubitable, even by someone who possesses the relevant concepts:

> In stating a truth of meaning (however one construes the notion), one is not stating a degenerate truth. To put this crudely: in explicating one's 'meanings', one is equally stating nondegenerate truths—'facts'. So giving a true explication is not separable from getting the facts right. It is a short step from this point to the observation that truths of meaning are dubitable (Burge 1986, 714).

2.2 Truths of Meaning and Externalism

How are we to understand the claim that stating truths of meaning involves stating 'non-degenerate' truths, genuine facts? To answer this question, we have to take a closer look at Burge's later externalism. Burge's first, and most familiar, defense of externalism occurs in "Individualism and the Mental", where Burge argues that the meaning of an individual's words, and the contents of her thoughts, depends on the social environment, more specifically, on the linguistic conventions of her community (Burge 1979). In Burge's more recent writings, however, his focus has shifted from the social environment to the physical one. Burge now emphasizes the role physical examples play in our linguistic practices. He discusses a central set of linguistic expressions, what he calls "empirically applicable terms"—terms that apply to empirically observable objects and events, such as 'house', 'chair', and 'walk' (Burge 1986; 1989; and 1993). When we try to give characterizations that capture the meaning of these terms, Burge suggests, we consider examples of what we take to be archetypical applications of the term, and try to arrive at "factually correct characterizations" of these empirically accessible entities (Burge 1989, 705). The use of examples ensures that our explications are dependent on empirical facts and can be doubted, even by the most competent speakers; it ensures that there is a potential gap between our conventional or practice-based definitions, our attempts to explicate the meaning of our terms, and the real definition of the term. In this sense, thus, truths of meaning are not knowable a priori.

This shows, according to Burge, that we need to distinguish between two notions of meaning: On the one hand a practice-based notion of meaning, "conventional meaning"; on the other hand a notion of meaning tied to the nature of the external phenomenon in question, what Burge calls 'translational meaning' (Burge 1986, 714–5; 1989, 181; 1993, 317). Conventional meaning, Burge suggests, is determined by the use of the most competent speakers, and it provides a norm for ideal competence: We *should* use our words in accordance with the use of the most competent speakers. Translational meaning, by contrast, transcends use, and determines the correctness of the conventional meaning characterizations. It can be articulated through exact translation and through such trivial thoughts as "my word 'tiger' applies to tigers", but the speaker need not be able to give any further articulation or explication of it. Corresponding to this distinction, Burge suggests, is a distinction between conceptions and concepts: My *conception* of a given object, a knife say, is determined by the explications I would give; my *concept* of a knife, by contrast, depends on the actual nature of the object in question. Concepts, therefore, correspond to translational meaning, not to conventional meaning, and this allows for the possibility that conceptual truths are dependent on external facts and empirically discoverable.

To illustrate this Burge offers a thought-experiment concerning an empirically applicable term, 'sofa' (Burge 1986, 707 f.). In this experiment we are invited to imagine the following. A in the actual world, and B in a counterfactual world, use the word 'sofa' competently. However, both proceed to develop non-standard theories about the objects in their environment called 'sofas', and start to doubt the truth of the statement "Sofas are furnishings to be sat upon". A's doubt, as it turns out, proves unfounded: It is indeed part of the nature of sofas, in the actual world, that they are furnishings to be sat upon. B's doubts, however, prove to be correct: The objects that B is confronted with look like sofas but are, in fact, works of art and would collapse under a person's weight. This implies, according to Burge, that "there are no sofas in B's situation, and the word form 'sofa' does not mean sofa" (Burge 1986, 708). A and B, despite being physically identical ('for all intents and purposes'), mean different things by 'sofa' and have different 'sofa'-concepts.

The important difference between this thought-experiment and the 'arthritis'-one, as Burge himself emphasizes, is that in this experiment there is no appeal to linguistic conventions and the speaker is not said to have an incomplete grasp of the conventional meaning of the term in question. In "Individualism and the Mental", recall, the claim that 'arthritis' has a different meaning in the counterfactual community than in the actual one, depends on the idea that there is a difference in conventions between the two communities: In the actual community it is a definitional truth that arthritis afflicts the joints only, whereas in the counterfactual community, the word is used more widely to apply to rheumatoid ailments of the joints as well as of the ligaments. The individual in the actual community uttering "I have arthritis in my thigh" is therefore exhibiting an incomplete understanding of the conventional meaning of 'arthritis'. By contrast, in the 'sofa'-experiment the difference in meaning derives not from a difference in conventions, but from a difference in the underlying nature of the objects referred to. A has not misunderstood the conventional meaning of 'sofa', Burge argues, but has simply developed a nonstandard theory about sofas. Burge suggests that this makes the argument "extremely comprehensive in its application", since nearly anything can be the topic of non-standard theorizing:

"Similar thought experiments apply to knives, clothing, rope, pottery, wheels, boats, tables, watches, houses" (Burge 1986, 709).

According to Burge, therefore, the upshot of Quine's attack on analyticity is not that there are no truths of meaning, but that truths of meaning depend on the empirical features of the objects referred to. This dependence on the external objects implies that empirical discoveries may lead us to revise our meaning explications—even those given by the most competent speakers. Burge suggests a parallel with traditional rationalism. The characteristic tenet of rationalism, Burge says, is that by understanding conceptual relations one can gain deep and fundamental knowledge of the world (Burge 1992, 10). Endorsing an externalist account of meaning and concepts allows us to honor this idea, Burge suggests, since it frees us from the idea that truths of meaning are a mere reflection of our conventions.

Given this sketch of Burge's position on analyticity, let us turn to a closer examination of his neo-rationalist construal of truths of meaning. I shall focus on two questions: What are the motivations behind Burge's neo-rationalism, and what implications does it have for meaning and concepts?

3. *A Posteriori Analyticity: Motivations*

Burge's principal argument in favor of his "neo-rationalist" position derives from the possibility of rationally doubting conventional definitions. In A's community it is part of the conventional characterization of the meaning of 'sofa' that sofas are furnishings to be sat upon. Nonetheless, Burge says, when A comes to doubt the truth of this characterization, his doubts are not irrational: He is not linguistically confused, nor is he ignorant of expert opinion concerning sofas. Rather, A's doubts concern empirical facts and he has simply developed a testable, nonstandard theory (Burge 1986, 711). This shows, Burge suggests, that the conventional meaning characterization 'Sofas are pieces of furniture meant for sitting' cannot be vacuously true, but must be informative. Otherwise, A's doubts would indeed be irrational (Burge 1986, 715).

Burge puts this point by saying that 'thought corrects meaning', and he draws a parallel with traditional rationalism: "Our cases develop a theme from the Socratic dialogues: Thought can correct meaning. ... If new empirical facts or new insights are imported into the discussion, the background assumptions of normative characterizations may be undermined, and the characterizations themselves may be shown to be mistaken" (Burge 1986, 714). When we attempt to characterize the meaning of our words, Burge argues, we typically engage in rational argumentation of the sort displayed in Plato's dialogues: Purported definitions are examined and criticized, and better ones emerge until some form of reflective agreement is reached. To account for this dialectic, Burge argues, the positivist conception of truths of meaning must be rejected in favor of a conception according to which truths of meaning are simultaneously truths of fact and can be subject to rational debate.

Now, it is of course correct that the positivist conception of analyticity does not, in this sense, allow for the rational dubitability of definitions. However, the question is why Burge believes there is any need to go beyond Quine in this respect. After all, Quine has no difficulties explaining the rational dubitability of conventional definitions: We can rationally doubt purported definitions since meaning is not determined by isolated definitions but holistically, by overall 'theory'. In short, conventional definitions can be doubted since they are not in any sense definitional truths, but empirical truths, albeit very central and entrenched ones.

It is clear that one reason Burge considers it important to move beyond Quine is that he worries that Quine's point about the dubitability of definitions mainly applies to scientific discourse. The lessons drawn from holism, Burge writes, depends on the possibility of fundamental changes in scientific outlook, but such changes are not common in ordinary discourse: "We use definitions for many artifact terms, for example, that are not at all likely to be overturned. So it is less clear that the Duhem-Quine points about the falsifiability of definitions extend to ordinary discourse" (Burge 1993, 323). To explain how such definitions nonetheless may be dubitable, Burge suggests, we need to appeal to externalist aspects of meaning. Purported definitions are dubitable because their truth depends on the nature of the objects referred to. For instance, Burge says, someone can think that chairs must have legs, and come to realize that this meaning characterization is incorrect, through exposure to examples (such as ski-lift chairs). It is this dependence on examples, and not just the epistemic holism, that allows for the possibility of doubting a definition.

Again, however, it is unclear why there is any need to move beyond Quine. After all, if indeed "All chairs have legs" is merely a deeply entrenched empirical claim, and not a definitional truth in the positivist sense, then it is as rationally dubitable as any scientific claim, and can be overthrown by future empirical discoveries. It may be that ordinary claims of this sort are less likely to be overturned than scientific claims, but that does not impinge on their rational dubitability. Moreover, the thesis that meaning is determined holistically applies equally to ordinary terms, and this allows for the possibility of revising ordinary claims, even those that are taken to be central.[3] In addition, although ordinary terms are less theory-dependent than scientific ones, it is simply not the case that the use of ordinary terms is isolated from scientific theories and discoveries, nor is it at all clear how the two types of discourses are to be demarcated. Consider the familiar example of the discovery that whales are mammals—a discovery that led to a revision in a widespread everyday belief, i.e. the belief that whales are fish.

If, therefore, the goal is to explain the possibility of rationally doubting the truth of a conventional definition then, again, it seems that the simplest solution is simply to endorse something like Quine's view. There is no need to add Burge's rationalist element. It might be thought, however, that in a deeper sense Quine simply cannot make sense of the dialectic Burge appeals to. After all, if Quine is right and there are no truths of meaning, one might wonder how there could *be* such a thing as a rational dialogue concerning meaning characterizations.

However, it is not clear that this worry is well grounded either. Even if it is granted that there are no analytic truths, it might be useful for certain purposes to attempt to characterize the central aspects of the use of our terms. The result of such efforts will not be truths of meaning in any sense, but empirical statements that we cannot today, in our current epistemic position, conceive of giving up without a change in meaning. Nonetheless, such 'meaning characterizations' can serve a function similar to that of analytic statements. Thus, if a person rejects these statements, without providing any further justification, we have reason to conclude that she has failed to grasp the meaning of our words. But new discoveries may emerge, showing that what we took to

---

3. Of course, it is controversial, to say the least, exactly how the distinction between theory change and meaning change is to be drawn on a holistic picture of meaning. I cannot enter this debate here, but suffice it to say that if one takes meaning to be determined holistically, one can allow for the possibility that even a very central belief could be revised without a change in meaning. For an illuminating discussion of meaning holism see Pagin 1997.

be an immutable truth in fact is not. Consider again the discovery that whales are mammals. Prior to that discovery, presumably, a person who rejected this belief would not be considered a competent speaker. In this sense, the statement "Whales are fish", could usefully be employed as a characterization of the meaning of 'whale'.[4] Once the discovery was made this statement was rejected, and one way to describe this would be to say that the empirical discovery led to a change in 'meaning characterizations' (although not, therefore, in meaning).

It is therefore not correct that accounting for the type of rational 'meaning discourse' that Burge emphasizes requires appealing to his neo-rationalist truths of meaning. Central empirical claims will serve just as well. Next, I want to argue that not only is the notion of a posteriori truths of meaning poorly motivated philosophically, but that its implications are very problematic as well.

4. *A Posteriori Analyticity: Implications*

4.1 *Essentialism*

As we have seen above, Burge holds that the correctness of a purported meaning characterization depends not on our conventions but on facts about the physical environment. This is the reason truths of meaning are not vacuous and can be rationally doubted. The question, however, is how empirical facts of this sort can generate truths of *meaning*, as opposed to purely empirical truths. That is, assuming that Burge is right and we need to move beyond Quine, what sense are we to make of the suggestion that empirical features of the objects referred to generate truths of meaning? The question can be put in terms of the thought-experiment: Why should it be concluded that 'sofa' has a different meaning in B's world? Of course, the sofas around here are such that they do not break when we sit upon them, but why can't we simply say that they make lousy sofas in B's world?

Burge, at points, suggests that there is a perfectly innocuous reply to this question: The reason 'sofa' should be said to have different meanings in B's world and in ours, is simply that 'sofa' has a different

---

4. Putnam expresses a similar idea when he appeals to the notion of stereotypes (Putnam 1975, 250).

extension in the two worlds. Indeed, the principle that a difference in extension makes for a difference in meaning is made the cornerstone of Burge's externalism. Thus, Burge writes that modern externalism has its roots in the theory of reference, since this work (by Kripke, Putnam and others) bears on the meaning of terms and on the identity of concepts: "For the meaning of a wide range of non-indexical terms and the nature of a wide range of concepts are dependent on the referent or range of application in the sense that if the referent were different, the meaning of the term, and the associated concept, would be different ..." (Burge 1993, 318).[5]

However, the reasoning here is less innocuous than it might at first seem. First, in one sense, Burge's principle is simply not true. After all, our word 'sofa' does have a different extension in several "synonymy worlds". For instance, there is a possible world in which all sofas happen to be made of leather but this may still be a world in which 'sofa' has the same meaning as in the actual world. Consequently, the fact that 'sofa' has a different extension in the counterfactual world, does not yield the externalist conclusion that the word has a different meaning and expresses a different concept in that world.[6] To get this conclusion, the claim must be, not that 'sofa' has a different extension in the two worlds, but rather that the objects in B's world are not even within the extension of our term 'sofa'—*these objects are simply not sofas*. If this is so, then it does seem to follow that 'sofa' in B's world must have a different meaning, and express a different concept, than 'sofa' in our world. However, this means that our original question, why it should be concluded that 'sofa' has a different meaning in B's world than in A's, simply has been transformed into a new question: Why should it be concluded that there are no sofas in B's world?

This shows clearly that there is no innocuous reply to our initial question. The empirical facts that meaning characterizations depend upon cannot be 'mere' empirical facts, but need be facts concerning the essential properties of the objects in question. The reason that there are no sofas in B's world, on Burge's view, must be that the objects in B's world do not share the properties essential to our sofas—i.e. they cannot be sat upon. Again, the essential quality of this property does not

---

5. For this principle, see also Burge 1979, 75; and Burge 1989, 181.
6. For a discussion of this see Häggqvist 1996,177. See also my paper, "A Unifying Principle of Externalism?", submitted MS.

derive from our conventions, according to Burge, but from the nature of our sofas. Underlying Burge's later externalism is therefore a form of Aristotelian essentialism.[7]

This commitment to essentialism, of course, is hinted at when Burge speaks of reviving the Aristotelian notion of real definitions. However, at the same time Burge seems to shun the talk of essences and necessary properties. For instance, in "Intellectual Norms and the Foundations of Mind" Burge suggests that the key animating idea behind the paper is that some necessarily true thoughts can be doubted, but adds in a footnote that the argument need not rest on an assumption about necessity. He continues: "What we need are general thoughts or statements so central to the correct identification of a type of thing, property, or event, that, under ordinary conditions, if the thought failed to apply to some given entity x, we would correctly and almost automatically refuse to count x as an instance of the type" (Burge 1986, 698). But this cannot be right. If it is not a necessary truth that sofas are furnishings to be sat upon then, again, we have not been given any reason to believe that the objects in B's world are not sofas. That we would "almost automatically refuse" to count these objects as sofas, does not suffice to show that they are not sofas—in particular, it does not do so if one holds, as Burge does, that our speech community may be mistaken in its meaning characterizations.

Burge's later meaning externalism, therefore, depends on a form of essentialism. Of course, it is a familiar enough claim that the belief in a posteriori necessity brings with it a commitment to a non-trivial form of essentialism[8], and it would be surprising if the belief in a posteriori analyticity did not, in the same way, rest on essentialism. However, leaving general concerns about essentialism aside, there are reasons to worry about the very radical expansion in the scope of essentialism that Burge's position implies.

---

7. It is not obvious, of course, exactly how Aristotle's essentialism is to be construed. But leaving details aside, it is generally agreed that Aristotle held that the definitional features of a kind depend not on our practices, but on the essential, underlying features of the kind in question. See David Charles (2000) for an interesting discussion of Aristotle's views on definitions, meaning and essences. Charles emphasizes that Aristotle's essentialism differs from contemporary essentialism in that it does not rely on any a priori assumptions about the essential properties of a given kind (Charles 2000, chapters 2 and 3). In this respect Burge can fairly be said to be an heir of Aristotle.

8. See for instance Salmon 1982.

Kripke's thesis concerning a posteriori necessity, recall, is limited to two types of terms: names and natural kinds. Consider, however, some of the examples Burge gives of terms whose meanings depend on the physical environment: 'sofa', 'baby', 'chair', 'knife', 'house', 'bread', 'mud', 'stone', 'tree', 'edge', 'shadow', 'walk', 'fight', 'eat', etc. If Burge's externalism depends on essentialism, it follows that on his view not only natural kinds have underlying essences, but almost everything—artifacts, events, natural phenomena that do not constitute natural kinds, etc. The question is whether we can make sense of this. In the case of natural kinds, the externalism is driven by the widely shared view that what characterizes natural kinds is that they possess a certain underlying, microstructural property that unites and explains a set of superficial properties that we associate with the kind in question.[9] Because the underlying property is essential to a natural kind, the reasoning goes, there is a potential gap between our conceptions of the kind in question and its real, underlying nature. However, it is very difficult to apply a similar form of reasoning in the case of Burge's examples. What sense are we to make of the idea that sofas, knives, clothing, rope, pottery, tables, watches, etc. have an essence given by 'nature itself', independently of our classificatory practices? Even an essentialist about natural kinds will presumably hesitate to endorse an essentialism of this promiscuous sort.

It is therefore clear that Burge's neo-rationalism rests on unusually strong essentialist assumptions. This, I think, is not an accident. If one rejects analyticity in the positivist sense, and tries to replace it with an a posteriori notion of analyticity, one needs to endorse a form of generalized Aristotelian essentialism. The essentialism simply replaces the conventionalism. We have, as it were, come full circle. In *Two Dogmas*, recall, Quine starts out with a discussion of Aristotle, and he suggests that the Aristotelian notion of essence was the forerunner of the modern notion of meaning. As Quine famously puts it: "Meaning is what essence becomes when it is divorced from the object of reference and wedded to the word" (Quine 1951, 22). What Burge illustrates, one might say, is Quine's point once more, only this time in reverse; i.e. that "essence is what meaning becomes when it is divorced from the word and wedded to the object of reference".

---

9. I discuss this further in my paper "Naming Natural Kinds", forthcoming in *Synthèse*.

It is not necessary to pursue the topic of essentialism further here. Instead, let us assume, for the sake of argument, that this type of essentialism can be defended, and that it provides a solid ground for Burge's a posteriori analyticities. This takes me to the final question of this paper: What are the consequences of making facts about synonymy and conceptual connections a posteriori?

4.2 *A posteriori truths of meaning and cognitive role*

An important motivation behind Burge's neo-rationalism, as we have seen above, is the idea that we need to account for the rational dubitability of definitions. The emphasis on rational dubitability is reminiscent of Frege, and Burge employs Frege's assumption that a difference in dubitability implies a difference in belief content. For instance, he says, "force is mass times acceleration" is informative and hence dubitable, whereas "force is force" is not—one can believe the latter, without believing the former. Consequently, the contents of the two beliefs are different and there is a sense in which the defined terms do not have the same meaning, do not express the same concepts, i.e. the sense of translational meaning or 'cognitive value' (Burge 1993, 317). In fact, Burge suggests an explicit parallel with Frege's reasoning. The argument for distinguishing conventional meaning from cognitive value, he says, "is a variant of Frege's for distinguishing senses from one another and from denotation" (Burge 1986, 715).

Despite this reference to Frege, it is a serious question whether Burge's externalist rationalism is compatible with Frege's appeal to cognitive role. Frege's assumption that differential dubitability implies a difference in thought content, I want to suggest, conflicts with Burge's externalist claim that concepts and belief-content are individuated in terms of the nature of the object referred to, rather than by the speaker's conceptions of things.

Consider the individual who believes that all chairs must have legs. Assume that she takes 'chair' to be synonymous with something like 'piece of furniture with legs, meant for sitting', and that she would judge 'chairs are pieces of furniture with legs ...' as no more dubitable than 'chairs are chairs'. Thus, from her perspective 'chair' and 'piece of furniture with legs ...' play the same cognitive role. On Burge's view, however, the fact that the terms play the same cognitive role does not show that they express the same concept, since what concept 'chair' really expresses depends not on the individual's conceptual explications, but on empirical features of the objects called 'chair'. Thus, it is quite possible that her definition is false, and if this is the case it follows that there is a difference in the contents of the two beliefs despite the fact that the individual takes them to be equally dubitable. Conversely, an individual may consider two statements to have a different dubitability, although, on Burge's view, they express the same belief. This is the case in Burge's original thought experiment, where the individual doubts the truth of "Arthritis is a rheumatoid disease of the joints only" but not, presumably, of "Arthritis is arthritis". On Burge's view, 'arthritis' is synonymous with 'rheumatoid disease of the joints only', and so the two statements express the same belief, despite the fact that the individual doubts one but believes the other. In general, this difficulty arises whenever an individual doubts what turns out to be a conceptual truth, a very common phenomenon on Burge's view: The conceptual equivalence suggests there is a sameness in belief content, whereas Frege's test suggests that there is not.

There is therefore a real tension between Burge's externalist account of concepts and his appeal to rational dubitability as a test for difference and sameness in belief content.[10] The problem is that it is the speaker's *conceptions* of things that account for cognitive role, and correspond to Fregean Sinn, not the externalistically individuated concepts. This implies that despite what Burge says, he cannot employ Fregean considerations to motivate the distinction between conventional meaning and translational meaning. Of course, Burge is quite right in suggesting that if one combines Frege's test with the assumption that conventional definitions are dubitable, then it follows that conventional definitions do not, after all, spell out synonymy relations. However, as argued above, this point can be granted without taking the further step of appealing to the idea that truths of meaning are a posteriori, and Fregean considerations can never be used to motivate that further step. Applied to Burge's example of "Sofas are furnishings meant for sitting", what Frege's test shows is merely that 'sofa' and 'furnishings meant for sitting' express different concepts, not that we need to introduce a further, de re notion of a concept.

---

10. Scott Kimbrough makes this point in a discussion of Burge and Frege. The anti-individualist, Kimbrough argues, is committed to "the possibility that equivalences of content

This also brings out the fact that Burge is closer to the positivist outlook than he would like to recognize. What makes for the rational dubitability of definitions, on Burge's view, is not really the idea that definiens expresses a different concept than definiendum, but, rather, the idea that an individual can think with a concept that she only incompletely understands. When A doubts the truth of "Sofas are furnishings …" he doubts a conceptual truth, which is to say that he expresses an incomplete understanding of the concept of 'sofa'.[11] His non-standard theory about sofas, in fact, expresses a non-standard or incomplete grasp of the concept of *sofa*. If this were not the case, if A fully grasped the concept of 'sofa', his doubts would indeed be irrational. Since, therefore, the rational dubitability of a definition, on Burge's view, depends on the assumption that the individual has an incomplete grasp of the concept in question, his view is rather similar to that of the positivist. After all, the positivist too can grant that an individual may doubt a definition without irrationality, assuming that the individual does not have a full grasp of the concepts in question. Of course, *if* one holds there are conceptual truths, then it is rather plausible to say that an individual who doubts such a truth thereby expresses an incomplete understanding of the relevant concepts. However, the fact that Burge has to fall back on this idea makes his position less interesting since, in effect, it means that he has not succeeded in presenting an alternative account of how it can be possible rationally to doubt definitional truths.

It is clear that Burge could simply give up his commitment to Frege and grant that externalist concepts cannot account for cognitive role. I shall not speculate why Burge insists on appealing to Frege. However, the conflict between Fregeanism and Burge's externalism, I think, points to a general difficulty with trying to apply Kripke's strategy to

---

may be discovered", and this possibility is denied by the "differential dubitability test" (Kimbrough, 1998, 478).

11. The assumption of incomplete understanding plays a central role throughout Burge's writings. For instance, in "Belief and Synonymy", Burge suggests that the possibility of incomplete understanding allows for the rational dubitability of traditional analyticities such as "A vixen is a female fox" (Burge 1978). Similarly, the assumption of incomplete understanding plays a crucial role in "Individualism and the Mental" (I discuss this at some length in Wikforss 2001). The only difference between 'early' and 'late' Burge is that in his earlier writings the possibility of incomplete understanding depends on the idea that individuals may have an incomplete grasp of their own conventions, whereas in his later writings, it depends on the idea that concepts are individuated in terms of the external objects.

analyticity and divorce analytic truths from their traditional epistemic connection.

For an illustration of this, recall Quine's criticisms of modal logic and how the Kripkean strategy fits into that story. Quine's main complaint is that modal contexts are referentially opaque, and that this causes difficulties for the interpretation of the variables employed in quantification in modal contexts. For instance, the following argument appears invalid, since although (i) and (ii) are true, (iii) is, intuitively, false:

(i)   Necessarily Phosphorus = Phosphorus
(ii) Phosphorus = Hesperus
(iii) Necessarily Phosphorus = Hesperus[12]

Now, these problems spotted by Quine presuppose, as do Quine's arguments in *Two Dogmas*, that the relevant notion of necessity is that of analyticity, in the positivist sense. This, again, was not an arbitrary assumption on Quine's part, since the defenders of modal logic that Quine was after made the same presupposition. However, if modal logic abandons the analytic construal of necessity an efficient strategy for dismissing Quine's worries presents itself: Make the necessity reside in the objects themselves, rather than in their descriptions, and the charge of opacity can be met. The arguments cited above will then be perfectly valid, and the impression that they are not can be dismissed as a mere epistemic issue.[13]

This, of course, is precisely the move Kripke makes in his *Naming and Necessity* (1972). On Kripke's view, (iii) only *appears* false, since the necessity in question has nothing to do with meaning in the traditional sense and is therefore not knowable a priori. The appearance of contingency, Kripke suggests, is due to the fact that we associate certain

---

12. Quine's original example used a definite description, 'the number of planets'. However, as Stephen Neale has recently argued, Quine's point can equally well be made in terms of names, thereby circumventing the effort to meet his objection by appealing to the idea that sentences containing definite descriptions and a modal operator are ambiguous, depending on whether the description is construed as having a wide or a narrow scope (Neale 2000, 293).

13. It should be pointed out that Quine anticipates this move, but dismisses it on the grounds that it presupposes essentialism: "the invidious distinction between some traits of an object as essential to *it* (by whatever name) and other traits of it as accidental" (Quine 1962, 184).

reference-fixing descriptions with the name in question, 'the star that appears in the morning' and 'the star that appears in the evening', and that the contents of these descriptions are only contingently related.[14] Kripke puts this point, as is well-known, by distinguishing conceivability from possibility. It is conceivable, Kripke says, that the Morning star is not identical to the Evening star, in the sense that it is conceivable that the first star in the morning is not identical to the first star in the evening, but it does not follow that it is possible that the Morning Star is not identical to the Evening Star (Kripke 1972, 142–3).

The problem with making the same move in the case of analyticity should now be apparent: The epistemic aspect is not so easily dismissed. Kripke's strategy presupposes that the necessity in question is not one of meaning, does not reside in our descriptions. This allows him to explain modal mistakes by appealing to associated concepts and the cognitive roles these play. Once analyticity is made a posteriori as well, however, this explanatory strategy is blocked. That is, once conceptual necessities themselves are such that we can be ignorant of them, the appearance of contingency cannot be explained the way Kripke does. I think this is a perfectly general problem, one that applies not only to Burge's position, but that anybody faces who wishes to defend an a posteriori conception of analyticity. Kripke's strategy with respect to necessity cannot be repeated in the case of analyticity without encountering serious difficulties concerning the epistemic perspective. A posteriori analyticity, I surmise, will therefore not meet with the success that a posteriori necessity has.

In conclusion, a posteriori analyticity is not well-motivated philosophically, the way a posteriori necessity arguably is. Moreover, a posteriori analyticity relies on a problematic form of essentialism, and leads to difficulties in accounting for the connection between concepts and cognitive role, a connection that Burge himself wishes to respect. To the extent one agrees with Quine and is wary of the traditional, a priori conception of analyticity, therefore, one is better off giving up analyticity altogether than trying to reconstrue a non-epistemic, a posteriori conception of it.[15]

---

14. As Michael Della Rocca puts it: "the objector is mistaking a contingent relation between the properties of being the morning star and being the evening star for a contingent identity between the things that do in fact have these properties" (Della Rocca 1996, 8).

15. Thanks to Adam Green, Sören Häggqvist, Kathrin Glüer-Pagin, and Peter Pagin

REFERENCES

Boghossian, Paul 1996: "Analyticity Reconsidered", *Noûs* 30, 360–391.

Burge, Tyler 1978: "Belief and Synonymy", *Journal of Philosophy* 75, 119–138.

—1979: "Individualism and the Mental", *Midwest Studies in Philosophy*, eds. P. French, T. Uehling, and H. Wettstein, Minneapolis, 72–121.

—1986: "Intellectual Norms and the Foundations of Mind", *Journal of Philosophy* 83, 697–720.

—1989: "Wherein is Language Social", *Reflections on Chomsky*, ed. A. George, 175–191.

—1992: "Philosophy of Language and Mind: 1950–1990", *Philosophical Review* 101, 3–51.

—1993: "Concepts, Definitions, and Meaning", *Metaphilosophy* 24, 309–325.

Charles, David 2000: *Aristotle on Meaning and Essence*, Oxford.

Della Rocca, Michael 1996: "Recent Work. Essentialism: Part 1", *Philosophical Books* 37, 1–89.

Häggqvist, Sören 1996: *Thought Experiments in Philosophy*, Stockholm.

Kimbrough, Scott 1998: "Anti-Individualism and Fregeanism", *Philosophical Quarterly* 48, 470–482.

Kripke, Saul 1972: *Naming and Necessity*, Cambridge, Mass.

Neale, Stephen 2000: "On a Milestone of Empiricism", In: *Knowledge, Language and Logic*, A.Orenstein and P. Kotatko (eds.), Dordrecht, 237–346.

Pagin, Peter 1997: "Is Compositionality Compatible with Holism?", *Mind & Language* 12, 11–33.

Putnam, Hilary 1983: "'Two Dogmas Revisited'", In his *Realism and Reason*, (*Philosophical Papers*, Vol. 3), 87–97.

Quine, Willard Van 1951: "Two Dogmas Of Empiricism". In his *From a Logical Point of View*, Cambridge, Mass. 1953, 20–46.

---

for very helpful comments on various versions of this paper. Special thanks to Tyler Burge for a very interesting and rewarding discussion in response to the presentation of an earlier version of this paper at Humboldt University, Berlin, September 2001.

—1962: "Reply to Professor Marcus", Reprinted in his *The Ways of Paradox*, Cambridge, Mass. 1966, 177–184.

Salmon, Nathan 1982: *Reference and Essence*, Oxford.

Wikforss, Åsa 2001: "Social Externalism and Conceptual Errors", *Philosophical Quarterly* 51, 217–231.

II.
NECESSITY, SYNONYMY, AND LOGIC

THE LINGUISTIC DOCTRINE REVISITED

Hans-Johann GLOCK
University of Reading

Summary

At present, there is an almost universal consensus that the linguistic doctrine of logical necessity is grotesque. This paper explores avenues for rehabilitating a limited version of the doctrine, according to which the special status of analytic statements like 'All vixens are female' is to be explained by reference to language. Far from being grotesque, this appeal to language has a respectable philosophical pedigree and chimes with commonsense, as Quine came to realize. The problem lies in developing it in a way that avoids the powerful objections facing previous versions of the linguistic doctrine. I argue tentatively that this can be done by reconciling Wittgenstein's claim that such statements have a normative role with Carnap's concession that they are true.

My aim in this paper is to explore the possibility of rehabilitating a version of the linguistic doctrine of necessary truth, a view associated with Wittgenstein and the logical positivists. I shall tentatively argue for the following theses:

I. Analytic propositions do *not* describe a special kind of reality (whether it be abstract entities beyond space and time or the most abstract or general features of physical reality);
II. Rather, their special (necessary, a priori) status has to be explained by reference to *language*, and, more specifically, by reference to the meaning of expressions and hence to the way they are used.

The linguistic theory was allegedly refuted such a long time ago, that many people have forgotten the arguments against it. Even fewer people remember the arguments in its favour. For this reason, I shall in the main proceed constructively, by putting the *positive case* for the linguistic doctrine. As regards scope, I shall focus on *analytic* propositions, albeit in a broad sense. This broad sense includes not just propositions that can be reduced to logical truths by substituting synonyms for synonyms, but also definitions, including so-called implicit definitions. I shall not, however, try to account for the propositions of logic and mathematics. More specifically, I shall *not* argue for the following positions associated with the logical positivists:

> *General linguistic doctrine*: all strict, i.e. logical necessity is rooted in language or meaning.
> *Analytic theory of logical necessity*: only analytic propositions in the strict sense can be logically necessary.
> *Analytic theory of a priori knowledge*: only analytic propositions in the strict sense can be known a priori.
> *Conventionalism*: if a proposition is rooted in language or meaning, it is arbitrary, that is to say, there are no compelling reasons for or against accepting it.
> *Lingualism*: analytic propositions are rooted in language rather than in a conceptual scheme that is independent of or prior to language.

My defence of the linguistic doctrine has the following structure. Section 1 deals with an assumption of the linguistic doctrine, namely that analytic propositions can be distinguished from synthetic propositions in the first place. It also explains what I mean by an analytic proposition. Section 2 argues that the linguistic doctrine is implicit in or favoured by our common sense understanding of analytic propositions. In section 3, I relate some of the prima facie plausible considerations that have moved eminent philosophers in the direction of a linguistic doctrine.

In the remainder of the paper, I discuss three different attempts to spell out the linguistic doctrine, namely Ayer's verbal theory according to which analytic propositions are statements about linguistic use (sct. 4), Carnap's view that they are true by virtue of meaning or convention alone, i.e. follow from linguistic rules (sct. 5), and Wittgenstein's normativist view that they are themselves rules rather than descriptions (sct. 6). I shall argue that the most promising version of the linguistic doctrine combines elements of the latter two positions. Analytic propositions can be said to be true, but their truth consists in their having a normative status within a certain linguistic practice. This position can be defended against some prima facie compelling objections, because it seeks to explain not the truth of analytic propositions, but their necessity, the fact that nothing would count as contravening them. There remains the question of whether it falls foul of the atemporal nature of truth and necessity (sct. 7).

1. *What I mean by 'Analytic' or 'Conceptual' Statements*

I shall make an assumption that will strike many contemporary philosophers as outrageous, namely that a distinction can be drawn between analytic propositions in a wide sense and so-called synthetic propositions, e.g. between

(1)   All vixens are female

on the one hand,

(2)   All vixens can contract hydrophobia

on the other. Of course, this idea has been vigorously criticized by Quine. In 1953 he wrote: "analyticity, I have argued elsewhere, is a pseudo-concept which philosophy would be better off without" (1976, 171). But pseudo-concepts, like the pseudo-propositions of the *Tractatus* or the pseudo-problems of the logical positivists, have an intriguing capacity for reasserting themselves. Sure enough, in 1974 Quine was whistling a different tune. He countenanced a definition of "analytic" that went beyond his previous notion of "stimulus analytic" sentences, i.e. of sentences that are accepted under any circumstances by all speakers, such as "Lions roar" or "There have been black dogs". Analytical sentences are those which are learned together with language, that is to say, their non-acceptance signifies that a person has failed to learn the meaning of these expressions: "a sentence is analytic if *everybody* learns that it is true by learning its words" (1974, 79; see also 1986, 93–5).

According to Quine, this may "approximate the layman's intuitive conception" of analyticity (1994, 52–3). Yet he also insists that this conception does not have the epistemological and metaphilosophical importance traditionally accorded to it, and that, in fact, it lacks "explanatory value" (1976, 113; see also 1960, 66–7; 1993, 54–5; Hookway 1988, 37–46, Gibson 1988, 93–6). One of his complaints is that the distinction concerns only the acceptance of the beliefs in question and hence does not capture an "enduring" trait of the truths thus "created" (1976, 119–21; 1986, 95). But this defect can be remedied. For Quine wantonly introduced a genetic element into his definition that is easily jettisoned. Whether a sentence counts as analytic should not depend on how it came to be accepted (whether it was accepted as part of language acquisition). Rather, it should depend on its *subsequent* status. What counts is whether in a linguistic community rejecting the sentence is generally regarded as a criterion of having failed to understand it.

Contrast the following two propositions

(3) My five-year-old daughter understands Russell's theory of types
(4) My five-year old daughter is an adult

To (3) we would typically react with *disbelief* and by demanding evidence. By contrast, we *fail to understand* (4) and will demand an explanation of what, if anything, the speaker means by an adult (see Grice/Strawson 1956, 150–1). In other words, our typical reaction to (3) is "I don't believe what you say" (provided that we take the statement to be in earnest), whereas our typical reaction to (4) is "I don't understand what you mean" (provided that we do not take it as shorthand for "My five-year old daughter *behaves* like an adult"). This contrast is firmly established in our conceptual scheme. It is evident in the difference between terms like 'doubt' and 'incredible' on the one hand, terms like 'misunderstanding' and 'unintelligible' on the other, terms that have an established and clear use.

The sincere refusal to acknowledge an analytic proposition is a criterion *either* for not understanding at least one of its constituents, *or* for deliberately employing that constituent in a new sense. On this basis, one can define a class of propositions that I shall label *broadly analytic* or *conceptual*. A sentence *s* expresses a (broadly) analytic or conceptual proposition:

a. if a speaker x sincerely denies or rejects *s*, this shows *either* that x has failed to understand *s*, *or* that x is deliberately employing *s* in a novel sense.

Roughly the same point can be expressed without reference to linguistic acts:

b. mere grasp of the meaning of *s* suffices for being justified in accepting *s* (Boghossian 1997, 334; see also Künne 1983, ch. 5.4–5).

Whether the resulting distinction has the significance traditionally bestowed upon it depends on what that significance is supposed to be. No workable distinction will accommodate all the disparate claims made by the various proponents of an analytic/synthetic distinction (see Bealer 1998). Nevertheless, the distinction introduced here is a legitimate and useful instrument of sober philosophizing. In any event, I shall assume that my rehabilitation of the linguistic doctrine will not founder simply because it is entirely unclear what type of proposition it tries to account for.

2. *The Linguistic Doctrine and Common Sense*

Even conscientious critics of the linguistic doctrine often assume that it is accepted only by philosophers who are in the grip of a discredited ideology like logical empiricism, with its neurotic hostility to the Platonist invocation of abstract entities and to the Kantian idea of pure reason (e.g. Pap 1959, 162).

This is a prejudice, not only because the linguistic doctrine has been accepted by eminent philosophers for very different reasons, but also because of its proximity to common sense. In order to illustrate this point, I shall use a quotation. To make matters worse, it is from a poet rather than a philosopher, and that poet is German rather than Anglo-American.

> Sagt Hänschen Schlau zu Vetter Fritz,
> "Wie kommt es, Vetter Fritzen,
> Dass grad' die Reichsten in der Welt,
> Das meiste Geld besitzen?"
>   (Gotthold Ephraim Lessing)

It is notorious that German humour does not travel well. Nonetheless, here is my rendering of Lessing's joke:

> Says Jack Wiseguy to Cousin Fritz:
> "How come, Cousin Fritz,

that of all the people in the world
it is the richest that have the most money?"

Ordinary speakers of German and, dare I hope, of English, will find this funny because Jack Wiseguy's question betokens ignorance. This much will be granted on all sides. But I think that we can be more specific, and note that the ignorance in question is *linguistic*. Outside of philosophy, no one would say that Jack Wiseguy displays a risible ignorance of the Platonic form *the richest*, or of the intrinsic modal nature of reality, or of the holistic web of our beliefs. Rather, people would say that he does not know what the phrase "the richest" means. What amuses us is this: Jack Wiseguy thinks he is asking a profound question, one to be answered by reference to certain features of those people that are the richest; in fact, however, he is merely displaying his failure to understand the phrase "the richest".

The truth of a proposition like

(5)   The richest person in the world has the most money

appears to be simply due to language, to what we mean by "the richest". "The richest" simply means *those who have the most money*. If Jack Wiseguy had known this, he would not have asked his question. He might have asked instead how come that Bill Gates of all people has the most money. This would have been a substantial question, to which the answer is presumably that Bill Gates has an unbelievable knack for marketing mediocre computer software. By contrast, for a competent speaker it makes no sense to ask why the richest person in the world has the most money, because the co-applicability of "the richest" and "has the most money" is guaranteed by their meaning.

You might be tempted to point out that (5) can be understood as *de re* rather than *de dicto*, in which case it is tantamount to

(6)   Bill Gates has the most money.

As our reaction to Lessing's joke shows, however, this is not how we *in fact* understand statements like (5) and the questions with which they are correlated.[1] Moreover, this is unsurprising. We tend to use words

---

1. In discussion, Saul Kripke pointed out that "Why do most people live in cities?" is stan-

carefully, and for a reason. If we want to make a substantial statement or ask a substantial question, we must phrase it in the appropriate manner, namely a manner that leaves open a substantial issue.

Laymen and -women regard analytic propositions like (5) as verbal, connected to language or meaning in a special way that empirical truths are not. At any rate, this is Quine's view: "The analytic is what the layman calls 'just a matter of words'" (1994, 52; see also 1960, 66–7). We need not accept this simply on Quine's authority, considerable though it may be. The point is confirmed by the way we standardly explain linguistic jokes of the kind exemplified by my opening quote, and by our reactions to the denial of analytic propositions (see Naess 1953).

That the special status of analytic propositions is due to the meaning of their constituent expressions is therefore the view of common sense (pace Yablo 1992, 881). This already suggests that the almost universal condemnation of the linguistic doctrine is excessive and problematic. Philosophers ignore common sense and ordinary use at their peril, not because it is the last word, but because it is the first word, as Austin put it, at least on philosophical issues (1970, 185). Common sense can be wrong, but it can hardly be bizarre or ludicrous. This may even be an analytic proposition in its own right. And even if it is not, past experience suggests that in the great clashes between philosophy on the one hand and common sense on the other, it is the former rather than the latter that tends towards the bizarre and ludicrous. Unfortunately, one popular alternative to common sense philosophy seems to be "Common Non-sense Philosophy" (a term Brentano used for German idealism).

3. *The Philosophical Proponents of the Linguistic Doctrine*

The linguistic doctrine is not just implicit in common sense. It has also been advanced by a small but distinguished group of philosophers that goes back at least to Hobbes. According to *De Corpore*, the axioms of all scientific demonstration are definitions. Definitions, furthermore, do not capture the essence of things, as Aristotle thought, they are nothing

---

dardly understood as a substantial question, in spite of the fact that cities are defined as those areas with the highest concentration of people. But the substantial question that we associate with this form of words is, roughly "Why do more than 50% of the population live in areas of highest concentration?' rather than "Why is the density of population greatest in cities?".

but "settled significations of words", "truths constituted arbitrarily by the inventors of speech, and therefore not to be demonstrated" (1.3.9). "For it is true, for example, that *man is a living creature*, but it is for this reason, that it pleased men to impose both those names on the same thing" (1.3.8). If the term "living creature" had been made to mean something different, *stone*, let us say, it would not be true to say that man is a living creature.

Locke pursued a similar line. According to him, propositions like

(7) Roses are roses

or even

(8) Roses are flowers

are "trifling" rather than "instructive". For a speaker who uses them does not state "a real truth and conveys with it instructive real knowledge", but instead "trifles with words" (*Essay concerning Human Understanding* IV.viii). Analytic propositions, Locke holds, are "only verbal ... and not instructive" (1990, 23).

Two ideas emerge, which correspond closely to my theses (I) and (II). First, analytic propositions are vacuous, they tell us nothing about reality; secondly, they owe their truth to meaning or language alone. In the twentieth century, these ideas received a more precise formulation. According to the *Tractatus*, empirical propositions depict a possible state of affairs, truly or falsely. They are a posteriori, because to establish whether they are true, we must have recourse to reality. By contrast, the propositions of logic are "tautologies". They *say nothing* about reality, since they are compatible with every possible situation. Unlike

(9) It is raining,
(10) Either it is raining or it is not raining

says nothing about the weather, because it combines empirical propositions in such a way that all factual information cancels out. "I do not know anything about the weather when I know that it is either raining or not raining" (Wittgenstein 1961, 4.461).

Some philosophers, including Russell and Quine, have maintained that propositions like (10) tell us something about the most pervasive traits of reality (Quine 1970, 15; Harman 1999, 128). By this token, even (10) says something about the weather, something that we can know about the weather, namely that it is such that it is either raining or not raining.

However, by parity of reasoning *everything* is such that it is either raining or not raining. If (10) says something about the weather, it also says something about everything. But if it says something about everything, it certainly says *nothing about the weather in particular*, which makes the claim that it is about the weather look vacuous. Even if this point were waived, it would be difficult to contradict Wittgenstein's claim that tautologies like (10) "give no information" about reality. "If fifteen, then fifteen!" is no more an answer to the substantive question "How many people will be present?" than "Take it or leave it!" is an order (see Glock 1996a, 280). Some opponents of the linguistic doctrine will respond to this kind of defence by defining notions like information in such a way that (10) can be said to provide information about reality. But this kind of procedure willy-nilly reinforces Hobbes' point: one can redefine terms in such a way that it is no longer false to say certain things. As regards the ordinary understanding of 'information', tautologies like (10) do not provide any information about reality, and do not count as answers to substantive questions.

Led by Schlick and Carnap, the logical positivists tried to extend the *Tractatus* approach to mathematics on the one hand, analytic propositions proper on the other. Analytic propositions also owe their truth to the meaning of symbols alone, except that in their case the relevant symbols go beyond the logical constants. In many ways, the linguistic doctrine still sets the agenda for contemporary debates about logical necessity. At the same time, however, it has been widely condemned. This condemnation is largely due to Quine's vigorous critique of the account of logical necessity associated with the logical positivists. In one respect, however, Quine is quite close to the linguistic doctrine. For him, there is no such thing as "metaphysical necessity" (1981, 174), or *de re* necessity. In so far as modality can be made intelligible, it "resides in the way we say things, and not in the things we talk about" (1976, 176).

Other critics of logical positivism are less harsh on the analytic/synthetic distinction than Quine, but even harsher on the linguistic doctrine. This holds of Arthur Pap in his still unsurpassed *Semantics and Necessary Truth*. David Hamlyn (1966) described Ayer's version of conventionalism as "so obviously false as to be ludicrously so". Paul

Boghossian and Chris Peacocke are gentle by comparison, when they characterize the doctrine as "bizarre" (2000, 7).

In some respects, this repudiation was to be expected. Any common sense view is liable to attract the ire of philosophers sooner or later, especially when they find remnants of it in the writings of their colleagues. But this is only part of the explanation. The positivists' extension of the linguistic doctrine from analytic propositions and tautologies of the propositional calculus to the predicate calculus and to mathematics is not underwritten by common sense, and it is beset by numerous problems. Furthermore, even as regards analytic propositions, it has proven difficult to spell out the initially plausible idea that they are rooted in language. It is to different attempts to do so that I shall now turn. I shall discuss three versions of the linguistic doctrine:

- The verbal theory, briefly espoused by Ayer, according to which analytic propositions are descriptions of or generalizations about linguistic usage (sct. 4)
- The idea of truth by virtue of meaning, associated especially with Carnap, which has it that they follow from linguistic conventions (sct. 5).
- Wittgenstein's normativist position, according to which analytic propositions do not follow from conventions, but are themselves rules for the meaningful employment of words (sct. 6).

4. *Ayer's Verbal Theory*

A simple, some would say simplistic, version of the linguistic doctrine was espoused by Ayer in the first edition of *Language, Truth and Logic*.

> They [analytic propositions] simply *record* our determination to use words in a certain fashion. We cannot deny them without infringing the conventions which are presupposed by our very denial, and so falling into self-contradiction. And this is the sole ground of their necessity (Ayer 1971, 112; my emph.)

In the second edition, however, Ayer distanced himself from the implication that analytic propositions are "a sub-class of empirical propositions" that "describe the way certain symbols are used"; "it is a mistake to identify *a priori* propositions with empirical propositions about language" (1971, 22; see also Quine 1976, 108).

Ayer is certainly right to concede that one must distinguish between an empirical statement to the effect that in a linguistic community *C* an expression *e* is used in a certain way *W*, and an analytic proposition. But from this it only follows that analytic propositions cannot 'record' our determination to use *e* in *W* if to record is here understood as stating that *C* is determined to use *e* in *W*. There are other possibilities. In his scathing attack, Hamlyn glosses Ayer as claiming "that analytic statements ... *reveal* our determination to use words in a certain way" (1966, 200; my emphasis). Ironically, this position is far more plausible than the one Ayer actually held. For the fact that we treat certain sentences as analytic does indeed reveal something about our determination to use words in a certain way.

Consider Putnam's claim that

(11) All cats are animals

is not analytic, because we would abandon it if it turned out that the things we call "cat" are radio-controlled automata (1975, ch. 15). Whether we would indeed react in this way will, in my view, depend on the circumstances. Whatever the circumstances, however, there is nothing incoherent in persisting to treat (11) as analytic, e.g. by maintaining that, unbeknownst to us, all cats have turned into automata, or even that what we used to regard as cats were never really cats. Those who pursue that line will simply operate with a different concept of a cat from those who abandon (11), namely one that applies to things with a certain property, rather than one that applies to things to which we have previously applied the label 'cat'. And by calling or treating (11) as analytic, they indeed reveal their determination to use 'cat' in a certain way. Similarly, if I were to insist that a just society must be one in which there is no material inequality, I would reveal my determination to use the term 'just' in a certain way.

It does not follow, however, that (11) describes our use of the term 'cat' or that it states our determination to continue in this use. For the fact that a certain utterance reveals something about its utterer does not show that it is a statement about the utterer. The utterance "Off with his head!" discloses something about the speaker's state of mind, yet it is not a piece of autobiography.

5. Truth by Virtue of Meaning (Carnap)

We should accept, therefore, that Ayer's version of the linguistic doctrine is untenable. Like him, we might then move on to the idea that analytic truths do not describe linguistic use, but follow from rules or conventions of linguistic use. On this view, all a priori truths are true solely in virtue of the meanings of their constituent words. *Logical* truths are tautologies which are true in virtue of the meaning of the logical constants alone, and *analytical* truths proper can be reduced to tautologies by substituting synonyms for synonyms. Thus "All bachelors are unmarried" is transformed into "All unmarried men are unmarried", a tautology of the form "(x) ((Fx & Gx) → Gx)". This conception of analytic propositions as those that can be derived from logical propositions with the help of definitions is nowadays often referred to as Frege analyticity (e.g. Boghossian 1997), although it goes back at least to Kant. What the logical positivists added is the idea that the truth of both logical propositions and analytic propositions proper is guaranteed by meaning alone and hence by linguistic conventions. Whereas the truth of logical propositions is guaranteed by the meaning of the logical constants that occur in them, the truth of analytic propositions is *also* guaranteed by the meaning of other constituent terms of those propositions. The positivist account was first elaborated by Carnap (1937), but a more succinct summary is provided by Ayer's recantation of his earlier verbal theory.

> Just as it is a mistake to identify *a priori* propositions with empirical propositions about language, so I now think that it is a mistake to say that they are themselves linguistic rules. For apart from the fact that they can properly be said to be true, which linguistic rules cannot, they are distinguished also by being necessary, whereas linguistic rules are arbitrary. At the same time, if they are necessary it is only because the relevant linguistic rules are presupposed. Thus, it is a contingent empirical fact that the world "earlier" is used in English to mean earlier, and it is an arbitrary, though convenient, rule of language that words that stand for temporal relations are to be used transitively; but, given this rule, the proposition that, if A is earlier than B and B is earlier than C, A is earlier than C becomes a necessary truth (Ayer 1971, 22–3).

The positivist position can be seen as based on the following argument:

P₁   In the case of analytic propositions, meaning suffices for truth
P₂   Linguistic rules/conventions suffice for meaning
C   In the case of analytic propositions, linguistic rules/conventions suffice for truth

The argument is valid, but is it sound? For present purposes, I shall not scrutinize P₂. But I shall briefly remind you of its plausibility.

> ... a word hasn't got a meaning given to it, as it were, by a power independent of us, so that there could be a kind of scientific investigation into what the word *really* means. A word has the meaning someone has given to it (Wittgenstein 1958, 28).

One need not identify the meaning of an expression with its use in order to recognize that expressions owe their meaning to the use linguistic creatures make of them.

P₁ is the idea of truth in virtue of meaning alone. It implies that each individual truth involves a 'linguistic' and a 'factual' component or content, and that the latter is zero in the case of both logical and analytical truths. Quine has attacked this idea by appeal to semantic holism: individual propositions cannot be said to have either a factual or a linguistic component or content. This attack rests on two premises: first, that the content of an individual proposition would have to be identical with the evidence that counts for or against it (verificationist theory of meaning); secondly, individual propositions are not associated with a particular set of evidence (epistemic holism). Both premises rest on theoretical assumptions that are at least as problematic as the linguistic doctrine (see Glock 2003, ch. 3.2). For this reason, I shall leave the holistic objection aside and address instead a line of criticism that is less assuming and more internal.

This criticism questions the very idea that some propositions are true *solely* in virtue of the meaning of their constituents, independently of the world. As Waismann (1968, 124–5) pointed out, the phrase "true by virtue of meaning" is *prima facie* puzzling, since it is unclear how a proposition could follow from a meaning rather than from another proposition. Quine associated the phrase with the "myth of a museum" (1969, 27, see 19), Wittgenstein with the picture of "meaning-bodies" (1974, 54–8). What they condemn under these titles is the idea that there are meanings—abstract entities or mental processes—which coerce us (either psychologically or rationally) to hold on to analytic propositions, come what may.

In fact, however, the proponents of the linguistic theory were never committed to such a Platonist or mentalist myth. But without it, the idea of truth by virtue of meaning boils down to the claim that necessary propositions are true by virtue of *definition*: they follow from the definitions of their constituents. This takes us back to the proposal that analytic propositions are either logical truths or reducible to logical truths by substituting synonyms for synonyms. But this proposal faces three objections.

Objection 1
This objection dogged logical positivism from its inception. Non-empirical statements like

(12) (x) (y) (x is warmer than y → y is not warmer than x)

or

(13) Nothing can be green and yellow all over

resist such reduction, since the ingredient terms are not definable in the appropriate way. Consequently, they would have to be classified as synthetic a priori.

Both Wittgenstein (1974, 184) and Carnap (1956, 226–8) developed a response to this objection. Statements like (12) and (13) need not be reducible to logical truths with the aid of definitions. For they do not *follow* from definitions; rather, they *themselves* are implicit definitions or explanations of our vocabulary for thermal qualities and colour. Like definitional truths, (12) and (13) are *conceptual*. Unlike contingent statements, which apply concepts to make statements of fact, they are *constitutive of our concepts*. They determine how certain terms are to be used, and thereby they also determine the meaning of these terms (what concepts they express).

Objection 2
The second difficulty was first pointed out by Quine. Standard definitions cannot create truths, since they are simply conventions of abbreviation which license the replacement of a definiendum by a definiens. Conse-

quently, definitions only transform truths, they cannot create them. For example, given the definition

(14) Bachelors are unmarried men

one can transform the analytic truth

(15) All bachelors are unmarried

into the logical truth

(16) All unmarried men are unmarried.

"What is loosely called a logical consequence of a definition [e.g. (15)] is therefore more exactly describable as a logical truth [e.g. (16)] definitionally abbreviated" (Quine 1976, 79).

The fact that this procedure presupposes logical propositions is not fatal to the version of the linguistic doctrine that I am defending, since the latter does not purport to explain logic. But the objection that definitions are simply incapable of creating truths would be, if it could be sustained. Quine himself grants, however, that there is a kind of convention capable of creating truths. Unlike "discursive definitions", which simply record pre-existing relations of co-extension or synonymy, "legislative postulates" or "implicit definitions" are capable of creating truths. Adopting propositions on the basis of "deliberate choices", which are justified only "in terms of elegance and convenience", renders those propositions true by convention (1976, 117–20). In this fashion, we can even render logical truths true by convention. We define the meaning of the logical constants *a novo* by specifying that certain propositions in which they occur are to be true and others to be false. The former "become true by fiat, by linguistic convention" (1976, 89–91; see 1990, 49–60).

At the same time, both Quine and Pap have denied that legislative postulation redeems the linguistic doctrine. They deplore that this procedure can be extended beyond logic and mathematics to empirical science.

> But if the method of specifying the meaning of a term T by saying that T is meant in such a way that statement S containing T is true justified the assertion that the truth expressed by S is conventional, then any true state-

ment could be made out as a conventional truth (Pap 1959, 170; see Quine 1976, 100–2, 121–2).

From my perspective, however, this consequence is perfectly acceptable. It means that we can extend legislative definition beyond what we currently accept as logical or even analytic truths. For example, we might simply stipulate that "bachelor" is to be used in such a fashion, that all sentences of the form

(17) If x is a bachelor, then x is unmarried

are to be true (presupposing a prior assignment of meaning to "if ... then" and "unmarried"). In that case, (17) might be said to be true by linguistic convention.

Of course, we could also extend the procedure to include forms of words that are now used empirically, such as

(18) If x is a bachelor, then x is unhappy

But, to use Quine's own words, all this would show is that in addition to analytic propositions being true by convention, "it is likewise a matter of linguistic convention *which* propositions we are to make analytic and which not" (1990, 64). Conventionalists can happily accept that we are at liberty to adopt statements as analytic even within empirical science—such as Carnap's meaning postulates (1956, Suppl. B)—namely for the sake of accommodating the empirical evidence.

Objection 3
At the same time, Quine's own discussion intimates reasons against his initial concession that legislative conventions, at any rate, are capable of creating truths. "Verbal usage is in general a major determinant of truth" (1976, 108, see 113, 116). For *any* sentence s, s is true iff for some p, s says that p and p. All that conventions do is to determine what a sentence *says*; whether what it says is true is another question, to which linguistic conventions are irrelevant. Therefore, a sentence cannot owe its truth-value exclusively to meaning or conventions. Granted, if it pleased humans to apply the term 'living creature' to stones, it would no longer be true to *say*

(19) Man is a living creature

But the proposition that we now express through (19) would still be an analytic truth.

Stephen Yablo (1992) calls this "the Lewy point", "with doubtful historical accuracy". The qualification is sapient, since the point goes back at least to C. I. Lewis (1946, ch. 5; see Lewy 1976, ch. 5; Boghossian 1997, 334–6). Heroically braving the risk of further correction, I shall refer to it as the Lewis-Lewy objection. I also want to elaborate it in a slightly different way. What could it mean for a convention to *create* a truth? Of course, we can choose to *assume* that a certain proposition is true, in the course of constructing hypotheses, or for the sake of argument. But this does not *render* that proposition true. In the sense in which, for example, the fact that the cat is on the mat might be said to render true the statement that the cat is on the mat, conventions cannot be said to render anything true. The only truths conventions could "create" are truths such as "In 1795 France adopted the metric system", which are precisely not true by convention (see Baker/Hacker 1985, 234; Glock 1996).

6. *The Normativist Position*

These points militate against the view that necessary propositions are truths following from meanings, conventions, or definitions. But they do not rule out linguistic accounts in general. Carnap's and Wittgenstein's idea of treating some analytic propositions as implicit definitions suggests a different version. Analytic propositions do not *follow* from the meanings of their component signs, as the classical positivist picture suggests, they partly *determine* or *constitute* them. For example, the axioms and rules of logic implicitly define the logical constants; they determine their meaning, rather than proceeding from them. Whether a specific transformation of symbols is licensed or not is one aspect of the correct use and hence of the meaning of the terms involved. For example, that we treat "~~p ↔ p" as a tautology and infer "p" from "~~p" contributes to the meaning of "~". If we treated "~~p ↔ ~p" as a tautology and inferred "~p" from "~~p", the meaning of "~" would change correspondingly. The idea resurfaces in contemporary conceptual role semantics: "if some expressions mean what they do by virtue of figuring in certain inferences and sentences, then some inferences and sentences are *constitutive* of an expression's meaning what it does, and others aren't" (Boghossian 1997, 353).[2]

We can extend this position to analytic propositions. For example,

(15) All bachelors are unmarried

is partly constitutive of the meaning of the term "bachelor". It is an analytic proposition not because we can transform it into a logical truth by substituting synonyms for synonyms, as Frege analyticity has it, but because it is semantically constitutive in this way. (15) has its status independently of "All unmarried men are unmarried", because it provides a direct license for substituting "unmarried man" for "bachelor" in empirical statements like "Kant was a bachelor".

But what is the precise status of implicit definitions or conceptual statements? According to Boghossian (1997, 348–56), it is conventional that we express a logical truth by assigning the value "true" to a sentence like "~~p ↔ p" ; but the truth so expressed rests on facts about a "logical object" that obtain even if we no longer treat the sentence as true. This option avoids the idea of truth by convention. But it is a version of Platonism, and it may well lead us back to the myth of a museum. In any event, it undermines the very idea behind implicit definitions. Implicit definitions cannot at the same time be both definitions that *constitute* meaning or concepts and statements about and *validated* by meanings or concepts.[3]

---

2. This account implies that any change in necessary propositions amounts to a partial modification of at least one of the concepts involved. This consequence was welcomed by Wittgenstein, but may be implausible for some necessary truths, such as less central mathematical propositions. Still, the proofs of such propositions provide us with new non-empirical grounds for the application of mathematical terms (Glock 1996a, 226–31). Once we accept the Pythagorean theorem, having a hypotenuse the square over which is identical with the sum of the squares over its two catheters becomes a necessary condition for something being a right-angled triangle. In any event, the implication is plausible with respect to central logical and mathematical propositions. For example, the move from "~~p ↔ p" to "~~p ↔ ~p" clearly alters the meaning of "~". More importantly still, it holds of analytic propositions as I defined them. If rejection of such a proposition betokens ignorance of meaning, the communal rejection amounts to a change in the meaning of one of the constituent terms.

3. According to Boghossian, Kripke shows these claims to be compatible: the statement "S is one metre long", where S refers to the standard-metre, is both a definition and a factual statement. It must be granted that this form of words can be used both to express as a norm that ties the unit 'one metre' to the length of a particular rod at a particular time and to express a statement about the length of a particular rod. But it cannot fulfil both roles at the same time. In so far as it is a factual statement, it *presupposes* that the term 'one metre' has been

A second option is conventionalism à la Carnap. It avoids the myth of a museum by insisting that *we confer* necessary status on certain sentences by employing them as implicit definitions. At the same time, it holds on to the idea that they are truths, albeit truths determined by conventions. But the Quinean objections count against this compromise. Conventions are incapable of creating truths. What conventions can do, however, is to *establish rules*.

This idea underlies Wittgenstein's position. If necessary propositions do not record extra-linguistic necessities but constitute meaning or concepts, then they must be *normative* rather than *descriptive*. Although their linguistic appearance is that of statements of fact, their actual function is to express linguistic rules, standards for the correct or meaningful use of words. Analytic propositions can neither be confirmed nor confuted by experience, because linguistic rules antecede matters of fact. (15) cannot be overthrown by the putative description "This bachelor is married", since the latter incorporates a nonsensical combination of signs. (15) is conceptually necessary simply because we would not *call* anybody both 'married' and 'bachelor'. Given our linguistic rules, it makes no sense to apply both terms to one and the same person.

This account avoids both the myth of a museum and the idea of a special truth by convention. We can remove a sentence from the scope of empirical refutation by using it normatively rather than descriptively. But in that case we have not created a *fact* or *truth*, but *adopted* a linguistic *norm*. At a superficial level, at least, it avoids the Lewis-Lewy objection. That conventions cannot render anything true is no objection to the linguistic doctrine, if analytic propositions are themselves rules rather than truths created by conventions. Conventions cannot render what a sentence says true, but there is no reason to deny that they can accord a normative status to a sentence.

Alas, the normativist position faces other serious difficulties. The most immediate is that it seems to run counter to the linguistic facts. Unlike rules, analytic propositions are *about* vixens, colours, and bachelors, etc., not about words. Furthermore, they are expressed by declarative sentences, hence they can be *true*, stand in logical relations, and can be known (e.g., Waismann 1968, 66–7, 136–7).

---

defined. And in so far as it is a definition, it is not factual, i.e., it is not validated by any facts, but by our fiat. If 'one metre' is defined as whatever length S has, then 'S is one metre long' cannot be refuted by facts.

In my view, however, this difficulty is not insuperable. As far as *aboutness* is concerned, the linguistic doctrine fares no worse than other much more popular accounts. According to Frege, for example, (15) is about the complex concept (function) *if x is a bachelor then x is unmarried*, to which it ascribes the property of taking the value true for all arguments. Taken at face value, however, (15) is about none of these arcane things, it is about bachelors, or about all bachelors.

I am not suggesting that we should take the grammatical form of (15) at face value. But what is sauce for the Fregean goose must be sauce for the Wittgensteinian gander. If it is possible to disregard the grammatical form of (15) in order to bring out its inferential powers, why should it not be possible to disregard that grammatical form in order to bring out its special normative role vis-à-vis the meaningful use of 'bachelor'?

More importantly, Wittgenstein's distinction between rules and statements of fact is based on function rather than linguistic form. It does not reduce analytic propositions to empirical propositions about linguistic usage. One must distinguish between the expression of a rule and an empirical proposition to the effect that a community follows certain linguistic rules, what von Wright calls a "norm proposition" (1963, viii). Unlike the latter, the former need not be a meta-linguistic statement. A meta-linguistic statement like

(20) 'Bachelor' means (the same as) 'unmarried man'

a standard definition like

(14) Bachelors are unmarried men

and an analytic proposition like (15) all have similar normative functions:

– they lay down what counts as intelligible description of reality
– they establish internal relations between concepts (the concept of being a bachelor and the concept of being unmarried) and propositions
– they license transformations of empirical propositions (from "Wittgenstein was a bachelor" to "Wittgenstein was unmarried").

Whether a sentence expresses a rule depends not on its grammatical appearance, but on its *role on an occasion of utterance*, on whether in the particular case it is used as a standard of correctness. For example, the sentence "War is war" *could* be used to illustrate the law of identity, but is typically used to express a questionable moral view (Wittgenstein 1967, 221).

As far as the *declarative* nature of analytic propositions is concerned, it should be noted that many non-linguistic rules are expressed in the indicative mood. One example is provided by what Bentham called "the dominative tense" (see Baker/Hacker 1985, 41), as in

(21) The Prime Minister will form a cabinet within two weeks of a general election

An even clearer example is provided by a

(22) The chess-king moves one square at a time

This also provides a crucial clue as to the difficulty that analytic propositions are *true*. It is correct that we do not ordinarily call rules true. On the other hand, (22) is standardly used to express a rule, yet there is no strain whatever in saying that it is true or about the chess-king.

(22′) It is true that the chess-king moves one square at a time

is perfectly compatible with

(22*) It is a rule that the chess-king moves one square at a time

What is infelicitous is only the combination of the two operators, for example in

(22#) The rule that the chess-king moves one square at a time is true

One possible explanation is that the two operators "it is true that ..." and "it is a rule that ..." cast (22) in different and incompatible lights. (22*) brings out the normative force of (22), whereas (22′) is akin to a norm proposition. It is not, however, a statistical claim about the behaviour of chess-players. Rather, it is typically a claim that (22) is indeed the rule. The role of the truth-operator is to affirm that this rule is in force (whether or not it is heeded by all, or even by a majority).[4]

7. *Uncompelling Postscript*

This observation takes us to the crucial question, namely whether being about and being true *amount to the same thing* in the case of analytic propositions as in the case of synthetic propositions (see Baker/Hacker 1985, 276). In my view, the answer to this question should be negative. An analytic proposition is true not in the sense of saying how things in fact are, but in the sense of being a rule that is indeed constitutive of the meaning of a word in a certain linguistic community.[5]

For one thing, the typical role of an analytic proposition like (15) is not to make a true statement of fact about bachelors, but to explain the meaning of 'bachelor'. This is why we do not verify (15) by investigating the marital status of people we regard as bachelors, and why its sincere denial betokens not *factual ignorance* but *linguistic misunderstanding*.

For another, unlike synthetic propositions, an analytic proposition like

(13) Nothing can be green and yellow all over

cannot be understood as denying a genuine possibility. In order to do so it would have to be possible to specify the possibility they seem to exclude. But this possibility cannot be coherently specified.

---

4. Another problem is how to make sense of inferences involving analytic propositions. Of course, various systems of deontic logic account for logical relations between imperatives and norms. But the question is whether any of them captures the normative character of analytic propositions. A non-formal rumination must suffice here.
    (P_1) All vixens are foxes
    (P_2) All foxes are animals
    (C) All vixens are animals
can be rendered as
    (P_1') It makes no sense to apply 'vixen' while withholding 'fox'
    (P_2') It makes no sense to apply 'fox' while withholding 'animal'
    (C) It makes no sense to apply 'vixen' while withholding 'animal'.

5. An analytic proposition is not a norm proposition, but the proposition *that an analytic proposition is true* is at the very least closely related to a norm proposition.

> It is queer that we should say what it is that is impossible ... In speaking of that which is impossible it seems as though we are conceiving the inconceivable. When we say that a thing cannot be green and yellow at the same time we are excluding something, but what? Were we to find something which we described as green and yellow we would immediately say this was not an excluded case. We have not excluded any case at all, but rather the use of an expression (Wittgenstein 1979, 63–4).

Wittgenstein concludes that propositions like (13) do not exclude or negate a genuine possibility. Rather, they ban a certain combination of words as meaningless from our language. What analytic propositions exclude is a move within a language-game, akin to the proposition "you cannot castle in draughts".

Coming from a very different angle, the same point was made by Ernest Nagel (1949). It is a mark of analytic propositions that we maintain them no matter what facts turn up. And we specify what we meant by these propositions in such a way as to render them compatible with whatever facts turn up. Take

(23) Every tone is characterized by exactly one pitch

Suppose we object to this by appeal to chords or overtones. Then someone who treats (23) as analytic will reply that neither chords nor overtones are properly describable as tones.

At this point the Lewis-Lewy objection once more raises its head. The normativist must concede that analytic propositions can be true; but, the objection ran, the appeal to linguistic conventions or practices cannot explain truth. If my account of truth for analytic propositions is correct, however, the objection fails. For an analytic proposition to be true, I argued, is for a certain rule to be in effect. And what rules are in effect depends on linguistic conventions or practices. It might be replied that this linguistic explanation of truth for analytic propositions is simply untenable, since analytic propositions must be true in precisely the same way as empirical propositions. But this response ignores a crucial point.

The appeal to rules accounts for necessity and apriority rather than factuality. It explains not why bachelors *are* unmarried, or the *fact* that bachelors are unmarried, but why *nothing counts* as a married bachelor. And nothing counts as a married bachelor because we use 'married' and 'bachelor' in ways that preclude their application to one and the same person. By pain of idealism, the way we use expressions cannot make it the case that certain individuals are unmarried (see Boghossian 1997, 336; Yablo 1992, 381). What it establishes is a *de dicto* connection, between those to whom we apply the term 'bachelor' and those to whom we apply the term 'unmarried'.

Consider Pap's example of a legislative definition, namely that we specify that

(R) 'red' means that colour C for which "the city buses running on Broadway are C" is true

Pap asks the rhetorical question: "Is the fact that the city busses running on Broadway are red, then, a result of linguistic convention?".[6] But the rhetorical force of this question is owed to the fact that we understand the term 'red' that occurs in it in its customary sense, which is independent of the colour of the buses running on Broadway. (R) cannot and does not purport to explain why the buses on Broadway have the same colour as ripe tomatoes. Rather, it stipulates that 'red' is to mean whatever colour the buses actually running on Broadway have. If that colour is what we now call 'blue', then the rule will have the consequence that 'red' applies to blue things. If the buses have no uniform colour, then 'red' will apply to all those things that have these various colours. Whether in that case 'red' is still what we call a colour term is a different matter. The rule stipulates that whatever has the same colour as the buses running on Broadway is to count as 'red'. What the appeal to convention explains is why, given the new rule, nothing counts as a bus running on Broadway that does not also count as red.

The Lewis-Lewy objection was based on the need to distinguish the following two

A. The sentence *s*, as presently used, expresses an analytic truth
B. The proposition that is at present expressed by *s* is an analytic truth

---

6. Pap 1959, 170. In a similar fashion, Davidson (1984, 269) writes that even if there were necessary and sufficient conditions for the application of a term, it would not follow that these conditions are conventional. "We all agree that horses must have four legs, but it is not a convention that horses have four legs". It would be a convention, however, that nothing that doesn't have precisely four legs *counts* as a horse.

and on the idea that (B) is entirely independent of (A). But there is an analogous distinction for norms

A' The sentence s, as presently used, expresses a rule of language L
B' The rule that is at present expressed by s is in effect in language L

The normativist must grant the distinction between a rule and the sentence expressing it. He must also grant that as the expression of a linguistic rule the analytic proposition itself need not, and in general will not be tensed. However, there is no obstacle to saying that the validity of the rule can be tensed, and hence subject to change. We can express a linguistic rule differently, without thereby suspending it. However, we can also suspend the rule, and it would be wrong to insist that the rule is still in effect, even if our linguistic practices have changed. Although a rule need not be obeyed by all, or even by a majority, it cannot be in effect, if no one invokes it as a standard of correctness (see Glock 1996a, 328).

The rule expressed by (22) would no longer be in effect if chess evolved so that the king moves two squares at a time. Similarly, as things are

(24) All red things are coloured

is a rule for the use of 'red'. But if a community drew a sharp distinction between warm and cool colours, and confined 'colour' to the latter, this would no longer be a rule. It won't do to say that a mere shift in language has taken place, and that even for those people it would be necessary that whatever is red is coloured (e.g. Yablo 1992, 878). For this amounts to a *petitio principii* against the linguistic doctrine. In the envisaged community, there is no necessity to apply the term 'coloured' to all the things to which they apply 'red'. What is true is this: it makes no sense for us to withhold the term 'coloured' from the things they call 'red'. But this merely means that 'red' as used by us is a colour term, whatever they say. Being a rule is not atemporal and independent of linguistic use in the same sense as being true is.

The matter can also be expressed in a different manner by going back on one point in our definition of analyticity, namely the idea that analyticity is a feature of propositions. Truth is a feature of what is expressed by sentences, but perhaps analyticity is best regarded as a feature of sentences: it indicates that they have a special, normative function. And this role is obviously something that sentences can lose, subject to the vagaries of our linguistic practice. The price to be paid for this manoeuvre is the acknowledgement that talk of analytic *propositions* and analytic *truths* is strictly speaking elliptical. *Au fond* it is sentences that are analytic, namely if they are used to express a rule that is constitutive of the meaning of a word.

I want to draw two lessons from these reflections. First, at least as regards analytic propositions it is worth revisiting the linguistic doctrine. Perhaps a version of it can be defended against the numerous and vigorous criticisms brought against it. Wittgenstein's normativist position, in particular, is not as outlandish as it may seem, and can perhaps deal with the Lewis-Lewy objection. At any rate, the linguistic doctrine must contain at least a kernel of truth. No account of analytic propositions can be deemed satisfactory unless it can explain the common sense conviction that these propositions have a special connection to language, meaning or linguistic use.[7]

BIBLIOGRAPHY

Ayer, Alfred J. 1971: *Language, Truth and Logic* [1936], Harmondsworth.

Austin, John Langshaw 1970: *Philosophical Papers*, Oxford.

Baker, Gordon and Peter Hacker 1985: *Wittgenstein: Rules, Grammar and Necessity*, Oxford.

Bealer, George 1998: "Analyticity", in: E. Craig (Ed.), *The Routledge Encyclopedia of Philosophy*, London, 234–239.

Boghossian, Paul 1997: "Analyticity", in B. Hale, B. and C. Wright (Eds.) *A Companion to the Philosophy of Language*, Oxford, 331–68.

Boghossian, Paul and Chris Peacocke 2000: "Introduction", in P. Boghossian and C. Peacocke (Eds.), *New Essays on the A Priori*, Oxford, 1–10.

Carnap, Rudolf 1937: *The Logical Syntax of Language*, London (German edn. 1934).

— 1956: *Meaning and Necessity*, Chicago.

---

[7]. For comments on previous drafts I should like to thank Peter Hacker, Wolfgang Künne and Geert Keil, as well as audiences in Berlin and Bologna.

Davidson, Donald 1984: *Inquiries into Truth and Interpretation*, Oxford.

Gibson, Robert F. 1988: *Enlightened Empiricism: an Examination of W.V. Quine's Theory of Knowledge*, Tampa.

Glock, Hans-Johann 1996: "Necessity and Normativity", in H. Sluga/D. Stern (Eds.), *The Cambridge Companion to Wittgenstein*, 198–225.

— 1996a: *A Wittgenstein Dictionary*, Oxford.

— 2003: *Quine and Davidson on Language, Thought and Reality*, Cambridge.

Grice, Paul and Peter Strawson 1956: "In Defense of a Dogma", *Philosophical Review* 65, 141–58.

Hamlyn, David 1966: "Contingent and Necessary Statements", in: P. Edwards (Ed.), *The Encyclopedia of Philosophy*, London, Vol. 2, 198–205.

Harman, Gilbert 1999: *Reasoning, Meaning and Mind*, Oxford.

Hookway, Chris 1988: *Quine*, Cambridge.

Künne, Wolfgang 1983: *Abstrakte Gegenstände*, Frankfurt am Main.

Lewis, Clarence Irving 1946: *An Analysis of Knowledge and Valuation*, La Salle, Ill.

Lewy, Casimir 1976: *Meaning and Modality*, Cambridge.

Locke, John 1990: *Drafts for the Essay Concerning Human Understanding and Other Philosophical Writings* Vol. 1, Oxford.

Nagel, Ernest 1949: "Logic without Ontology", in: E. Feigl and W. Sellars (Eds.), *Readings in Philosophical Analysis*, New York, 191–210.

Naess, Arne 1953: *Interpretation and Preciseness*, Oslo.

Pap, Arthur 1958: *Semantics and Necessary Truth*, New Haven.

Putnam, Hilary 1975: *Mathematics, Matter and Method: Philosophical Papers Volume 1*, Cambridge University Press.

Quine, Willard van Orman 1960: *Word and Object*, Cambridge/Mass.

— 1969: *Ontological Relativity and Other Essays*, New York.

— 1970: *Philosophy of Logic*, Cambridge/Mass.

— 1974: *The Roots of Reference*, La Salle/Ill.

— 1976: *Ways of Paradox and Other Essays*, Cambridge/Mass.

— 1981: *Theories and Things*, Cambridge/Mass.

— 1986: "Reply to Herbert G. Bohnert", in L.E. Hahn and P.A. Schilpp (Eds.), *The Philosophy of W. V. Quine*, La Salle, Ill., 93–5.

— 1990: "Lectures on Carnap (Harvard University, November 1934)", in R.

Creath (Ed.), *Dear Carnap, Dear Van: The Quine-Carnap Correspondence and Related Work*, Berkeley, 47–103.

— 1994: "W. V. Quine: Perspectives on Logic, Science and Philosophy: Interview with B. Edminster and M. O'Shea", *Harvard Review of Philosophy* IV, 47–57.

Waismann, Friedrich 1968: *How I See Philosophy*, New York.

Wittgenstein, Ludwig 1961: *Tractatus Logico-Philosophicus* [1921], London.

— 1958: *The Blue and Brown Books*, Oxford.

— 1967: *Philosophical Investigations*, Oxford.

— 1974: *Philosophical Grammar*, Oxford.

— 1979: *Wittgenstein's Lectures, Cambridge 1932–1935*, Oxford.

von Wright, Georg Henrik 1963: *Norm and Action*, London.

Yablo, Stephen 1992: "Review of A. Sidelle: Necessity Essence and Individuation", *Philosophical Review* 101, 878–81.

QUINE AND THE PROBLEM OF SYNONYMY

Peter PAGIN
Stockholm University

Summary
On what seems to be the best interpretation, what Quine calls 'the problem of synonymy' in *Two Dogmas* is the problem of approximating the extension of our pretheoretic concept of synonymy by clear and respectable means. Quine thereby identified a problem which he himself did not think had any solution, and so far he has not been proven wrong. Some difficulties for providing a solution are discussed in this paper.

1. *Synonymy in the* Two Dogmas *framework*

At the end of section three of *Two Dogmas*, Quine decides to turn his back on what he calls 'the problem of synonymy'. By then he has spent two sections on discussing what synonymy might amount to, dismissing first *definition* and then *interchangeability salva veritate* as candidates for explaining it. In a sense, he does the right thing, for the discussion of synonymy in *Two Dogmas* is really a digression.

Quine's main target, or one of his two main targets, is analyticity. But, as Tyler Burge (Burge 1992, 4–10) and Paul Boghossian (Boghossian 1997, 335–7), among others, have pointed out, there are several notions of analyticity in *Two Dogmas*. The first notion (1951, 20) of an analytic truth is that of a truth grounded in meaning independently of matters of fact. The second (1951, 23), is that of a truth that can be turned into a logical truth by putting synonyms for synonyms. The third and last notion (1951, 43) is that of a truth that holds come what may, as opposed to a synthetic truth that holds contingently on experience. At no point does Quine comment on the relations between these different notions, and it is not easy to know what he thought.

The first and the third of these are different but closely related, the one concerning independence from facts and the other independence from experience. These notions are directly relevant to the holism Quine proposes in section six. They are relevant to his discussion of the nature of science, of the relation between theory and experience, and of that between theory and the world. The second analyticity notion, however, does not really belong in this framework. By the definition of the second notion, logical truths are unproblematically analytic. But Quine is explicit about rejecting the analytic/synthetic distinction, or the existence of analytic truths, when talking of the first notion—independence from facts—and of the third notion—independence from experience. So logical truths wouldn't qualify as analytic in any of those two senses. From Quine's own point of view, the second notion is not really compatible with the other two.[1]

But if that is so, what is, after all, the problem of synonymy? If Quine is right about analyticity in the first and third sense, then a logical truth like

(1)   All unmarried men are unmarried

is not true independently of matters of fact, nor true independently of experience. But then we will not get any such sentence either by interchanging synonyms in a logical truth. Specifically, on the assumption that 'unmarried man' is synonymous with 'bachelor', this will hold of

(2)   All bachelors are unmarried.

(2) is hardly more independent of facts or experience than (1) is, and hence it isn't analytic in any of the two central senses. Because of this, it does not really matter to Quine's rejection of analyticity, in the first or third sense, whether we have an adequate definition of synonymy or not. Even if a definition can be devised that is respectable from a Quinean point of view, Quine's criticism of the first and third notion remains intact. The literature has not always been clear on this point.

---

1. More precisely, the following four sentences are jointly inconsistent: 'all analytic sentences are true independently of matters of fact', 'no sentence is true independently of matters of fact', 'all logical truths are analytic sentences', and 'there are logical truths'. Analogously with 'unrevisable' instead of 'true independently of matters of fact'.

The synonymy discussion does, therefore, even though motivated by Carnap's writings, stand out as a digression. It is, however, a digression of considerable independent interest.

2. *The problem of synonymy in* Two Dogmas

The problem of synonymy, as it is conceived in *Two Dogmas*, is that of explaining what synonymy is, without making use of any other notion that is as much in need of explanation as synonymy itself. So stated, however, the problem is not very well defined. Are we supposed to *analyze* the concept of synonymy (if such there is)? Or are we to provide a systematic *reconstruction* of our intuitive, pretheoretic conception of synonymy (if such there is)? Or are we to provide a reconstruction that as far as possible approximates the *extension* of our intuitive conception? I guess the last of these alternatives is most like what Quine had in mind. At least it is Quinean in spirit. Take what we have in the way of clear and respectable means of defining or explaining, and see if we can come up with a definition that at least approximately agrees in extension with what we are disposed, pretheoretically, to count as synonyms. It is plausible, I think, to see Quine as attempting this in sections two and three of *Two Dogmas*, but in fact, as we shall see shortly, Quine accepted deviations from the pretheoretic conception, thus making the problem easier.

In section two Quine correctly dismisses the appeal to definition. In section three he turns to interchangeability. In a nutshell, he reasons as follows: "First, we propose that two expressions are synonymous just if they can be interchanged *salva veritate* in all linguistic contexts, except where they are mentioned rather than used. But, if the language providing these contexts is extensional, then coextensive expressions meet this condition. Coextensiveness, however, falls short of (cognitive) synonymy. To compensate, we can either enrich the language by adding the adverb 'necessarily', or strengthen the condition, from interchangeability *salva veritate* to interchangeability *salva analyticitate*. These two options are in fact equivalent, for prefixing 'necessarily' to a sentence is just another way of saying that it is analytic. But now we have been moving in a circle, for an explanation of analyticity is what we wanted in the first place". To this one can add, in the light of later sections, that the strenghtening to interchangeability *salva analyticitate* doesn't do much good for synonymy if there aren't any analytic sentences to begin with.

Now, it doesn't require genius to notice that Quine has left many options unconsidered here. He hasn't considered alternative enrichments of the language, nor alternative interpretations of the modal adverb, even though he has discussed both at other places. In particular, however, he hasn't considered alternative properties to be preserved by an interchange.

We can in fact extract such a candidate property from Quine's own holistic picture of science, i.e. of total science as a fabric with theoretical sentences in the interior and with experience-confronting sentences at the periphery (1951, 42–3). The relevant property is then, to use Quine's own metaphor, the *distance* to the periphery. That is, two expressions count as synonymous just if any substitution, in any use-context, of the one by the other results in a sentence having the same distance to the periphery as the original sentence. This is interchangeability *salva distantia*. As Quine himself explains it, (1951, 43), the distance to the periphery consists in the relative likelihood of giving up the sentence in the face of recalcitrant experience. What is preserved, then, by the interchange of synonyms, is the subject's willingness to make revisions. For instance, if I hold 'brother' and 'male sibling' as synonymous, then I am as unwilling to give up

(3) Brothers are male siblings

as I am to give up

(4) Brothers are brothers.

I need not think that (4) is *immune* to revision, but I will be very unwilling to give up this and any other logical truth. I am then equally unwilling to give up sentences produced from logical truths by interchange of synonyms. This proposal has been worked out in greater detail elsewhere (Pagin 2001). Distance to the periphery is not a metric, but a position in a strict partial order of being *less revisable than*. The most revisable sentences are at the periphery, and the least revisable ones in the center.

If the language in question is extensional, then, given a few natural rationality constraints on revisions, the synonymy relation will be different from logical equivalence, but it will *not* be more strict than logical equivalence. That is, logically equivalent expressions count as synonymous. Because of that, this definition will deviate from intuitive synonymy judgments. This much deviation did not bother Quine, however, who wrote that

> Statements may be said simply to be cognitively synonymous when their biconditional (the result of joining them by 'if and only if') is analytic (1951, 32).

A biconditional whose immediate parts are logically equivalent is a logical truth, and logical truths are, by the second notion, analytic. So Quine would accept logically equivalent sentences as synonymous. He also accepted disposition talk. Indeed, the *less-revisable-than* ordering relation is more or less formulated by Quine:

> [...] in this relation of "germaneness" I envisage nothing more than a loose association reflecting the relative likelihood, in practice, of our choosing one statement rather than another for revision in the event of recalcitrant experience (1951, 43).

The proposal therefore seems to be a solution to the problem of synonymy, as Quine presumably conceived it at the time of *Two Dogmas*.

3. *The problem recast*

Nonetheless, there is reason not to be satisfied with such a solution, and not only because of the remaining deviation from pretheoretic synonymy judgments. After all, synonymy is supposed to be sameness of *meaning*, or at least intralinguistic sameness of meaning. So there is reason to ask what the preservation of relative revisablity has to do with meaning, and to answer this question we need to have at least some idea of what meaning might amount to.

Quine's own preliminary suggestion of interchangeability *salva veritate* is not itself formulated in isolation from any idea of meaning. After all, why would interchangeability *salva veritate* be even a candidate for a synonymy relation? The answer, I guess, is twofold. First of all, there is an assumption that semantics is *compositional*: the meaning of a complex expression is determined by the meanings of its parts and its mode of composition. Simplifying a little bit, it follows, as Carnap remarked (1956, 121–2), that a substitutivity, or interchangeability, principle holds: replace an expression by another expression with the same meaning, and the meaning of the whole remains the same. For two expressions to have the same meaning, i.e. to be synonymous, it is then necessary that interchanges in larger expressions—where they are used, not mentioned—are meaning preserving. The most conservative option is to make this a sufficient condition as well. Then the meaning of a single expression can be identified with the contribution it makes to the meaning of larger expressions containing it.

Secondly, there is an assumption that *truth* depends on meaning. Even if there are other determinants of truth value than facts and linguistic meaning—and we know that because of indexicality, at least, there are—two sentences with the same meaning, as potentially used by the same speaker at the same time, should have the same truth value. If again we take a conservative line on sentence meaning, we can identify it with *truth conditions*. For what Quine in *Word and Object* called "eternal sentences" we can be even more conservative and identify sentence meaning with truth value. The result will be that two expressions are synonymous just in case they are interchangeable *salva veritate*. It is unlikely that this idea of synonymy could have anything going for it without these, or closely related, background assumptions about meaning.[2]

Still, there have been at least two reasons for preferring talk of synonymy at the expense of explicit talk of meaning. One is that the concept of meaning is badly defined and very difficult to characterize, and that we have reason to be skeptical about including meaning entities in our ontology. Quine exemplifies both attitudes already in *Two Dogmas* (1951, 22). The constructive idea, expressed by Quine in several passages (e.g. 1960, 201), is then that if we manage to make the synonymy relation precise, we can simply identify meanings with equivalence classes of synonymous expressions, since those would serve as counterparts to synonymy as well as anything else, and if synonymy can't be made precise, then we should reject meaning entities anyway.

---

2. The connection between synonymy, compositionality and truth is highlighted by the problem of belief sentences. Benson Mates (1950), later supported by Tyler Burge (1978), claimed that intuitively synonymous expressions need not be interchangeable salva veritate in belief contexts, and Mates took that to be a problem for the concept of synonymy. By contrast, Jeff Pelletier (1994), who also endorsed the claim of substitutivity failure, took it to be a problem, not for synonymy, but for the compositionality of natural language. In both cases, however, the connection between these concepts is reaffirmed.

But this option is not, I think, acceptable. First, if synonymy is understood as just *intralinguistic* sameness of meaning, as it usually is, then we get the odd result that two expressions belonging to different languages also differ in meaning, in virtue of that fact alone, regardless of similarity in usage. For their respective meanings will be different equivalence classes of expressions, each being a class of expressions of one language only. The relation of interlinguistic sameness of meaning will be well defined, but it will have an empty extension. Second, if we stick to the idea of compositionality, the meaning of the whole, and thus the truth value of a sentence, should depend on the meaning of the parts. But it is quite implausible that membership in a class of synonymous expressions is *that* very property of an expression that helps determine the truth value of a sentence containing it. Taking meanings to be equivalence classes of synonymous expressions is putting the cart before the horse; sameness of meaning should depend on meaning, not the other way around.

The second reason, however, challenges this order from considerations of determinacy. Given any intuitive idea of meaning properties, we run a risk—maybe a high risk—that the assignment of meaning properties to expressions remains indeterminate. Several different meaning distributions over the expressions of a language may be equally well supported by the facts and the principles that jointly determine what is right. By contrast, the intralinguistic synonymy relation, as governed e.g. by the idea of interchangeability, will be uniquely determined. Because of this, the objection concludes, we can make good sense of synonymy talk even if meaning is indeterminate. Therefore, we should stick to the former.

It is of course correct that substantial ideas of meaning properties and meaning assignment induce the risk of indeterminacy. And it is true that the intralinguistic synonymy relation can be made determinate even if the meaning assignment isn't. But the right conclusion isn't that we should skip talk of meaning. Rather, the right conclusion is that the dependence of synonymy on meaning must be generalized. What we should say isn't simply that two expressions are synonymous just if they have *the* same meaning, but that they are synonymous just if *any* correct distribution of meanings over the language will assign the *same* meaning to both expressions. This definition indeed makes the synonymy relation determinate, even if meaning assignment itself is not (provided it *is* determinate whether or not a given meaning distribution is correct), and gives the simple definition as a special case if it is.

Given such an understanding of the relation between synonymy and meaning, is there a problem of synonymy, beyond the problem of knowing what meaning is? I think there is, and I think it is pretty much parallel to Quine's problem. For Quine, the problem was to match *pretheoretic* ideas of synonymy with what can be explained by clear and respectable means. We can phrase the remaining problem in similar terms: the problem is to match intuitive ideas of synonymy with our best (clear and respectable) account of meaning. Will our pretheoretic judgments of intralinguistic sameness and difference of meaning be supported by our best account of linguistic meaning?

What will be the nature of our best account? I think there is no good alternative here to following Quine, Donald Davidson and many others at least two steps on the way. First, meaning is language-independent. That is, there is no good sense to a notion of meaning which doesn't even allow expressions of different languages to be *compared* for sameness or difference in meaning. Second, what meaning an expression has is essentially connected with how speakers manage to communicate with the help of that expression. That is, a meaning property plays a role for what is communicated by means of expressions having that property. Even though the second point may be a little more controversial than the first, I don't think either is much disputed.

So far, there is not much to conclude about synonymy. Meaning properties may, for all that has been said so far, involve *more* than what is relevant for communication. There may be (perhaps small) differences in meaning that don't matter for communicative success. In that case synonymy, being the complete lack of difference in meaning, is not relevant.

However, at this point I prefer to follow Quine and Davidson, and Michael Dummett, a third step, parting company with others. I shall assume that what isn't relevant for success of communication isn't relevant for meaning either. Meaning properties *are* properties that play a certain role in an account of successful communication.[3] That is, if the interchange of two expressions α and β cannot make a difference

---

3. Note that there is nothing behaviorist about this choice. I don't think that successful communication can be understood in behaviorist terms (cf. Pagin *unpublished*). Moreover, I do not even assume here that it is always knowable whether communication succeeds or not.

to communicative success in any possible context, then α and β are synonymous.

Given this assumption, we can recast the problem of synonymy as follows: does success or failure of communication ever depend on synonymy according to pretheoretic standards? If it doesn't, then there is no theoretic basis for pretheoretic synonymy. And then there is a problem of synonymy, i.e. pretheoretic synonymy.

When turning to intersubjectivity for the basis of meaning, the first place to look is naturally Quine's account in *Word and Object*.

4. *Synonymy and radical translation*[4]

It is a common view, I think, that in *Word and Object* Quine took the critique of meaning, and thus of synonymy, one step further. It is not just that intuitive synonymy cannot be made clear sense of; according to our best approximation of interlinguistic meaning, there cannot be such a thing. That is the lesson of the indeterminacy of translation, according to this view.

This is a mistake, however. Since intralinguistic synonymy can survive indeterminacy of meaning, it can also survive indeterminacy of translation (the reason is given in the appendix). But the problem of synonymy doesn't end there. In a sense it only begins.

In *Word and Object*, Quine proposed the basic translation condition, for observation sentences, to be a matching of stimulus meanings. However, as stimulus meaning was defined (Quine 1960, 32–3), in terms of a pair of classes of stimulations, it is not something that can be shared between speakers. For a stimulation is a stimulation of a person's nerve endings, and as long as two persons don't share nerve endings, they don't share stimulations. Quine discussed this in lectures in 1965, later published as "Propositional Objects". He there rejects the appeal to homology of receptors as a solution, "not only because full homology is implausible, but because it surely ought not to matter" (Quine 1969, 157). He briefly considers appeal both to a looser idea of resemblance of stimulations, and to an idea of similarity of "barrages of outside forces" (ibid., 159), but ends the paper with speaking of the

---

4. Sections 4 and 5 are digressive illustrations of the basic conflict. The main reasoning picks up with section 6.

intersubjectivity of stimulus meaning as a problem.

The problem resurfaces more than twenty years later, at the Quine conference in St Louis 1988, with Davidson's "Meaning, Truth and Evidence". Davidson notes that if translation is to be based on similarity of stimulus meaning, then strange results are possible:

> [...] let us imagine someone who, when a warthog trots by, has just the patterns of stimulation I have when there's a rabbit in view. Let us suppose the one-word sentence the warthog inspires him to assent to is 'Gavagai!'. Going by stimulus meaning, I translate his 'Gavagai!' by my 'Lo, a rabbit' though I see only a warthog and no rabbit when he says and believes (according to the proximal theory) that there is a rabbit (Davidson 1990, 74).

Because of the possibility of such discrepancies, according to Davidson, Quine's account—i.e. what Davidson calls the 'proximal theory'—leads to skepticism (Davidson 1990, 74). Either way, it clearly seems that in the circumstances imagined by Davidson, the right translation would be 'Warthog', not 'Rabbit'. What matters seems to be the shared, distal stimulus, not the unshareable proximal one.

This seems to have been Quine's own conclusion. In *Pursuit of Truth* he says:

> The view that I have come to, regarding interpersonal likeness of stimulation, is rather that we can simply do without it. The observation sentence 'Rabbit' has its stimulus meaning for the linguist and 'Gavagai' has its for the native, but the affinity of the two sentences is to be sought in the externals of communication. The linguist notes the native's utterance of 'Gavagai' when he, in the native's position, might have said 'Rabbit'. So he tries bandying 'Gavagai' on occasions that would have prompted 'Rabbit', and looks to natives for approval. Encouraged, he tentatively adopts 'Rabbit' as translation (Quine 1992, 42).

So, stimulus meaning is still there as the best respectable approximation to the intuitive idea of meaning, but translation isn't based on correlating instances of it.

The consequence of this choice is a certain tension between synonymy and the correctness of translations. The synonymy relation will be intrapersonal and based on internal facts, while the translation relation will be interpersonal and based on external facts.

To illustrate this, let's adapt an example of Carnap's (1956b, 236–40). Carnap, in "Meaning and Synonymy in Natural Languages", was concerned with the possibility of empirical methods for determining the meaning a speaker attaches to a particular expression. For the extension of a particular predicate, within a surveyable region, the method consisted in simply eliciting a response from the speaker, as to whether he wanted to apply the predicate to a particular object or not. Carnap acknowledged some difficulties, because of the possibility of factual error on the speaker's part, and because of the general problem of induction in trying to project the total extension from the extension in a limited region.

An additional problem is introduced when it comes to determining intension. Carnap considers two hypotheses about what the German speaker Karl means by the word 'Pferd': on the one hand *horse*, and on the other *horse or unicorn*. Since unicorns don't exist, the two hypotheses determine the same extension, and they are therefore empirically equivalent in predicting the applications of the predicate by the speaker. A version of this example can illustrate the present difficulty. For assume that Karl has two words, 'Pferd' and 'Schmerd', and that the stimulus meanings are different: Karl is disposed to assent to 'Pferd' after stimulations typically caused by horses, and to assent to 'Schmerd' after stimulations typically caused by horses *as well as* to stimulations that would be caused by animals looking like unicorns. Because of this difference, the two words must be counted non-synonymous for Karl.

However, it is not clear that they should be differently translated, if the correctness of translation is determined by the speaker's dispositions with respect to distal stimuli. For with respect to distal stimuli, the speaker has the same disposition to apply both terms, the disposition to apply it to horses, and to nothing else, since there is nothing else to which he is disposed to apply either of them.

Carnap tries to solve his problem by indirect methods: we can describe unicorns to Karl and ask whether he would apply his term to it, and we can show him a picture of a unicorn. The first method can work, of course, if we already have a well established translation manual for a large fragment for Karl's language, but if the problem afflicts all predicates, this cannot be assumed for a solution of the problem. The second method might be decisive as well, but it need not, for strictly speaking Karl is disposed to assent after stimulations from unicorns, not from pictures of unicorns. After all, my disposition to assent to 'unicorn' is not the same as my disposition to assent to 'picture of unicorn'. The picture method should work if it gave Karl the *illusion* of seeing a unicorn, but that is not so easily accomplished.

It is even more difficult than that, since for the sake of determining the correct translation between Karl's use of 'Pferd' or 'Schmerd', and George's use of the English 'horse', we would need to provide *both* speakers with an illusion of a unicorn, in order to see whether there would be any difference between their dispositions to assent to their respective words. But this is not enough either, for it is also required that the illusion is suitably *shared*. There must be a shared distal stimulus that would elicit the reactions of both speakers. It would not be enough to directly stimulate the nerve endings of each.

In this particular case I guess the normal intuition is that translating 'Schmerd' with 'horse' is simply wrong, and we would look for methods for finding this out without a direct inspection of proximal stimulations. But even if this is right, it is not so clear in the general case. For one speaker may have two terms, *a* and *b*, differing slightly in (proximal) stimulus meaning, even though it is practically impossible, or even nomically impossible, that any *distal* stimulus would cause a proximal stimulation of the one kind that is not also a proximal stimulation of the other kind. These terms are non-synonymous for the speaker. But with respect to *distal* stimulus meaning, they may both be translatable into the same expression *e* of another speaker, e.g. 'rabbit', and it is not obvious that either of the translations should be considered incorrect. The difference in stimulus meaning between *a* and *b* need not be relevant to the translation of them into another speaker's language. Regardless of what we should say in any particular case, there seems to be a general tension between the intrapersonal requirement of sameness of proximal stimulus meaning and the interpersonal requirement of sameness of distal stimulus meaning. If intralinguistic synonymy depends on the first, and *meaning* proper on the second, there is a genuine conflict.[5]

---

5. This is not to deny that we can expect a high degree of covariance. In general, if one person finds objects *x* and *y* (or situations *x* and *y*) perceptually similar, then so does the next person. Largely overlapping standards of perceptual similarity, between persons, seem to be a prerequisite for largely successful linguistic communication. Since basic standards of perceptual similarity must be innate, Quine calls this interpersonal overlap "a preestablished harmony" (Quine 1995, 21; thanks to Geert Keil for reminding me of this passage). To the extent that synonymy judgments depend on perceptual similarity, we can therefore expect widespread interpersonal agreement in synonymy judgments. Note that perceptual similarity is distinct from similarity of stimulations.

5. *A Fregean example*

The conflict mentioned above may have the consequence that intralinguistic synonymy is a stricter relation than sameness of meaning. That is, two expressions may have the same meaning, but still not be intralinguistically synonymous. But if that can happen, what kind of relation is intralinguistic synonymy? You might think that this conflict is a result of rather specific ideas about stimulus meaning, or linguistic behaviorism in general. But this is not obviously the case.

There may, on the contrary, be a general tension between the need for intrapersonal semantic distinctions and the need for interpersonal semantic sameness. Such a tension is exemplified in Frege's ideas of sense. As Frege presented it, a linguistic expression expresses its sense, and the sense is what contains the mode of presentation of the referent. The mode of presentation of an object to a particular speaker corresponds, on common interpretations of Frege, to how the speaker *knows* or *thinks about* the referent. How the speaker thinks of an object may be more or less idiosyncratic, and Frege himself provides an example, in "Der Gedanke" (1918, 24–6), of two speakers communicating about a third person, presented to each of them in a different mode. The two speakers, Leo Peter and Herbert Garner, will then associate different propositions with the sentence

(5)   Dr Gustav Lauben has been wounded

since they associate different senses with the proper name, even though the reference is the same. On Frege's view, there is a communication failure, and he even claims that the two speakers don't speak the same language (Frege 1918, 25). In Frege's example, it is a mere coincidence that the two ways of determining the reference yield the same result, but that feature can be changed. We may assume that because of e.g. the social context the two speakers are justified in believing that under the name 'Dr Gustav Lauben' they understand the same person, regardless of differences in mode of presentation. We may also assume that their respective modes of presentation are so related that it is impossible for them to pick out different referents given shared background knowledge of the speakers.[6] In such a case, it is strongly counterintuitive to say

---

6. For example, suppose that for Leo Peter the name 'Dr Gustav Lauben' is associated

that communication fails. If this intuition is right, then communication can succeed despite interpersonal differences in Fregean sense.

The introduction of sense is motivated by concerns of individual psychology. We need an account of differences for a single person in cognitive value between the sentences

(6) $a = a$
$a = b$

and we need an account of substitution conditions of expressions in propositional attitude contexts. In both cases, possible mental states of a single person—knowing the one thing but not the other; believing the one thing but not the other—need to be accounted for, and the concept of sense is the core of the account. Sameness of sense (for non-indexical expressions) is, if anything is, synonymy in Frege's theory. The need for differences in sense goes beyond what is needed for communicative success.

This shows that the semantic tension between the intrapersonal and the interpersonal exists even in a more mentalistic setting. It does not show that there is problem with intralinguistic synonymy, partly because of the rather natural Fregean motivation for the distinctions between senses, and partly because we have considered only communicative success in a particular case. The tension will become acute only when we have distinctions between sense that *cannot ever* make a difference between communicative success and failure. But it seems the tension is in fact acute, for it seems that an account of pretheoretic synonymy will have to appeal to features of the individual speaker that cannot matter to communicative success.

6. *Synonymy and communication*

First, what does it mean in general for intrapersonal synonymy to be relevant to communication? It cannot amount to the following idea, that

---

with the mode of presentation of being the physician who lives on the second floor, and that for Herbert Garner the name is associated with the mode of presentation of being the physician who delivered the second child of the emperor. Suppose, finally, that both know that the physician who lives on the second floor is the physician who delivered the second child of the emperor.

synonymy between two sentences in the speaker's language guarantees that if communication with a hearer succeeds with the one sentence, then it succeeds with the other. This isn't the right idea, for synonymy, no matter how strict—as long as it can hold between different sentences—cannot guarantee that success is preserved by interchanges. The hearer may simply know the meaning of just one of the sentences.

Rather, I think it should be understood the following way. Whether a particular communicative event, involving a speaker, a hearer and an utterance, is successful depends on the hearer's response. The response can be e.g. that of thinking that it is a beautiful night, following an utterance of the sentence 'it is a beautiful night'. When the response is appropriate, e.g. because the hearer came to think just the same thought as the speaker expressed by the utterance, communication succeeds. Then, let's call two sentences *communicatively equivalent* just if the same hearer response, or responses, would be appropriate whichever of the two sentences would be used by the speaker. Intuitively, the same thing is communicated with the two sentences; that is, it *is* the same thing as far as communication is concerned.

Now we can say that synonymy is relevant for communication just if synonymy between sentences coincides with communicative equivalence. For subsentential expressions it must hold that they are synonymous just if a substitution of the one for the other produces a sentence synonymous with the original sentence. This is the adequate condition on synonymy, for if synonymy is a stricter relation than communicative equivalence, then two sentences need not be synonymous for being communicatively equivalent, and so the added similarity that synonymy contributes makes no difference to communication. If synonymy is a more inclusive relation, then different things are communicated with synonymous sentences, and so synonymy fails to represent what matters to communicative success.

What does matter to communicative success? Clearly, a difference in truth conditions between sentences can matter. It need not always matter, but if e.g. two predicates have different application conditions, there are at least some sentential contexts in which that difference is crucial to what is communicated. Suppose for a moment that truth conditions, say in the sense of possible worlds truth conditions, is what in general matters to success. That is, if the hearer reacts by thinking a thought which is false in some possible circumstances where the speaker's thought is true, then communication has failed. By the present proposal of how synonymy matters to communication, this would mean that synonymy is relevant just in case synonymy between sentences coincides with identity of possible worlds truth conditions. However, it is common wisdom that synonymy is more narrow than identity of truth conditions. For instance, the two sentences

(7) Pigs grunt

(8) Pigs grunt and $2+2=4$

are true in the same possible worlds, but by pretheoretic standards, they are not synonymous. So if truth conditions are what matters to communication, then synonymy doesn't.

But surely more does matter to communication than possible worlds truth conditions, even if we abstract from all pragmatic aspects. For instance, it does make a difference whether I make you think that $2+2=4$ or that $16 \times 7 = 112$, even though both hold in all possible worlds. The most natural way to represent this difference is to let thought content be individuated by semantic *structure*. Intuitively, the components of the thought that $2+2=4$ are different from the components of the thought that $16 \times 7 = 112$ (except for the identity relation), and that is a reason for distinguishing between the thought contents as wholes, too.

The linguistic counterpart of structured thought content is structured meanings, and the classical definition of a synonymy relation based on semantic structure is Carnap's definition of *intensional isomorphism* (Carnap 1956, 56–7). Briefly stated, for two expressions to be intensionally isomorphic, they must have the same syntactic structure, and corresponding *simple* constituents must have the same intension. If we apply these ideas and find that, first, sameness of structured thought content is necessary and sufficient for communicative success, and, second, that two sentences are communicatively equivalent just if they are intensionally isomorphic, and, thirdly, that intensional isomorphism coincides with synonymy, then we do have the result the intrapersonal synonymy is relevant for communication.

However, in so far as we are concerned with pretheoretic synonymy, the result is negative. Carnap himself notes that the expressions 'brother' and 'male sibling' are not synonymous by the standard of intensional isomorphism (1956, 61), simply because one is simple and the other complex. But 'brother' and 'male sibling' is one of our stock examples of pretheoretic synonymy.[7]

It might also be the case that two simple expressions can have the same intension without being synonymous by pretheoretic standards, even though I don't know of any uncontroversial examples. One kind of example, although controversial, would be proper names, if one would combine the view that names are rigid designators with the view that names have Fregean senses. Given that they are rigid, coreferring names have the same possible worlds intension, but they can still differ in sense, and hence be non-synonymous.

Either way, it seems clear that pretheoretic synonymy does not coincide with intensional isomorphism. Neither does it seem easy to save this equivalence by some sophisticated syntactic theory. The idea would be that the criterion of intensional isomorphism should not be applied to surface structure, but to an underlying level of syntactic form. Some examples of apparent synonymy combined with surface structural difference can be plausibly handled this way. For instance, the sentences

(9) The police brought in the criminal

(10) The police brought the criminal in

would count as intuitively synonymous, and they can plausibly be seen as sharing an underlying structure.[8] Applying the criterion at that level would make them come out isomorphic. Similarly, if the underlying form of 'brother' in fact is the same as that of 'male sibling', then the two expressions would count as intensionally isomorphic despite the surface difference. But I can see no good reason for thinking that general principles of syntactic theory would make *all* pretheoretical synonyms

---

7. In Pagin 2003 I suggest a somewhat relaxed synonymy relation (dubbed 'μ-congruence') that allows a simple expression to be synonymous with a complex one, but otherwise is close to Carnap's. It is far from clear how that notion measures up to intuitions (it has been rejected as counterintuitive by a couple of linguists). The matter is discussed in the final section of Pagin 2003.

8. (10) is derived from (9) by the separation transformation T^{op}_{sep} of Chomsky 1957, 75–76. In the days of transformational grammar it was argued, especially by Katz and Postal (1964, 30–70), that all interpretation of complex expressions, i.e. by so-called projection rules, apply to *underlying* phrase structures. Thus, any singulary grammatical transformation, like from (9) to (10), is taken to be meaning preserving. In later theories, sentences are synonymous that share (interpreted) LF.

share an underlying structure. Rather, there is good reason to suspect that this could only be achieved by a series of *ad hoc* stipulations.

7. *Beyond semantic structure*

So far the result has been negative. However, even if we cannot represent pretheoretic synonymy by semantic structure, there must be some feature of the speaker's linguistic dispositions that singles out synonymy pairs from other pairs, beyond his disposition to call the members 'synonymous'. One such feature might be the sameness and differences between dispositions to revise judgments, which would be in accordance with the proposal in section 2. I am going to argue, however, that such a proposal does not meet the condition that meaning is to be relevant for the success of linguistic communication. In fact, the argument will be more general: *no* account of synonymy that goes beyond semantic structure will make the synonymy relation relevant for communication. The basic reason is that it is too implausible that the thought contents of speaker and hearer agree as far as semantic structure and that yet the communication fails.

Assume that there is some relational property type S of expressions such that any two expressions sharing S type property are synonymous. The S type property may be what was suggested in section 2, i.e. what an expression contributes to the revisability conditions of sentences containing it. It can be some *normative* property, such as that of being stipulated to have a certain relevance for linguistic commitments etc. It can be a property that depends on the linguistic competence of the individual speaker, or a property that depends on general norms or regularities in the speech community. It will not matter which. All that matters is the assumption that two sentences can have different S properties, and hence be non-synonymous, even though sharing semantic structure, or have the same S property, and hence be synonymous, even though differing in semantic structure.

To consider an example, suppose that for speaker A

(11) x is to the left of y

is synonymous with

(12) y is to the right of x

for any uniform replacements of the variables. That is, an instance of (11) has a certain S property s* for A iff the corresponding instance of (12) has s* for A. Suppose, further, that this doesn't hold for speaker B. For B, any two corresponding instances of (11) and (12) will be necessarily equivalent, but they will not be synonymous.[9]

Now B says to A

(13) Elsa is to the left of Arnold

and we may suppose that communication is successful. A understands what B says. The question now is whether communication would have been successful if B had said instead

(14) Arnold is to the right of Elsa.

For B, (13) and (14) are equivalent (they will have the same truth value with respect to all possible circumstances), but they are not synonymous. Assuming that synonymy is relevant to communication, they are not communicatively equivalent, in the sense of the previous section. That is, the hearer response that is appropriate for a B utterance of (13) is not appropriate for a B utterance of (14). However, for A, the two sentences are synonymous, and hence the hearer response of A will, again on the assumption that synonymy is relevant to communication, be the same for both utterances. Then, since communication was, by assumption, successful when B used (13), it would have *failed* had B instead used (14).

If the example is acceptable, two things are to be concluded. First, since the pretheoretic synonymy relation is allowed to vary between speakers, or between communities, pretheoretic synonymy in general is distinct from communicative equivalence. If A's synonymy relation does coincide with communicative equivalence, then B's doesn't (it makes too fine distinctions). If B's synonymy relation coincides with

---

9. If you have taken the S type to be a type that depends on what the speech community is like, you should here take A and B to come from different communities. These two communities can then be assumed to be completely alike except insofar as the S type properties, or some S type properties, are concerned.

communicative equivalence, then A's doesn't (it makes too coarse distinctions). This holds regardless of how the communication in the example is evaluated.

Second, it is not reasonable to take the communication, by either (13) or (14) to have failed. We assumed that the S type properties go beyond truth conditions and semantic structure. Therefore, we can assume that as A and B understand the two sentences, they will have the same truth value in all possible circumstances. The same will hold for *any* pair of alternative instances of (11) and (12): communication between A and B cannot succeed with both members of the pair, even if A and B agree on possible worlds truth conditions of both members.

But this conclusion is too implausible. What more could be demanded for successful communication than that the meanings of all the parts of the sentence, and the structure of the sentence, uniformly contribute to determining truth conditions that will be the same as understood by both speakers?[10] Setting the standards of success higher than that is simply a mistake. Such standards would deviate so much from common sense standards of communicative success that at best this would amount to a stipulation of a new meaning for the very expression 'communicative success'.

If this is right, then there cannot be any S type property, beyond semantic structure, that underlies synonymy. But maybe this verdict is premature. After all, if synonymy matters to communication, it is enough that the difference between A and B with respect to (11) and (12) *can* lead to communicative failure at some point when these expressions are involved. It should not be required that it lead to failure in the very instances of the schemata. But if not in the instances, where?

Maybe we should consider sentences like

(15) If Elsa is to the left of Arnold, then Arnold is to the right of Elsa.

For A, (15) would come out as analytic, in the sense of being transformable into a logical truth by replacing the occurreence of (14) with

---

10. Clearly, (11) and (12) are semantically equivalent in the sense that every shared substitution (same term for same variable) produces instances with identical truth conditions. Therefore, it makes sense to count (13) and (14) as equivalent in semantic structure. Still, it is also possible to count them as not sharing semantic structure, e.g. since a direct application of the intensional isomorphism criterion gives the result that corresponding parts are not even coextensive.

a second occurrence of (13). For B, since the two are not synonymous, (15) would be non-analytic in this sense. Should we not say, then, that communication between A and B by means of (15) would fail? Again, I think there is no good reason to do so, and the same good reason as before not to. Classifying (15) as analytic for A and as non-analytic for B is simply a consequence of classifying (11) and (12) as synonymous for A and as non-synonymous for B. The former stands and falls with the latter, and does not add anything of its own.

Perhaps A is disposed to *call* (15) 'analytic', while B is not so disposed, but this does not show that there is any difference in how they interpret (15). All it shows is that either they understand (15) differently, or one of them makes a mistake, or they understand 'analytic' differently. Without a good reason for the first or second alternative, the third is the best choice. Similarly with calling (11) and (12) 'synonymous'.

But couldn't one say that for A (15) is a *conceptual* truth, while for B it is non-conceptual? I think there is no basis for this either. There is a good sense in which (15) is a conceptual truth for both A and B: the truth of (15) depends essentially on the semantics of the relational expressions, the conditional form, and the coreference of the singular term occurrences. As long as this is preserved, the singular terms can be varied *salva veritate*. For both A and B, then, the truth of (15) depends in this sense on the relational concepts, and not on the terms. But even so, it is left open whether (11) and (12) stand for, or express, the same or different concepts. Moreover, if they express different concepts, it is still left open whether the necessary equivalence depends on meaning alone, or if it depends on the nature of the corresponding properties (and it is left open whether this distinction makes sense).

All in all, (15) can't make the difference. It should be clear that nothing would change in this respect by prefixing (15) with 'necessarily'. But maybe belief contexts offer a decisive factor. For A, by assumption, would be disposed to assign the same truth value to

(16) Zeno believes that Elsa is to the left of Arnold

(17) Zeno believes that Arnold is to the right of Elsa

while it would be conceivable for B that one be true and the other false. So in this case, the difference would result in possibly divergent truth value assignments. Therefore, for B but not for A, there must be a difference in content between (16) and (17), and since this difference depends only on the difference between the embedded sentences (13) and (14), these must have a different content for B but not for A.

But this cannot work either. If synonymy makes a difference for belief contexts, then synonymy must already make a difference in other contexts as well. For if (16) is true and (17) false, then the beliefs expressed by (13) and (14) must *already* be different. If beliefs expressed by the two sentences are different, then the sentences are not communicatively equivalent to begin with, for it would be a misunderstanding to interpret an utterance of the one as expressing the belief that would be expressed by uttering the other. But if the beliefs are different, we want to know what it is that makes them different. The difference in belief content cannot *arise* only at the level of the belief sentence themselves. If B does hold that (16) and (17) differ in truth value, or that they could differ in truth value, there is a further question of what this attitude is based on.[11]

The conclusion is that belief contexts do not offer a reason for making meaning distinctions beyond difference of semantic structure. There seems to be no good reason for the view that (11) and (12), for instance, could be synonymous for one speaker or speech community but just necessarily equivalent for another. If the communication condition is adequate, then there seems to be no good reason for assuming the existence of an S type property of the kind suggested.

Quine was perhaps wrong insofar as overrating the importance of the problem of synonymy to his overall theme of analyticity. He was wrong, I believe, in thinking that the problem of synonymy, as he conceived it in *Two Dogmas*, could not be solved. He was right, however, in pointing out the difficulty of saving or even approximating our pretheoretic notion, or notions, of synonymy by clear and respectable means. He was right, that is, in pointing out that there is a problem of synonymy. Moreover, his negative attitude to the prospects for solving it may in the end be borne out.

---

11. Indeed, for Mates (1950) and Burge (1978), (16) and (17) could differ in truth value *even if* (13) and (14) are synonymous.

Appendix: Synonymy and indeterminacy of translation

Quine's thesis of the indeterminacy of translation rules out non-linguistic meanings, such as propositions as the meanings of (eternal) declarative sentences, that can be shared by expressions of different languages. Quine himself is explicit about that at the end of § 42 of *Word and Object*. The reason is simple. The assumption to be reduced to absurdity is that correct translations are meaning preserving. Then suppose we have two correct translation manuals M_1 and M_2 between languages L and L*. A translation manual is a definition of a recursive translation relation. By the indeterminacy thesis we can choose M_1 and M_2 so that the following holds: a sentence *s* of L is translated by M_1 into *s'* and by M_2 into *s''* of L*, but *s'* and *s''* "stand to each other in no plausible sort of equivalence however loose" (Quine 1960, 27). So, *s'* and *s''* do *not* have the same meaning. But, by the assumption of meaning preservation both *s'* and *s''* have the same meaning as *s*. Given the transitivity of identity they also have the same meaning as one another, and so we have a contradiction. Hence, the assumption is false. Correct translations aren't meaning preserving. Even if there are propositions and other meanings, they are not determinately assigned to linguistic expressions.

If Quine is right, then, determinate interlinguistic sameness of meaning has to go, but there are still two questions about *intra*-linguistic synonymy. First, is the possibility of a well-defined synonymy relation compatible with the indeterminacy of translation? Second, if so, can it approximate our intuitive synonymy judgments?

Let's consider the first question. Our situation is pretty analogous to that in section 3, where we generalized the definition of synonymy to accommodate indeterminacy of meaning. The analogous solution would be this: we define two expressions e_1 and e_2 of language L to be synonymous just if it holds of any correct manual M, with L as the source language, that $M(e_1) = M(e_2)$. That is, they are mapped on the same expression by any correct manual M with L as the source language. Although this generalization accommodates the indeterminacy, it is not acceptable as it stands. For the target language may contain synonymous expressions, too. The simplest way of handling this complication is to take a manual to define in general a many-many relation and then to require the following: two expressions e_1 and e_2 of language L are synonymous just if it holds of any correct manual M, with L as the source language, and any expression e in the target language, that $M(e_1, e)$ iff $M(e_2, e)$ (that is, e_1 and e stand in the translation relation M just if e_2 and e do). Call this 'translational synonymy'.

Note that this proposal does accommodate indeterminacy. To take Quine's example of indeterminacy of reference, the term 'gavagai' of L can go into both 'rabbit' and 'undetached rabbit part' of English, by different manuals, but no single correct manual M would translate 'gavagai' with *both* of the English expressions. Thus, by the definition proposed, 'rabbit' and 'undetached rabbit part' are non-synonymous, as desired.

Could we then simply *define* intralinguistic synonymy this way? There are two problems with this suggestion. First, without a correct and complete set of criteria for the acceptability of a translation manual, we don't have a complete definition of synonymy. We don't know under what conditions of linguistic use two expressions of a language *should* be translated the same by any correct manual. Quine himself doesn't propose any complete set, just a short list of desiderata, at the beginning of § 15 of *Word and Object*. And in later writings he is even less specific (cf. 1992, 48).

The second problem is that we don't yet know whether what would be defined this way would be *synonymy*, or anything even close to it. It is pretty clear that we can claim two expressions to be synonymous if they are assigned the same *meaning* by any acceptable distribution of meanings over the language, but it is not so clear that we manage to approximate a pretheoretic understanding of synonymy by the condition that the two expressions be *translated* the same. We need to know more about the relation between meaning and translation. More precisely, under what relation between translation and meaning does the sameness-of-translation definition of synonymy imply the sameness-of-meaning definition?

To illustrate, assume that for any correct manual M, an expression e_1 of L is translated by M into expression e of L^* just in case any meaning that can be correctly assigned to the one also can be correctly assigned to the other. Assume further that for both e_1 and e_2 of language L and for e of L^* it holds that they can be assigned meanings m_1 and m_2. Then, by the first assumption both e_1 and e_2 are translated by any correct manual M into e. In this way e_1 and e_2 can meet the conditions of the sameness-of-translation definition of synonymy. However, it is still possible that no *single* correct meaning distribution over L will assign

e_1 and e_2 the same meaning. It may be that any total assignment will give m_1 to e_1 just if it gives m_2 to e_2, and *vice versa*. So the conditions of the sameness-of-meaning definition aren't met. The two expressions are translation synonymous but not (meaning) synonymous.

The situation changes, however, if the relation between meaning and translation is tightened. For suppose it holds that a manual M is correct just if any correct total distribution of meanings of the source language is also a correct total distribution over the target language under the correlation M. More precisely, for a manual M between L and L^* and a total distribution D of meanings over L, define an M+D-induced distribution of meanings of L^* M(D) so that $M(D)(e) = D(e_1)$ just in case $M(e_1,e)$. Then we can assume M to be correct just in case M(D) is a correct distribution over L^* whenever D is a correct distribution over L.

Now the deviant translation example above is ruled out. For although there is, by assumption, a correct total distribution assigning m_1 to expression e of L^*, no total distribution assigns m_1 to both e_1 and e_2 of L. Therefore no correct manual M translates e with *both* e_1 and e_2.

In fact, it is as easy to see that with this tightened condition on the relation between meaning and translation, translational synonymy does imply meaning synonymy. For suppose that e_1 and e_2 are translation synonymous. Then, by definition, any correct manual M such that $M(e_1, e)$ is also such that $M(e_2, e)$. Under the tightened relation between meaning and translation it holds that if D is a correct meaning distribution over L, then the induced distribution M(D) is a correct meaning distribution over L^*. Therefore, it holds that $M(D)(e) = D(e_1)$ and $M(D)(e) = D(e_2)$, and hence that $D(e_1) = D(e_2)$. Since this holds for arbitrary correct M and D, the expressions are meaning synonymous if they are translation synonymous.

Whether this tightened relation really holds depends on the details of the correctness conditions of translations, which remain to be specified. Nonetheless, we can conclude that the indeterminacy of translation itself is no obstacle to having a well defined intralinguistic synonymy relation.[12]

---

12. Earlier versions of this paper were presented at the conference *Fifty Years of Empiricism Without Dogmas*, Humboldt University at Berlin, September 2001, and at the philosophy of language seminar at the department of philosophy, Stockholm University. I am grateful to comments from the participants on those occasions, and especially to Paul Boghossian, Kathrin Glüer, Geert Keil and Åsa Wikforss.

REFERENCES

Boghossian, Paul 1997: "Analyticity", in: B. Hale and C. Wright (Eds.), *A Companion to the Philosophy of Language*, Oxford, 331–368.

Burge, Tyler 1978: "Belief and Synonymy", *Journal of Philosophy* 75, 119–38.

— 1992: "Philosophy of Language and Mind 1950-1990", *The Philosophical Review* 101, 3–51.

Carnap, Rudolf 1956: *Meaning and Necessity*, 2nd. ed., Chicago.

—1956b: "Meaning and Synonymy in Natural Languages", in: Carnap 1956, 233–47.

Davidson, Donald 1990: "Meaning, Truth and Evidence", in: R. Barrett and R. Gibson (Eds.), *Perspectives on Quine*, Oxford, 68–79.

Frege, Gottlob 1918: "Der Gedanke. Eine logische Untersuchung", *Beiträge zum deutschen Idealismus* 2, 58–77. In English as "The Thought. A Logical Inquiry", translated by A.M. and Marcelle Quinton, in P. F. Strawson (Ed.), *Philosophical Logic*, 17–38. Page references to the translation.

Katz, Jerrold and Postal, Paul M. 1964: *An Integrated Theory of Linguistic Descriptions*, Cambridge, Mass.

Mates, Benson 1950: "Synonymity", *University of California Publications in Philosophy* 25, 201–26. Reprinted in L. Linsky (Ed.), *Semantics and the Philosophy of Language*, Urbana 1952, 111–38.

Pagin, Peter 2001: "A Quinean Definition of Synonymy", *Erkenntnis* 55, 7–32.

— 2003: "Communication and Strong Compositionality", *Journal of Philosophical Logic* 32, 287–322.

— *unpublished*: "What is Communicative Success?".

Pelletier, Jeffrey 1994: "The Principle of Semantic Compositionality", *Topoi* 13, 11–24.

Quine, Willard V. O. 1951: "Two Dogmas of Empiricism", *The Philosophical Review* 60, 20–43. Reprinted in his *From a Logical Point of View*, third edition, Cambridge, Mass. 1980, 20–46. Page references to the reprint.

— 1960: *Word and Object*, Cambridge, Mass.

— 1969: "Propositional Objects", in his *Ontological Relativity and Other Essays*, New York, 139–60.

— 1992: *Pursuit of Truth*, 2nd ed., Cambridge, Mass.

Quine, Willard V. O. 1995: *From Stimulus to Science*, Cambridge, Mass.
Salmon, Nathan 1986: *Frege's Puzzle*, Cambridge, Mass.

LOGIC AND ANALYTICITY

Tyler BURGE
University of California at Los Angeles

Summary

The view that logic is true independently of a subject matter is criticized—enlarging on Quine's criticisms and adding further ones. It is then argued apriori that full reflective understanding of logic and deductive reasoning requires substantial commitment to mathematical entities. It is emphasized that the objectively apriori connections between deductive reasoning and commitment to mathematics need not be accepted by or even comprehensible to a given deductive reasoner. The relevant connections emerged only slowly in the history of logic. But they can be recognized retrospectively as implicit in logic and deductive reasoning. The paper concludes with discussion of the relevance of its main argument to Kant's question—how is apriori knowledge of a subject matter possible?

Quine's *Two Dogmas of Empiricism* changed the course of philosophy.[1] The defeat of logical positivism freed philosophy to pursue topics to which it had seemed to be closed. Quine's arguments, albeit primarily ones outside the famous paper, subverted the notion of analyticity that had buttressed the positivist view of mathematics and logic. This notion had functioned to close off mathematics and logic from philosophical reflection, and to sever a main route to rationalism and metaphysics. Quine reopened the route, but declined to develop it. The route invites development—especially its epistemic branch. I first survey Quine's criticisms of analyticity in order to evaluate and celebrate his achieve-

---

1. An ancestor of this paper was given to commemorate the fiftieth anniversary of "Two Dogmas of Empiricism" at a conference in Berlin, during the fateful part of September 2001. I am grateful to Tony Martin for advice and instruction on several issues in sections IV–VI, and to Calvin Normore for help on the pre-Leibnizean historical issues discussed in Appendix II.

ment. Then I consider the place of logic in knowledge of the world. I will argue that in a complex way logic is apriori associated with substantial ontological commitment.

I.

Three concepts of analyticity found a place in philosophy before Quine mounted his attack on the two dogmas of logical positivism. Quine opposed use of all three. Perhaps for this reason he did not bother to distinguish them. The three concepts are not equivalent. They demand different types of treatment. I begin by discussing them.[2]

I call the first the *containment concept* of analyticity. On this concept, a proposition or sentence is analytic if and only if its predicate is contained in its subject. This is Kant's official characterization of analyticity (Kant 1787, A 6/B 10). Leibniz and Kant thought that the truth of the relevant propositions can be demonstrated by analyzing the subject concept so as to find the predicate concept contained within it—as one of its components.

The second is the *logic-with-definitions concept*. On this concept, a proposition or sentence is analytic if and only if it is a truth of logic or can be derived by rules of logic from truths of logic together with definitions or exchanges of synonyms. Leibniz and Kant regarded this concept of analyticity as equivalent to the first, because they assumed that the business of logic was to analyze concepts.[3] Frege freed the logic-with-definitions concept from this assumption, and made this characterization of analyticity his official one (Frege 1884, section 3).[4] This concept carries no commitments about the nature of definitions or of truths of logic.

The third is the *vacuousness concept*. On this concept, a proposition or sentence is analytic if and only if it is true *solely* in virtue of its conceptual content or meaning: a subject matter plays no role in its

---

2. I distinguish these conceptions in Burge 1992.
3. It appears that Kant, at least, made an exception of certain basic principles of logic, such as the principle of non-contradiction. He counted these principles neither analytic nor synthetic. He thought that their truth could not be obtained by analysis—they were too basic.
4. For further discussion of these matters, including some discussion of Leibniz and Kant, see Burge 2000.

being true; its truth owes nothing to the world. Kant held that logic, but not mathematics, is analytic in this sense. The positivists attributed analyticity in this sense to both logic and mathematics. The vacuousness concept was the centerpiece of their defense of empiricism and their attack on allowing logic or mathematics to engender metaphysics.

The vacuousness concept is my main interest. I think that Quine's attack on it is substantively sound as well as dialectically successful. The dialectical success had a revolutionary effect on philosophy. Logical positivism had tried to extract philosophy from fruitless grandiosity and make it scientific. An effect of this attempt was to constrict philosophy and turn it from legitimate sources of reflection. This is why I see Quine's criticisms as liberating.[5]

The three concepts of analyticity are not equivalent. The logic-with-definitions concept is not extensionally equivalent to the containment concept because many logical truths do not hinge on containment relations among concepts. Many lack subject-predicate form.

The containment concept is not notionally equivalent to the vacuousness concept because it does not entail that containment truths are vacuous.[6] (By "*notional equivalence*" I understand conceptual identity.) Vacuity also does not entail containment. I believe that the containment and vacuousness concepts are not extensionally equivalent either. There are some containment truths ("*That* logical truth is a truth"); but no truths are analytic in the sense of the vacuousness concept.

The logic-with-definitions concept is not notionally equivalent to the vacuousness concept. Being a logical truth does not entail that a subject matter plays no role in its being true. The logic-with-definitions concept is not extensionally equivalent with the vacuousness concept. There are truths of logic, but no vacuously analytic truths.

Although the existence of logical truths suffices for there to be analytic truths on the logic-with-definitions concept, the motive for thus

---

5. Positivism made major *methodological* contributions—its use of logic and insistence on clarity, its interest in language and science, its building intellectual community. These contributions outweigh what I regard as its methodological mistakes—its aversion to traditional philosophical problems and its obsession with reduction, deflation, and dismissal. I believe that Quine deepened the methodological contributions, but passed on the methodological mistakes.

6. Leibniz held that all truths are analytic truths of containment. He also thought that all or most truths are substantive and are made true by the nature of the world. There is no inconsistency in these beliefs. Cf. Leibniz 1677.

counting logical truths analytic arose from assumptions associated with the containment concept. The idea was that all logical truths are deductively "implicit" in the axioms of logic. Frege knew that the containment concept does not apply to all logical truths, because of its narrow focus on subject-predicate form. He still thought that all logical truths are implicitly "contained" in the axioms, in the sense of being derivable from them (Frege 1879, section 13). This view is untenable for logics substantially stronger than first-order logic, by Gödel's incompleteness theorem. So although counting logical truths analytic under the logic-with-definitions concept is harmless, the historical motive for doing so has eroded. At least, the motive must be qualified to apply essentially only to first-order logic.[7]

As noted, Quine rejects use of all three concepts. He opens "Two Dogmas" by identifying the *first dogma* with belief in a distinction between analytic and synthetic truths. The vacuousness concept is evidently at issue. The first dogma is the view that there is a distinctive set of "... truths which are *analytic*, or grounded in meanings independently of matters of fact ..." (Quine 1953, 20). Quine proceeds to give little specific attention to the vacuousness concept.

The discussion of the first dogma centers on objections to attempts to explain the notions of meaning, synonymy, and definition. Quine seems mainly concerned with the role of these notions in the logic-with-definitions concept. Some objections lean on requirements of clarity and scientific purity by restrictive standards. Some provide insight into various types of definition and the ways that some types presuppose empirical beliefs. The objections bring out the difficulty of distinguishing between widely shared background knowledge and synonymy.

None of these objections shows that *meaning* or *synonymy* is a defective notion. I think that Quine's requirements on vindicating the relevant notions are inappropriate. The notions have cognitively worthwhile uses in ordinary discourse and in linguistics.[8] Quine's objections were,

---

7. This is a point pressed by Gödel. See Parsons 1995. Gödel had a looser conception of analysis. He regarded difficult axioms for resolving the question of the Continuum Hypothesis as possibly implicit in the concept of set. Yet Gödel did not seem to think of the concept of set as complex or as "containing" components.

Completeness only approximately demarcates the distinction between classical first-order and stronger extensional logics. For an interesting discussion of systems beyond classical first-order logic that have completeness theorems, see Barwise 1977, especially section 5.

8. I believe that Putnam was right to defend a limited use of the notion of synonymy in

however, dialectically effective; for his requirements on vindication were shared by his opponents.

In his attack on the first dogma, Quine so focuses on notions of definition and synonymy that he says little about the idea that logical truths or containment truths are "analytic". As I have said, he appears to ignore the key vacuousness concept almost entirely. These are expositional weaknesses of "Two Dogmas of Empiricism". Quine has a reason for his strategy, however. He thinks that his attack on the second dogma shows that the notion of meaning is cognitively useless. He regards this result as undermining the point of *any* concept of analyticity.

The *second dogma* is the "the belief that each meaningful statement is equivalent to some logical construct upon terms which refer to immediate experience" (Quine 1953, 20; cf. 40 f.).

Quine's argument against it, briefly stated, is this: Meaning is if anything confirmation or infirmation. Confirmation and infirmation are holistic; they apply to whole theories, not to statements taken individually. So meaning is if anything something that attaches to whole theories, not statements, much less words, taken individually.[9]

If sound, this argument would seem to undermine the containment and vacuousness concepts, and the synonymy aspect of the logic-with-definitions concept. So all three concepts are threatened by the argument. This is why Quine writes, "... the one dogma clearly supports the other in this way: as long as it is taken to be significant in general to speak of the confirmation and infirmation of a statement, it seems significant to speak also of a limiting kind of statement which is vacuously confirmed, *ipso facto*, come what may; and such a statement is analytic. The two dogmas are, indeed, at root identical" (Quine 1953, 41).

If it were sound, the argument that centers on confirmation would not undermine counting logical truths analytic, on the logic-with-definitions concept. It would simply eliminate further truths through exchange of synonyms. To maintain that logical truths are analytic under this concept, one need only distinguish logical truths from other truths in some way or other.

---

understanding language. Cf. Putnam 1962.

9. Quine later moderates these views, holding that meaning attaches to blocks of sentences in theories (Quine 1990, 13–17).

Quine can accept this view. Counting logical truths analytic in this sense amounts to counting them logical truths. Quine would make two cautionary points. He would urge that what counts as logic carries an element of stipulation. He thinks that the notion of a logical constant is applicable only relative to given languages: it is not a fully general or scientific notion (Quine 1970, 59). I do not accept this position, but I will not discuss it here.

Quine's second cautionary point would rest on expanding the confirmation argument: Meaning is if anything confirmation or infirmation. Confirmation and infirmation apply to theories, not statements taken individually. All theories face the tribunal of experience. So meaning attaches to empirical theories, not to individual statements.

The expansion of the holism argument asserts empiricism about confirmation. It implies that confirmation in mathematics and logic rests on sense experience. Meaning in these disciplines would depend on role in empirical theory. The cautionary point is that logical truths are just as much confirmed by experience and just as much about the world as truths in natural science. So traditional motives for distinguishing analytic and synthetic truths have no basis.[10]

I think Quine's holism about confirmation insightful and his rejection of the second dogma correct. But I think that both the original and the expanded argument against the second dogma are unsound. Quine had a gift for making these arguments exciting. The metaphors, slogans, and observations invoked to recommend them do not, however, make them cogent. Many of the large ideas in Quine's later philosophy—indeterminacy of translation, inscrutability of reference, ontological relativity, empiricism about logic and mathematics, opposition to non-behaviorist linguistics and psychology, naturalism about epistemology—result from extensions of his argument against the second dogma, combined with his strictures on scientifically acceptable notions. These theses are neither intuitively plausible nor impressively supported by argument. They seem to me no better grounded than the grandiose metaphysics of Whitehead or Bradley. They differ in their expositional clarity and in their motive to clear philosophy of all but natural science. They are, I think, no more worthy of belief.

---

10. This general line is not put in just these terms. But it is often present in Quine's writings—for example, in the last sections of Quine 1953, and in the last pages of Quine 1970.

I will discuss the two arguments from confirmation only cursorily. I think that they do not yield good grounds for rejecting use of *any* of the concepts of analyticity. Then I will turn to what interests me more—Quine's success in attacking the vacuousness concept.

Quine offers no argument that meaning is if anything confirmation. Linguistic meaning partly depends on there being inferential connections. But empirical meaning constitutively depends on other things—on causal relations to an environment, for example.[11] These relations hold independently of the individual's ability to conceptualize them, hence independently of the individual's means of confirming his beliefs. Anti-individualism shows how elements of meaning or content are constituted compatibly with wide variation in theory and confirmatory methods (Burge 1979a; 1982; 1986; 1990; and forthcoming; Putnam 1975; 1988). So meaning partly depends, constitutively, on relations to an environment that are largely theory independent.

The main point is that Quine gives no good reason to think that meaning *is*, if anything, confirmation, or that its partial dependence on inferential capacities makes it assignable only to discourses, not to words and sentences. The view is hardly antecedently plausible.

As to the second premise, Quine is right that empirical confirmation tests several claims together. But he provides no reason, from an account of actual scientific practice, to think that it follows that individual claims lack discrete content. He does not discuss confirmation in enough detail to account for the ways experiments target some claims differently from others. The falsity of the first premise (that meaning is, if anything, confirmation) remains the central problem.

The empiricist premise in the expansion of the confirmation argument—that all statements face the tribunal of experience—is again not argued anywhere in depth. The view rides the waves of assertion and metaphor. Logic and mathematics do not treat their axioms or theorems as hostage to natural science.[12] Knowledge of pure mathematics does not seem to depend on the role of mathematics in empirical explanation. Quine provides no grounds to think that the non-empirical reasons given in the pure mathematical sciences are inadequate on their own terms.

---

11. These relations ultimately depend on perception or interlocution, at least in empirical cases.

12. How mathematics is applied in natural science is largely an empirical matter. This is the lesson of the non-Euclidean geometries. It does not follow that principles of pure mathematics are justified empirically.

So both the spare argument and the expanded argument from confirmation against analyticity limp at every step. Quine does, however, advance powerful criticisms of the vacuousness concept of analyticity. I turn now to those criticisms.

II.

The idea that logic is a science of being is an old one. It dominates the history of logic. Aristotle, most medievals, Leibniz, Frege, Russell, and Gödel maintained versions of it. A contrary view emerged early. Kant credits Epicurus with proposing, against Aristotle, that logic merely supplies norms for thinking—a canon for thought, not an organon of knowledge about a subject matter (Kant 1800, 13). Kant took up this line, introducing the vacuousness concept of analyticity and applying it to logic (Kant 1787, A 55/B 79; A 58–9/B 83; Kant 1800, 94). Carnap and other logical positivists owe to Kant their view that logical truths do not depend for being true on a subject matter. They distinguish themselves from Kant by applying this view to mathematics as well as to logic, and by claiming that such truths originate in linguistic convention, pragmatic decision, or the like.

Quine's strongest arguments against use of the vacuousness concept of analyticity do not occur in "Two Dogmas of Empiricism". They occur in "Truth by Convention", "Carnap and Logical Truth", and *Philosophy of Logic*. I divide these into three arguments or argument-types.

The first argument, advanced in "Truth by Convention", attacks the view that the truth of logical truths is to be explained as a product of convention—hence as vacuous. Quine's counter-argument goes: To cover all logical truths, the supposed conventions must be general: there are too many logical truths to provide conventions for them individually. For particular truths to be true by some convention, they must follow from convention by logical inference. Relevant inferences are understood in terms of their role in preserving truth. Moreover, they are themselves associated with counterpart truths (conditionalizations of the inferences). Appeal to convention cannot explain logical truth since it must presuppose logic (Quine 1936, 97 ff.).

This argument showed that any explanation of logical truth presupposes logic. It devastates its intended target—truth by convention. But it does not defeat all versions of the view that logic is analytic under the vacuousness concept. Carnap waived any pretension to explain logical truth in terms of convention (Carnap 1937, 124). He simply postulated that logic is vacuous. He thought that such postulation best serves the interests of science.

Quine's second type of argument holds such postulation to be of no scientific value. In "Carnap and Logical Truth" Quine discusses three kinds of purported support for the view that logical truths are vacuously analytic. One kind notes that a sentence like "Brutus killed Caesar" owes its truth not only to the killing but to use of component words. It is suggested that a logical truth like "Brutus killed Caesar or it is not the case that Brutus killed Caesar" owes its truth not at all to the killing but purely to the meaning of words—here, "or" and "it is not the case that". A second consideration notes that alternative logics are treated as compatible with standard logic. They use familiar logical words with unfamiliar meanings. This point might be taken to show that logical truths owe their truth entirely to the meanings of logical words. A third consideration is that allegedly pre-logical people are best seen as mistranslated. Translation of someone as committed to a simple contradiction is bad translation. The point might again be taken to show that logical truths depend only on the meanings of logical words (Quine 1954, 101 f.).

Quine shows that all three considerations beg the question. Appeal to the obviousness of logical truths equally well accounts for them (Quine 1954, 105 f.). As to the first, one can just as well regard the logical truth as true not in virtue of the killing, but in virtue of more general obvious traits of everything.[13] No appeal to analyticity is needed. As to the second and third considerations, the obviousness of logical principles again suffices to account for translation practice. Quine writes, "For there can be no stronger evidence of a change in usage than the repudiation of what had been obvious, and no stronger evidence of bad translation than that it translates earnest affirmations into obvious

---

13. Quine switches here from truths of the form A or $\neg A$, to the truth of the sentence $(x)(x=x)$. This is perhaps because self-identity is more easily seen as a "trait" of things. Quine does not spell out how his point applies to the example from the propositional calculus that he began with. I think that it is dubious that the truth of the initial logical truth is independent of the killing. The truth *would have been* true even if the killing had not taken place, since the truth is necessary. But it does not follow, nor is it obvious, that the killing plays no role in the truth's being true. Simple reflection on the truth condition suggests that it does play such a role.

falsehoods" (Quine 1954, 106). The vacuousness concept provides no explanatory advantage in accounting for the phenomena.

I think these responses brilliantly insightful. To all appearances they are decisive. No genuine support has been given for using the vacuousness concept. I think that no support is forthcoming. In the absence of a reason to distinguish truths that do not owe their truth to a subject matter from truths that do, the use of this concept of analyticity should be rejected.

Quine's third type of argument against the vacuousness concept is more implied than supplied. It is suggested in *Philosophy of Logic*: "Logical theory ... is already world-oriented rather than language-oriented; and the truth predicate makes it so" (Quine 1970, 97). It is implicit in the remarks in "Carnap and Logical Truth" about truth depending on a subject matter, and in the concluding metaphor about the lore of our fathers (including their logic) being grey—black with fact and white with convention (Quine 1954, 105 f.; 125). It is suggested by the argument:

> How, given certain circumstances and a certain true sentence, might we hope to show that the sentence was true by virtue of those circumstances? If we could show that the sentence was logically implied by sentences describing those circumstances, could more be asked? But any sentence logically implies the logical truths. Trivially, then, the logical truths are true by virtue of any circumstances you care to name—language, the world, anything. (Quine 1970, 96).

The implied argument goes: Logical theory invokes the notion of truth. Truth is world-oriented. It entails successful relations of reference to or truth-of a subject matter. Any attempt to separate truth from a subject-matter must produce reasons. In the absence of such reasons, logical truths cannot justifiably be regarded as true independently of relation to a subject-matter.

This third argument is the positive counterpart of the negative second type. The argument indicates the deep relation between logical truth and truth of a subject matter. This relation supports associating truth with correspondence. Correspondence has been taken to require a relation between whole sentences or propositions and entities peculiar to them. It requires no such thing. "Correspondence *theory*" often masks pretension. Correspondence is too vague to explain truth. In a sense, nothing explains truth. But understanding truth requires applications of the notions of reference and truth-of. Indeed, understanding any of these three notions requires the others. Attempts to understand truth as "purely formal" or "solely in virtue of meaning" need not only good grounds. They need a reason to think that they are talking about truth at all.

I believe that this third type of argument is sound. It is in the spirit of many of Quine's remarks. There is a presumption of a role for a subject matter in understanding truth. Appeals to analyticity do not confront this presumption, nor do they provide good reasons for doubting it.

Quine's relation to this third argument is equivocal. I believe that he relies on it and often implicates it. But he resists stating it full voice. In his second group of arguments he writes, "We *can* say that ["Everything is self-identical"] depends for its truth on traits of the language (specifically on the usage of "="), and not on traits of its subject matter; but we can also say, alternatively, that it depends on an obvious trait, viz., self-identity, of its subject matter, viz., everything. The tendency of our present reflections is that there is no difference" (Quine 1954, 106). In the same passage where I find the third argument suggested, he writes, "Is logic a compendium of the broadest traits of reality, or is it just an effect of linguistic convention? ... [this question] has proved unsound; or all sound, signifying nothing." (Quine 1970, 96).

In these disclaimers Quine holds that "true in virtue of", "depends for its truth on", and "traits of reality" have no use in an explanatory theory. He regards such phrases as explanatorily empty: "Logic is true by virtue of language only as, vacuously, it is true by virtue of anything and everything" (Quine 1970, 97). After "Carnap and Logical Truth" he claims that reference and truth-of are indeterminate. This view requires separate argument. I do not accept it.

The disclaimers are in any case misleading. They fail to note the asymmetry between the two positions. "True in virtue of everything" is too vague to be explanatory. It is, however, connected to both intuitive and formal semantical notions of reference and being true of. It accords with the remark that truth implies "world orientation". "True solely by virtue of meaning" stands unconnected to any such basis. Quine's disclaimers are misleading also in that they can easily seem to be out of keeping with his own position. Logical truth by his lights is just as much about the world, about physical objects and sets, as is physics and mathematics.

III.

In what follows, I assume that logic is not analytic under the vacuousness concept. Like all truths, logical truths depend for their truth on relations to a subject matter. Dependence can be clarified by elaborating the role of "true of" in specifying connections between predicates and variables of quantification, on one hand, and objects, sets, or properties, on the other. Being true requires that sub-propositional elements like predicates bear relations to a subject matter.

Certain special features of logic have tended to provide fallacious encouragement to the view that logical truths are analytic under the vacuousness concept.

Logic seems to abstract from attributions specific to any entities. It does not represent the natures or distinguishing aspects of objects. It has been thought that any science must do this. Since logic does not, it abstracts from attributions to objects. This view has no force. The traditional idea is that logic presents structures or properties common to all objects. Its nature is *not* to specify distinguishing aspects of entities that it is about. To abstract from distinguishing aspects is not to abstract from all relation to a subject matter. Logic is distinctive in this respect.

A second special feature of logic is that it sets normative laws for thought. It has been held that in view of this feature, it says nothing about entities that thought is about. This claim is without force. Setting normative standards for thought is compatible with representing structural aspects of any subject matter for thought. The norms have traditionally been thought to get their purchase through connection to thought's function of aiming at and preserving truth.

A third feature that has encouraged use of the vacuousness concept is that logical truths remain true under substitutions of non-referring non-logical parts. Substituting "centaur" for all occurrences of a simple predicate in a logical truth yields a logical truth.[14] I wish not to go into this matter here. But the following point projects to wide applicability. "(x)(Centaur(x) → Centaur(x))" is true because the quantified conditional is true of everything.[15]

---

14. This is, of course, a variant on the first consideration that Quine criticizes in "Carnap and Logical Truth". Kant gives these arguments for analyticity from these three features of logic.

15. Of course, the cited proposition would remain true of everything whether or not

210

Let us return to the first feature of logic that I mentioned. Given that logic abstracts from attributions specific to any entities, how do we know that there are entities? Does logic provide this knowledge? Should it provide such knowledge, if it is to be an apriori science of being?

The axioms of first-order logic commit it to the existence of entities. The variables of quantification range over a non-empty domain. Non-denoting terms are idealized away. But the existence of free logics, allowing an empty domain, suggests that these points do not establish metaphysical conclusions.[16] One might see classical first-order logic as helping itself to presumption of an existing world.[17] One might conclude that knowledge of existence does not reside in logic, and that free logic best represents knowledge expressed in first-order logic.[18]

It is not obvious that it is a thinkable possibility that there be nothing. We can model fragments of language that fail to make contact with the world, by assigning them an empty domain. It does not follow that it is thinkable much less possible that there be nothing. It is doubtful, however, that one can arrive at any such conclusion from logical principles alone.

I shall pass over logics, like Frege's and Russell's, whose axioms carry strong specific commitments to objects.[19] Modern logics have

---

centaurs were included. That is necessity, not mere truth. The structure-dependent nature of the necessity is certainly relevant to understanding the logical truth, but it does not show that the world, the actual world, is irrelevant to the truth of the logical truth. Cf. note 13.

The logical truth can be known without knowing whether centaurs exist. That is knowledge, not truth. There are interesting issues here that need development. I believe, however, that knowing such truths does not depend on knowing exactly which conditions in the world make the truth true, or on knowing exactly how the truth condition is fulfilled. Cf. Burge 1974.

I think that the existence of non-referential representations, and the truth of propositions containing them, depends on there being referential representations. This is, I believe, a general principle that underlies anti-individualism. I shall not defend this view here.

16. For an example of such a free logic, see Burge 1974. This logic exhibits, I think, the fundamental world-dependence of all logical truth, even allowing for empty domains.

17. Cf. Quine's dismissive attitude toward the requirement that classical logic requires a non-empty domain, in Quine 1970, 52 f.. This attitude is, I think, plausible as a response to a quick inference from the existential commitments of classical logic.

18. See Appendix I—Logic: First-order? Second-order?

19. Frege grounded his commitments to logical objects partly in analogies that led him to postulate truth values as objects. He grounded these commitments partly in the belief that the notion of the extension of a predicate is a logical notion and that his comprehension principle, which connected extensions with predication, was a logical axiom. The analogies do not force ontological commitment (Burge 1986a). The comprehension principle led to

tended to avoid such axioms. To be sure, some thinkers do conceive of logic as having substantial ontological commitments to objects through its axioms. Some regard class theory or even set theory as logic. I have no animus against these conceptions. I will, however, follow standard conceptions of even second-order logic, on which logical principles are true in universes of one object—or no objects at all.

I believe that the standard conceptions have rationales. One is that denials of existence of objects do not seem to contradict principles of deductive reasoning.[20] Another is a normative argument closely related to the first: Logic concerns deductive inference. The principles of deductive inference apply in putative situations where there are few or no objects. They apply in impossible theories or suppositions in which apparently necessary entities (space, time, numbers) are treated as absent. Logical truths should remain true under conditions that can be deductively reasoned about. So logical truths should remain true under metaphysically impossible conditions, including small or empty domains, particularly insofar as these can be understood as sub-parts of structures that do exist. (It does not follow that the logical truths are made true by such conditions, or that their truth does not depend on actual conditions.)

This rationale accords with the intuitive notion *logical validity*—truth correctly explicable in terms of structure characterized by deductively relevant logical form. There may be other tenable conceptions of logic. Perhaps even under the conception that I pursue, there are other routes to existence (cf. note 21.) I shall not explore such routes here.

Logic's being made true by objects does not depend on yielding knowledge that they exist. It could provide knowledge about entities whose existence is knowable only by other means. Logic provides knowledge that whatever there is is self-identical. It might be left to other disciplines to show that there are entities that this knowledge applies to.

---

contradiction. Russell postulated an axiom of infinity as a logical principle, but simultaneously doubted that it had this status. Most subsequent logicians have found the doubt more congenial than the postulation—at least as regards principles of logic.

20. This intuition is a legacy of Kant's criticism of the ontological argument for the existence of God. The intuition is complicated by logics for demonstratives or indexicals, but I believe that these logics presuppose agency (demonstrations or uses) wherever they involve commitment to referents. Even in these cases, I do not believe that existence of agents or objects is a consequence of logical principles, but rather a presupposition of them.

Logic certainly yields no knowledge of the existence of subject-matter-specific kinds—neutrons, amoebae, thought events, symphonies. We know to apply logical structures to such entities only on non-logical grounds. So logic depends on other disciplines for knowledge of many of its applications to the world. Perhaps it so depends for all its applications.

The picture just sketched is as follows: Logical truths are about the world. Their truth depends on relations to entities. To know logical truths, we need not know the exact entities and structures in the world on which their truth depends. One can know the truths to be true by understanding that any entities or structures will fulfill their truth conditions. Other disciplines supply knowledge of existence. Logical truths are true of whatever there is. The existence of some entities, for example, the numbers, may well be necessary. Logic does not adjudicate that point. Existence is known through other means.

IV.

This picture may be accurate as far as it goes. Yet I am not satisfied with it. The dissatisfaction that I want to develop here arises from reflecting on how logic is actually done.[21] A standard semantics for logic requires a set of entities as domain of discourse, assignments of entities in the domain to the terms, and assignments of subsets of the domain to the predicates. Logic relies on a mathematically stronger and more committal meta-theory to systematize applications of its basic underlying notions—*logical validity* and *logical consequence*.

Such meta-theories are committed to mathematical entities. Although various nominalist proposals for doing without numbers or sets (in

---

21. One source of dissatisfaction that I will not discuss is this. The laws of logic are partly laws of predication and quantification. Predication and quantification are representational operations. They appear to apply to structural aspects of the world—the relation between objects and properties, the relation between quantities of objects and properties, and so on. These seem to be necessary aspects of the world. Logic seems committed to them regardless of what individuals fill these structures. That is, despite the methodological value of Quine's criterion for ontological commitment, it is not obvious that the ontological commitments of logic go purely through quantification on its variables. It is worth reflecting on whether ontological commitments reside in the logical constants and in predication (independently of just what is predicated). This is a complex and old issue. I think it near the heart of understanding logic as a science of being. I will not pursue this aspect of our topic here.

mathematics generally) have been advanced, none are, I think, at all plausible.[22] Apart from parochial ideology, I think it clear that standard, accepted mathematics is true and is committed to abstract entities. The mathematical commitments of the meta-theory of logic are relevant to whether ontological commitment is necessarily and apriori associated with reflective understanding of logic.

The key intuitive notions in understanding logic are *logical validity* of sentences or propositions and *logical consequence* in argument. These are certain conceptions of logical truth and formal deductive preservation of truth, respectively. Logical validity is truth grounded in or correctly explicable in terms of logical form and logical structure. The relevant truths have logical forms that bear semantical relations to entities in relevant structures "in the world". Correct explication of logically valid truth rests on such relations and structures. The relevant truth and truth-preservation are conceived as hinging partly on logical form; and the logical form is associated with semantical relations to structural features of subject matters.

The intuitive notions associate logical form and logical structure with a conception of maximum generality. Sometimes the intuitive notion *logical validity* is glossed as truth formally explicable in any structure, or truth under all conditions, or in all structures (but cf. notes 25, 30.) Similarly, for truth-preservation. The two intuitive notions presuppose conceptions of what count as *logical* forms and structures, and may vary with different conceptions of logic. The generality intuition conditions and helps guide what is to count as logical form and logical structure.[23]

The intuitive notions *logical validity* and *logical consequence* do not occur in logic, as notions expressed by logical constants do. When I say "within logic", I take logic narrowly, to include the axioms and rules of

---

22. I also do not take seriously fictionalism about mathematics, or denials that mathematical theorems are true. There are technically informed defenses of such views, but I find this sort of philosophy of mathematics so lacking in perspective on knowledge, truth, mathematics, and reason, as not to be worth tilting with. The philosophical motives for such views seem to me thin in relation to the enormity of the program they are supposed to motivate—assimilation of mathematics to fiction. I think that the assumption that mathematics is true and committed to mathematical entities is reasonable and widely held. I shall take it for granted.

23. Hanson 1997 holds that the intuitive concept of logical consequence is a hybrid of concepts of necessity, apriority, and formal generality. One can, of course, construct a hybrid concept of this sort. But I believe that doing so tends to blur matters more than to clarify them. I accept that logical consequences can be known apriori and that at least classical logi-

inference, not the meta-theory. The intuitive meta-notions help indicate the point of logic. They are needed for both intuitive and systematic reflective understanding of logic. They conceptualize intuitions that drive logic's formalizations.

As I will soon explain, the *intuitive* notions *logical validity* and *logical consequence* must be distinguished from the *theoretical* notions *model-theoretic logical validity* and *model-theoretic logical consequence*. The model-theoretic notions not only are not the same

cal consequences are necessities. But the notions of formality and generality have emerged as autonomous and fundamental in understanding deductive argument.

Hanson argues that none of the three elements in his hybrid concept suffices to explicate intuitions about logical consequence. He claims that the "most straightforward" version of a formal account of logical consequence validates arguments that are intuitively invalid. The formal account that he discusses is: "The conclusion of an argument is a logical consequence of the premises just in case no argument with the same logical form has true premises and a false conclusion" (366 f.). He gives two examples intended to show the inadequacy of this account. One turns on being agnostic about the truth of the claim that every number has a successor (368 f.). I believe that this example is not worth discussing.

Hanson's second example is more interesting: $(\exists x)(\exists y)(x \neq y)$, hence $(\exists x)(\exists y)(\exists z)(x \neq y$ & $y \neq z$ & $x \neq z)$. Hanson holds that the formal account takes the conclusion to be a logical consequence of the premise, for "the premise and conclusion ... are both true, and, on the usual way of classifying terms as logical and nonlogical, they contain only logical terms. Thus the premise and conclusion are true under all substitutions for their nonlogical terms ... and under all interpretations of their nonlogical terms." But he takes the conclusion not to be an intuitive logical consequence of the premise (368-371).

Everything Hanson says about this case seems true. But the intuitive notion *logical consequence* is more substantial than his rendering of it in his formal account (quoted in this note above). The intuitive notion is preservation of truth *grounded in* and (correctly) *explicable* in terms of logical form and logical structure. That is, the basis or ground for preservation of truth lies in logical form and logical structure. Since Frege believed that arithmetical structure *is* logical structure, he would have regarded the argument as valid—in virtue, of course, of other "logical" principles than those made explicit in the first-order argument. Let us assume with Hanson and most logicians, however, that arithmetic is not logic and that the conclusion is intuitively *not* a logical consequence of the premise. Intuitively, the problem with the argument is that its preservation of truth is not grounded in, or explicable in terms of, logical form and logical structure. There is nothing about the logical structure semantically associated with the conclusion that is intuitively grounded in the logical structure semantically associated with the premise. Arithmetic insures that (necessarily) the conclusion is true if the premise is. Indeed it insures the (necessary) truth of the conclusion. But neither the truth of the conclusion nor the connection between premise and conclusion is explicable from what we are hypothesizing to be *logical* form and structure. Standard model theory uses domain variation to account for this intuitive fact. But the intuition that model theory elaborates is that there is nothing about the *logical* forms in the argument, and the *logical* structures semantically associated with those forms, that grounds—or allows an explication of—preservation of truth in the argument.

as the intuitive notions. They do not replace them in our understanding of logic. (The intuitive notions concern a type of truth. The theoretical notions introduce a notion of *truth-in*. The notion *truth* is epistemically more basic than the notion *truth-in*.) The model-theoretic notions do, I believe, bear certain necessary connections to the intuitive notions. They yield systematic, formal elaboration of them. Whereas the intuitive notions help yield intuitive understanding of the point of logic and of various logical principles and inferences, the model-theoretic notions help provide systematic theoretical understanding of both the intuitive notions and the underlying logic.

The intuitive notions *logical validity* and *logical consequence* emerge from sufficiently mature reflection on the practice of ordinary object-level deductive inference. They are *internal* to this practice in the sense that applying them need not take account of information from outside that practice. They conceptualize the practice's own aims and activity by reflection on the practice alone. The same can be said of their more theoretical, model-theoretic counterparts.

By contrast, theories of the sociological functions of tribal practices introduce concepts that are not only not available to the practitioners. They would not be available to sophisticated reflection on the aims of the practice taken by itself. One would need empirical knowledge of societies and of human psychology to explain sociological functions (Burge 1975). This knowledge might attribute to the practice a point that is at odds with any aim that practitioners could arrive at by reflecting just on the cognitive and representational aspects of the practice.

The intuitive notions *logical validity* and *logical consequence* are not like that. Nor are their model-theoretic counterparts. It is certainly possible for beings to engage in deductive inference who do not understand what they are doing from a meta-perspective. Understanding requires an objectification and a correct meta-viewpoint that many who are competent in inference lack. It is even possible, I think, for higher animals and primitive people to engage in simple deductive inference but lack a *capacity* for meta-understanding.

Nonetheless, the notions *logical validity* and *logical consequence* have emerged as the key intuitive notions for understanding the practice and point of logic. They are not the only such notions. They emerged as pre-eminent only slowly in the history of logic.[24]

---

24. See Appendix II—A Sketch of the Key Intuitive Notions in the History of Logic.

Notions of proof, knowability from proof, strict implication, logical necessity, and other modal notions figured in the development of logic. When conclusions are logical consequences of their premises, they necessarily follow from the premises. Logically valid truths, at least in classical logics, are necessary truths. But the intuitive notions *logical validity* and *logical consequence* are not themselves modal notions, any more than they are proof-theoretic or epistemic notions. Logical validity is a notion of formal truth grounded in or correctly explicable in terms of logical form and logical structure. Excepting the notion of proof, no other notion has been as fruitful in understanding logic. None has yielded as extensive elaboration and systematization. To understand the aims and functions of deductive inference from inside the practice, one must employ the intuitive notions *logical validity* and *logical consequence*. They are part of any full intuitive reflective understanding of logic and deductive inference.

Applying the intuitive notions *logical validity* and *logical consequence* entails applying the notion of truth. Logical validity (of sentences or propositions) is a type of truth. Logical consequence is a type of truth-preservation. Both notions are meta-logical. Inasmuch as they are conceptions of types of truth or truth-preservation, they are *semantical* notions.[25]

---

25. Qualifications apply to the relation between the model-theoretic notions and truth. Model-theoretically valid formulas in pure first-order logic are schemas, not assertable sentences. Such schemas are not true or false. They are only true under all interpretations or true in every model. They are forms that yield truths only when they are made into assertable sentences by filling the schematic markers with non-logical constants. The schemas are, however, used to account for logical *truth* and deductive *preservation of truth*, not merely truth-in or truth-under. A logical truth like "Anything red and square is square" is both intuitively valid and model-theoretically valid. Model-theory aims at understanding such truths, and associated deductive inferences, by systematically elaborating the intuitive notions in a systematic semantics for logic.

One does well not to overestimate the closeness of relation between *true-in* or *true-under*, on one hand, and *true*, on the other. There are models—such as models with domains of one object—which logical truths are true in, but which are not really possible and thus play no role in making the truths true. Moreover, the intended model of a first-order theory may play no role in proving the consistency and completeness of the theory, even though all model-theoretically valid sentences in a first-order theory are true. Although the logic of a strong first-order set theory is provably complete, the theory may not *have* an intended *model*. Intuitive logical validity entails truth; and model-theoretic logical validity, at least for assertable sentences, *should* entail truth (cf. Appendix I, note 28, and the previous paragraph of this note). But proving model-theoretic logical validity need not depend on the intended model, if there is one—much less the "full reality" of the world. [*continued*, p. 218]

I intend "semantical notion" *broadly*. Narrowly, semantical notions apply to relations between *symbols* and what they refer to or otherwise represent. This standard usage often carries an assumption that symbols are the primary bearers of truth. One might hold instead that truth, logical validity, and logical consequence fundamentally concern non-linguistic propositions or thoughts. I will not rely on either position, but I want to allow for the latter one since I hold it. On this view, semantic meta-theory elaborates representational relations between components of propositions (components of thought contents) and entities. These are analogs of the narrowly semantical relations between symbols and what they refer to or are true of. The relations hold between representational propositional components and subject-matter entities. On my broad usage, these analogs are semantical relations. Similarly, because of their essential association with (analogs of) reference and truth-of, the notions *truth*, *logical consequence*, and *logical validity* count as broadly semantical notions whether or not they apply fundamentally to sentences, propositions, or thought contents.[26]

The key intuitive semantical notions are not identical with their model-theoretic counterparts. In the first place, logical validity is a type of truth; logical consequence is a type of truth preservation. The model-theoretic notions involve a closely related but different notion—*truth in* a model or preservation of *truth in* a model.

Logical validity and *logical consequence*, notions for types of *truth* and *truth*-preservation, remain the fundamental notions. Where model-theoretic logical validity or model-theoretic logical consequence applies directly to sentences or propositions that are true or false, the model-theoretic notions must be understood as entailing truth or truth preservation. Where the model-theoretic notions apply to schemas, their relation to truth is more circuitous, but still necessary.

26. One can treat Fregean propositions or thought contents on an analog of the model-theoretic way sentences are treated. A *proposition* is "model-theoretically" valid if every proposition that results from a logical-structure-preserving replacement of non-logical components, where the replacing components apply to individuals or (possibly null) sets of elements, within any set of elements to which the quantifiers are restricted (the analog of a domain of discourse), is true. The notion of truth, as applied to replacement propositions that are restricted in this way, would then be elaborated in terms of the semantics of the parts of the proposition—in a way parallel to the way the truth of a sentence in a model is elaborated. The truth of the whole proposition would be systematically explicated in terms of the semantical contributions of the parts. Note that the "model-theoretically" valid proposition need not be among the propositions, resulting from the replacements, whose being true makes it "model-theoretically" valid.

Secondly, the intuitive notions are inspecific or open-ended about the mathematics relevant to systematically explicating their notion of truth in terms of structure. The mathematics that has become standard is model theory. But other mathematics, for example, a theory in which domains are not sets but classes, or where numbers or functions take the place of sets, can systematize the intuitive notions—to all appearances equally well.

Thirdly, it is not obvious how to equip the model-theoretic notions so as to apply to truth-bearers containing semantical predicates (like "true") and yet avoid paradox. The model-theoretic notions are normally applied to sentences that do not contain semantical predicates. It is prima facie plausible that the intuitive notion *logical validity* applies to sentences or propositions that do contain semantical predicates.[27]

A fourth point applies if second-order logic is counted as logic. It is not mathematically trivial or inferentially immediate that intuitive consistency implies having a model in second-order logic. It seems intuitively consistent to assume the non-existence of certain large sets, inaccessible cardinals. This assumption would block any implication from the assumption of consistency of second-order Zermelo-Fraenkel set theory with the axiom of choice to the theory's having a model. Belief in inaccessible cardinals is a matter of mathematical postulation and discovery. Since the intuitive notion is not immediately and intuitively equivalent to the model-theoretic notion, since reasoning and theory would be needed to show the notions to be equivalent, and since the reasoning and theory would not merely analyze concepts contained in the intuitive notion, they are different notions.[28] Similarly, it is not

---

27. For discussion of the paradoxes, see Parsons 1974 and Burge 1979. The issue of how the notions of generality and structure that figure in the intuitive notions *logical validity* and *logical consequence* interact with the notion of truth is far from adequately understood.

28. This line is developed by Kreisel 1967. I am indebted to Tony Martin for improving my understanding of these matters. He gave the example of the putative non-existence of inaccessible cardinals blocking the connection between consistency and having a model. Although Martin accepts Kreisel's claim that the intuitive and model-theoretic notions differ, he holds that there is no known plausible *actual* counterexample to their being mathematically equivalent—at least that considerations regarding the lack of a universal set and the size of the set theoretic universe have yielded no such counterexample. This is because, for example, it is mathematically plausible that the relevant inaccessible cardinals exist and that the relevant reflection principle that yields a model whenever a sentence of second-order ZFC is true in the universe of sets, is true. Maintaining the connection between intuitive logical validity and model-theoretic validity in reflection principles is one motivation for

mathematically trivial or inferentially immediate that truth in all models of a sentence of second-order set theory implies its intuitive logical validity. This point follows almost immediately from the point that it is not mathematically trivial or inferentially immediate that intuitive consistency implies having a model.[29]

I emphasize that it does *not* follow from the fact a) that it is not mathematically trivial or inferentially immediate that truth in all models is equivalent to intuitive logical validity, that b) truth in all models in

---

research on large cardinals.

Boolos 1985, 83–87, also rejects identifying the model-theoretic notion of validity with the intuitive notion of validity, and thinks that there is no actual counter-example to mathematical equivalence, as opposed to notional or conceptual identity. I think that he incorrectly identifies the intuitive notion of validity with his notion of supervalidity, a non-semantical notion. Validity of sentences or propositions is conceptually a type of truth, and is essentially a semantical notion.

As will emerge, my main argument does not depend on whether model-theory or some analog can provide a mathematical *equivalent* for the intuitive notion *logical validity*. Model theory or some analog can be necessary for systematic reflective understanding of the intuitive notion *logical validity* even if an equivalence is not forthcoming. It provides systematic, example-based understanding.

29. Follows almost immediately: 1) Suppose that sentence A (in a second-order set theory) is intuitively consistent and that it is not trivial or inferentially immediate that A has a model. Then trivially 2) it is not trivial or inferentially immediate that A's lacking a model implies A's intuitive inconsistency. Trivially, 3) If A is intuitively inconsistent, then the negation of A is intuitively valid. Trivially, 4) A lacks a model if and only if the negation of A is model-theoretically valid. Suppose 5) A lacks a model. Then by 2), 3), 4), and 5), we have trivially 6) It is not trivial or inferentially immediate that if the negation of A is model-theoretically valid (true in all models), then the negation of A is intuitively valid. Thus the notion *truth in all models* is not the same as the intuitive notion *logical validity*.

My annoying insertions of "trivially" through the argument 1)–6) are meant to insure that the reasoning goes through across the operator "it is not trivial or inferentially immediate that".

Cf. Kreisel 1967 for Kreisel's somewhat different exposition of the same conclusion. The example from Martin (note 28) can, of course, be adapted to bear on validity instead of consistency. Boolos 1985, 83, gives a variant of the same claim: the truth of a statement of second-order set theory does not immediately or obviously follow from its model-theoretic validity. But truth follows immediately and intuitively from intuitive validity.

It must be emphasized that the Martin and Boolos points are relevant to distinguishing the intuitive notion *logical validity* from the notion *model-theoretic logical validity* only if second-order logic counts as logic. If second-order logic is not logic, as I am inclined to believe (cf. Appendix I), then the fourth consideration discussed in the text is irrelevant to whether intuitive *logical validity* is the same concept as *model-theoretic logical validity*. The first three considerations still apply. As will become clear, the main argument that I develop in this section and in sections V–VI does not depend on whether second-order logic counts as logic.

second-order set theory is not theoretically or mathematically equivalent with logical validity. The point is that the notion or concept *truth in all models* is different from the intuitive notion or concept *logical validity*.

The intuitive notion *logical validity applied to first-order theories is* mathematically equivalent to the theoretical notion *truth in all models of first-order theories*. Kreisel shows this as follows: Sentences that are derivable from the axioms and rules of first-order logic are intuitively valid. Intuitive logical validity is truth in all structures. So an intuitively valid sentence is true in all structures that are first-order models (i.e. intuitive validity applied to first-order theories implies first-order model-theoretic validity). By the completeness theorem, all sentences that are true in all models of first-order logic (model-theoretically valid in first-order logic) are derivable from the axioms and rules of first-order logic. So a first-order sentence is intuitively valid if and only if it is true in all models of first-order logic.[30] These restricted applications of intuitive validity and model-theoretic validity are equivalent.

Some modern explications of logical truth or deductive inference do not rely on the intuitive notions *logical validity* and *logical consequence*, or on any analog of model theory. There are characterizations strictly in terms of remaining true under substitution of non-logical constants. Such characterizations are not fundamental insofar as they leave unmentioned that the truth of logical truths is systematically explicable by reference to semantical contributions of sub-propositional compo-

---

30. Cf. Kreisel 1967 (reprint), 90 f. It is important to realize that the first step in this reasoning is not a step from a purely syntactical point about proof to an intuitive notion of logical validity. To understand the intuitive logical validity of the axioms and rules of first-order logic, one must consider the logical constants with their intuitive meaning. Kreisel is aware of this point. He takes Frege's axioms and rules of derivability as his paradigm of the first stage of the argument. For Frege, these axioms were, of course, *not* merely syntactic shapes, and the rules were not simply procedures for manipulating syntactic shapes.

Kreisel's second step—that intuitive logical validity is truth in all structures—appears intended as a conceptual identity or notional equivalence. I doubt that the step has this status, because I think it important to distinguish truth from truth-in (cf. note 25). Intuitive logical validity is a type of *truth*, not truth-in. Kreisel's argument goes through, however, even if the second step is conceived as some sort of strong intuitive equivalence, short of conceptual identity. In fact, the argument goes through if the second step is weakened to hold that intuitive logical validity entails truth in all structures.

I believe that reasoning analogous to Kreisel's applies to Fregean propositions or thoughts as distinguished from sentences (cf. note 26).

nents.[31] By themselves they have not led to the wealth of knowledge that semantical methods have led to. Their correctness is evaluated through semantical methods. This is evident in the completeness theorem for first-order logic. The use of syntactic, substitutional explications is parasitic on the more standard semantical notions—intuitive and model-theoretic.

The relatively syntactic explications are less general than model-theoretic explications. They depend on assumptions about the strength of the language—on its having enough and the right kinds of predicates.[32] Such assumptions are not guided by discernible principle. The relatively syntactic characterizations elaborate an aspect of our understanding of logical truth. But they do not elaborate the dependence of logical validity and logical consequence on the semantical fine-structure of logical truth and of deductive truth preservation. They do not elaborate the way logical truth, like all truth, depends on relations to a subject-matter.

Likewise, for non-semantical explications of logical truth or logical "following-from" in terms of strict implication or modality. Both reflection and the development of logic show that key intuitive notions in understanding logic are *logical validity* and *logical consequence*. They are notions of particular types of *truth* and *truth preservation*. The notion of truth presupposes semantical relations between sub-propositional contents (such as predicates) and a subject matter. So the notions of reference, truth-of, term, predicate, and object are constitutively associated with the types of truth attributed by the intuitive notions *logical validity* and *logical consequence*. The intuitive notions are doubly committed to the *structure* of these semantical relations. They are committed through the notion of truth. They are also com-

---

31. Cf. Quine 1970, 49–51. I disagree with Quine's preference for syntactical characterizations in this passage. His preference is associated with a tendency in his later work to favor relatively deflationary conceptions of truth. In Quine 1950, the section "Validity", Quine alludes to reasons like those I cite in the next paragraph for preferring the model-theoretic characterization. There he makes primary use of the model-theoretic characterization. The substitution idea goes back at least to Abaelard (cf. Appendix II). In most of its history, the idea has been associated with the intuitive notion *validity*, not cut off from sub-propositional semantical structure, as it has been in some twentieth-century uses of it.

32. Of course, even these relatively syntactical explications use the notion of truth. Moreover, as Quine points out (1970, 53–56), the exposition of these explications is committed to arithmetic, or that part of set theory that can model arithmetic. For further discussion of the language-dependence of the syntactical characterizations, see Boolos 1975, 50–53. Tarski made many of these points in his original paper, Tarski 1936.

mitted through their construal of logical truth and deductive inference as hinging on sub-propositional aspects of logical form.

Mathematical elaboration of applications of the intuitive notions *logical validity* and *logical consequence* is required in any systematic understanding of the notions. Mathematical elaboration of their applications for any logic beyond monadic predicate logic requires significant ontological commitments. Some sentences of first-order polyadic predicate logic are true in all finite universes but are not intuitively or model-theoretically valid. Their invalidity can be systematically and structurally explained only by appeal to an infinity of entities. Löwenheim's theorem entails that a sentence of first-order polyadic predicate logic is model-theoretically valid if and only if it is model-theoretically valid in the domain of positive integers. By Kreisel's argument—that model-theoretic validity and intuitive validity are equivalent for first-order logic —, application of the intuitive notions *logical validity* and *logical consequence* to first-order logic requires commitment to infinitely many mathematical entities.

Reflective understanding of logical validity and logical consequence is systematic in the completeness theorem for first-order predicate logic. The theorem is that all model-theoretically valid sentences in first-order logic can be proved in the logic. By Kreisel's argument, the theorem shows the same for all intuitively valid sentences in first-order predicate logic. There is room for variation in the exact mathematical commitments needed to prove the completeness theorem. But any such proof requires commitment to infinitely many mathematical entities.[33]

---

33. One can produce accounts of the semantical structure of first-order logical validity and logical consequence and prove obvious analogs of the standard completeness theorem for *model-theoretic* logical validity without using models. One can employ numbers with characterizations (or definitions) on those numbers, and a sufficiently strong semantical vocabulary—instead of sets. One can employ functions instead of sets, or proper classes instead of sets. One can avoid taking the domain to be a set. There are many mathematical possibilities. The intuitive notions *logical validity* and *logical consequence* employ a notion of unrestricted generality. Prima facie, more powerful mathematical systematizations will be more appropriate than less powerful ones because of the commitment to generality in the intuitive notion. In being more restrictive, the mathematically weaker methods are less good candidates, than standard methods, for conceptually natural systematization of the intuitive notions. Some of the weaker methods are parasitic on the standard model-theoretic method in the sense that no one would have come upon them if the completeness theorem had not been proved in the standard way. As I noted (notes 28, 29), it is a mathematically open question whether standard model-theoretic systematizations can model the generality

Summarizing our argument sketch: Full reflective understanding of logic and of deductive practice must use the intuitive semantical notions, *logical validity* and *logical consequence*. Systematic reflective understanding of the use and import of these notions must be mathematical, and thus committed to entities the mathematics is committed to. Even for first-order predicate logic, that commitment is to an infinity of mathematical entities. So full reflective understanding of logic and of deductive practice requires commitment to an infinity of mathematical entities.

The conclusion of this argument does not imply that first-order logic is committed through its bound variables to the existence of entities. The argument applies to free logics.

I quoted with approval Quine's remark that the truth predicate makes logical theory world-oriented. Systematic elaboration of application of the notion of logical truth must presume connection between logical truth and principles for predication of entities, and for grouping and partitioning entities in quantification. Whether or not the truths themselves are quantificationally committed to entities, explaining these matters systematically requires mathematics, which *is* so committed. The mathematical entities help exemplify the subject-matter structure of logical validity and logical consequence. They constitute a ubiquitous subject matter partly in virtue of which logic is true. Logical truths are true of everything. The relevant mathematical structures are, of course, not everything. But they necessarily inform everything else. This is why,

---

of the intuitive notions as applied to second-order languages. Perhaps other mathematical theories will be needed. Even if the standard systematizations do suffice, there will likely be different mathematical systematizations that are equally adequate, in something like the way that different mathematically equivalent explications are, by Church's Thesis, adequate to the mathematically inspecific notion of effective calculability. As I argued above in this section (the second consideration), the open-endedness of the intuitive notions' conceptions of generality and structure count against identifying the intuitive notions with the model-theoretic notions. I think it reasonable to think that no single mathematical explication is uniquely appropriate as explication or "model" of semantical structural relations involved in intuitive logical validity. I will say more about this in sections V and VI.

Of course, it is also a philosophically open question whether to count second-order logic as logic (cf. Appendix I). The important point is that even if one restricts logic to first-order logic, any systematic semantical elaboration of the intuitive semantical notions *logical validity* and *logical consequence* must be committed to at least an infinity of entities. These entities are clearly mathematical. For Löwenheim's theorem and discussion of minimal resources needed to prove the completeness theorem, see Kleene 1964, 389–398.

in meta-logic, they can be seen as representatives or models of other subject matters of which logic is true.

We know objects and properties that logic is about in various ways. Such knowledge derives from common sense, self-knowledge and reflection, physics and the special empirical sciences, and mathematics. Mathematics inevitably applies in these other domains. I have highlighted an application that is constitutively associated with systematic reflective understanding of logic. The application of logic within its own meta-theory to a ubiquitous mathematical subject-matter models logic's being true of more mundane objects and properties.

V.

Most of the components of the argument sketched in section IV are familiar. The ideas that logic is associated with a semantics and that the semantics is committed to mathematical entities are certainly familiar. Seen in broadest outline, the chain of connections in the argument is also familiar. Thus seen, the argument is easy and obvious.

Doubting its soundness is also easy and obvious. One might hold that logic is one thing and its mathematical meta-theory, quite another. One might think that ontological commitments of the meta-theory are completely independent of commitment to logic. I think, however, that the rational chain connecting the commitments is tighter than these dismissive lines suggest.

It is true, in a sense, that logic is one thing and its meta-theory is another. It is true that the ontological commitments of model theory go beyond the quantificational commitments of first-order logic. It is possible to accept the axioms and inference rules of first-order logic and doubt the ontological commitments of model theory. It is possible to "adopt" a free logic—one without any ontological commitments through its quantifiers or singular expressions. It is possible to regard "$2+2=4$" and all of set theory as false, because of their commitments to abstract objects. It is possible to engage in logical inference without having the intuitive concept *logical consequence*, much less its model-theoretic counterpart. These points do not threaten the argument I sketched. The argument concerns rational connections, not whether thinking requires, as a matter of logic or psychology, recognizing and accepting those connections.

In this section I highlight three claims in the argument I sketched. One is that the intuitive notions *logical validity* and *logical consequence* are necessary for reflective understanding of logic. The second is that they are broadly semantical notions. The third is that systematic reflective understanding of these intuitive notions, and through them systematic reflective understanding of logic and deductive reasoning, requires commitment to mathematics. In this section, I also state in more detail the argument sketched in section IV.

I have only a little more to say about the first claim. I noted that other notions figure in understanding logic. But it is hardly controversial that the intuitive notions *logical validity* and *logical consequence* provide essential insight into logic and deductive inference. It is hardly controversial that epistemic and modal notions have been less fruitful in developing and systematizing logic. Such notions certainly cannot replace the intuitive semantical notions. The availability of other notions—strict implication, provability, necessity, necessary truth, knowability from proof, preservation of truth on substitutions in non-logical positions—that mimic or partially coincide with the intuitive semantical notions should not distract from recognition that reflection on these latter notions yielded the practice, formulation, and understanding of logic as we now know it. The basic theorems about logic, beginning with the completeness theorem, derive from reflection on applications of these notions to deductive inference.

The second claim complements the first. A—I would say, the—central point of logic is to formulate principles that underlie deductive inference or proof and that systematize good deductive inference's preservation of truth by virtue of its formal properties. Such principles include truths that themselves depend on deductive form and structure. Both deductive truth-preservation and logical truth depend on and are to be explicated in terms of formal aspects of semantical fine-structure. Successful reflective understanding of logic requires the notions *logical validity* and *logical consequence* because they conceptualize this explanatory aim.[34]

---

34. Hartry Field seems to me to blur the points in this and the preceding paragraph. He rightly distinguishes intuitive notions from model-theoretic notions, but centers attention on intuitive notions of logical necessity and consistency (cf. Field 1989, 30 ff.). He misleadingly cites Kreisel in support of the view that the key intuitive notions in understanding logic are "neither proof-theoretic nor semantical" (Field 1989, 32). Kreisel holds that the key intuitive notions are not "semantical" only in the sense that they are not the notions of model-theory—a point on which all sides here agree. Kreisel does not hold that they are non-semantical in the

The third claim needs more comment. What is the relation between the intuitive notions *logical validity* and *logical consequence*, on one hand, and their model-theoretic counterparts, *model-theoretic logical validity* and *model-theoretic logical consequence*, on the other?

It is possible to make deductive inferences without having the intuitive notions or their model-theoretic counterparts. It is possible to have an intuitive understanding of logic through the intuitive notions without having the model-theoretic notions. The intuitive judgments, both within logic and about logic, are epistemically prior to model-theoretic elaboration of them (cf. Appendices I and II) . There are surely reciprocal epistemic relations between intuitive judgments about validity and the use of model-theoretic notions. But reflective intuitive judgments are usually determinative. Model-theory attempts to understand intuitive judgments systematically.

---

ordinary narrow (or broad) sense that I have discussed. He explicitly recognizes their semantical natures in the ordinary sense of "semantical". He glosses the intuitive notion *logical validity* as "truth in all structures" (cf. Kreisel 1967, reprint, 90). Field takes the fundamental intuitive notion for understanding logic to be implication, which he construes modally. He regards it a matter of choice and convenience whether to formalize the notion as an object-language operator or as a predicate (Field 1989, 34 ff.; 83 ff.). Implication construed as an operator is not a semantical notion. Implication construed as a predicate is, on Field's construal, a semantical notion. I think that the operator notion cannot serve as basis for full reflective understanding of logic *because* it is not semantical. It does not make explicit the connection between logical principles and truth. It cannot be used to reflect on the systematic ways that logical truth and deductive preservation of truth depend on semantical relations to subject matters. History (cf. Appendix II), logical practice, and reflection all indicate that the intuitive semantical notions *logical validity* and *logical consequence* are among the fundamental notions in understanding logic. No argument is given against this view. Whether "the" semantical notion *implication* is the intuitive notion *logical consequence* depends on whether its notion of truth-preservation is construed in terms of structure as opposed to modality. Intuitive notions of implication are notoriously multiform.

Field chooses the modal operator treatment of implication as the key notion for understanding logic. He takes the aim of logic to be that of finding out about logical necessity and possibility. He holds that model theory, like all mathematics, is only a not-literally-true instrument to aid discoveries of these matters (Field 1989 85 ff.; 112). But logic aims to systematize certain types of form-and-structure-dependent truth and truth-preservation. Citing one of its *other* aims—studying logical necessity—and seeing semantics as merely instrumental in achieving that other aim is analogous to claiming that natural science is concerned with prediction or observational adequacy, and then holding that its descriptive and explanatory claims are mere instruments, with no literal truth, for achieving prediction or observational adequacy. I have not argued against instrumentalism or fictionalism regarding mathematics. My argument concerns apriori connections among types of understanding whose commitments I assume to be sound.

At most, certain model-theoretic notions provide theoretically illuminating equivalences with the intuitive notions. Truth in all first-order models (model-theoretic logical validity in such models) is theoretically equivalent to intuitive logical validity of a first-order theory. It is an open philosophical and mathematical question whether the intuitive notion can be given *general* theoretical equivalences in something like the way the notion of effective calculability was provided with such theoretical equivalences in Church's Thesis (cf. Appendix I and notes 28, 29, and 33).

Modeling structures associated with applications of the intuitive semantical notions is, however, part of reflectively understanding them. Model theory yields understanding of the intuitive notions not by defining them, and not necessarily by yielding a precise *general* theoretical equivalence. It yields understanding by offering a systematic way to think of examples—models—of semantically relevant structures, particularly sub-propositional semantical structures, on which logical truth and deductive preservation of truth hinge. If the semantical paradoxes or the nature of set theory prevent one from doing better than this (by obtaining a general theoretical equivalence for logical validity and for logical consequence), one will still have gained essential systematic reflective understanding of the intuitive notions. As in empirical domains, understanding need not consist in theoretical identifications or reductions.

Over the next six paragraphs I give a fuller version of the argument sketched in section IV—the argument that reflective understanding of logic and deductive reasoning requires commitment to mathematics. I believe that each step in the argument is apriori.

The intuitive notions *logical validity* and *logical consequence* are necessary for intuitive reflective understanding of logic and deductive reasoning. Reflection shows that logic is centrally concerned with certain kinds of truth and truth preservation. These kinds turn partly on logical form and are correctly explicated in terms of very general structures, or entities in such structures. This concern is conceptualized in the notions *logical validity* and *logical consequence*.

Full reflective understanding of the intuitive notions and their applications must include understanding of sentential or propositional forms on which logical validity and logical consequence partly hinge. Logical validity and logical consequence depend, even in elementary deductive reasoning, on the natures of *sub-propositional forms*, including predicational and quantificational forms. So full reflective understanding of the notions *logical validity* and *logical consequence*, and their applications to elementary deductive reasoning, requires understanding how sub-propositional forms contribute to logical validity and logical consequence.

Full reflective understanding must include understanding of the *semantics* of sub-propositional forms. The notions *logical validity* and *logical consequence* are semantical. They are notions for certain types of truth and preservation of truth. Truth is necessarily associated with predicates' being true of entities and with other sub-propositional semantical relations. Truth can be fully understood only by understanding the relation between the truth of a whole sentence or proposition and the semantical contributions of its sub-parts.[35] Moreover, logical validity and logical consequence turn on the semantical contributions of sub-propositional elements. For both reasons, reflective understanding of logical validity and logical consequence must include semantical understanding of sub-propositional components.[36]

Full reflective understanding of the intuitive notions *logical validity* and *logical consequence*, including their applications, must be *systematic*. Any two sentences in a language or any two propositions might appear in a single argument. Applications of the intuitive notions turn on a relatively small number of formal features shared among many sentences or propositions (relatively small number because of the great generality of their application). So principles accounting for logical

---

35. I am well aware that I am not engaging with conceptions of truth that attempt to detach it from the notions *reference* and *truth-of*—for example, some that try to explain truth purely in terms of the truth-schema or in terms of agreeing with what is said. I regard such conceptions as quite obviously inadequate. There are objections to them which I believe have not been convincingly answered (for discussion of some of these, see Davidson 1990). But the conceptual relations between truth and sub-propositional semantical relations like reference and truth-of are sufficiently obvious that I believe that such deflationary conceptions are not serious candidates for fully understanding truth.

36. I believe that accounts of substitutional quantification that avoid a systematic account of the semantical relations involved in quantification are parasitic on our normal conception of quantification, which is constitutively associated with sub-propositional semantical relations (cf. note 35). I shall not argue the point. It has fairly widespread acceptance and considerable plausibility. Relatively "non-semantical" conceptions of quantification and truth are analogous to the relatively "syntactic" substitutional conceptions of logical truth (cf. notes 31 and 32). They are not fundamental. Invoking such alternatives to avoid ontological implications is in the tradition of invoking the vacuousness concept of analyticity.

validity and logical consequence must apply systematically across propositions, or sentences in a language.

Given the complexity of semantical relations between sub-propositional elements and subject-matter structures that are relevant to logical validity and logical consequence, systematic reflective understanding of these relations requires that the semantics be mathematicized and the structures taken to include mathematical structures. Systematic reflective understanding of the relations involved in relatively elementary logical inferences is impossible without invoking a mathematics rich enough to carry commitment to an infinity of mathematical entities (cf. note 33.) This is a rational matter, not simply a psychological matter. So systematic reflective understanding of elementary applications of notions fundamental to an intuitive understanding of logic is rationally committed to an infinity of mathematical entities. Logic, narrowly understood, does not claim that there are infinitely many entities. Its truths can be explicated in, and remain true in, smaller structures. But systematic reflective understanding of elementary intuitive judgments about logical validity and logical consequence demands such commitment.

Comparable systematic understanding can be achieved in semantical frameworks with different ontological commitments. Commitment to classical model-theory is not necessary. But commitment to a semantics including mathematics and to an infinity of mathematical entities *is* rationally necessary for a systematic reflective understanding of the intuitive notions, of logic, and of relatively elementary deductive reasoning.

VI.

Many traditional accounts construed reflective understanding as analysis of containment relations among concepts. I have argued that the model-theoretic concepts are not the same as the intuitive semantical notions. Are the model-theoretic concepts contained in the intuitive concepts *logical validity* and *logical consequence*? Certainly not. This negative answer has three aspects. One concerns the relation between the intuitive concepts and concepts for sub-propositional semantical structure. A second concerns the relation between the intuitive concepts and systematization of structure. A third concerns the relation between the intuitive concepts and the particular mathematics involved in model-theory. I shall discuss these aspects serially.

A conception of sub-propositional semantical structure is constitutively associated with the concept of truth. Having a concept of truth requires being able to apply it. Being able to apply it requires having a concept of proposition or sentence. Being able to apply the concept of truth to a proposition or sentence as such requires being able to conceptualize predications and to determine how predication affects truth, which in turn requires the concept *true of*. A similar point applies to the concept of singular reference. Reciprocally, having the concept *true of* requires having the concept of truth. The concept of truth is more basic in understanding the point of belief, judgment, and inference. The concepts *true of* and *refers to* are more basic in understanding how the truth and logical validity of propositions (or sentences) and preservation of truth in deductions depend on contributions of sub-propositional elements. I see no strong case that either of the concepts *truth* and *truth-of* contains the other. So although the intuitive concept *logical validity* is a concept of a certain type of truth, the concept *logical validity* does not *contain* concepts of sub-propositional semantical structure.

Although not containment-analytic, the conceptual connections here are deep and firm. One could not intuitively understand the notions *logical validity* or *logical consequence* yet be unable to recognize entailments between truth and predicates' being *true of* objects, or between truth and quantifications-on-predications' being true of some, all, or most objects. Intuitive recognition of logical consequence and logical validity requires recognition of formal aspects of propositions and arguments. So although the intuitive meta-logical notions do not contain concepts of sub-propositional semantical structure, they are constitutively associated with them.

The notions *logical validity* and *logical consequence* are constitutively associated with the notion of truth. The notion of truth is constitutively associated with notions of truth-of and reference. These notions are constitutively applicable to sub-propositional semantical structures. Intuitive recognition of such semantical structures can be implicit or confused. Specifying the forms and semantical structures of relational expressions and stacked quantifiers had to await Frege, two millenia after Aristotle. Specification required reflection on applying intuitive semantical notions in a range of inferences. This was Frege's methodological insight.[37] Still, the intuitive bases for systematizing

---

37. Cf. especially the introduction of Frege 1984 for a statement of the methodology. See

predicational and quantificational forms—and ways that semantical valuations turn on them—were available to apriori reflection, given the intuitive semantical notions, mastery of the inferences, and mastery of relevant logical categories (*predication, quantification*).

I turn to the second part of our answer. I think that an imperative to systematize is associated with the intuitive concepts *logical validity* and *logical consequence*. The obvious applicability of these concepts to any sentences or propositions, and to arguments containing any sentences or propositions, and the obvious fact that any given sentence or proposition shares logically relevant form with others, provide intuitive impetus to understand *systematically* the ways that logical validity and logical consequence hinge on sub-propositional semantical structure. Recognition of the need for system derives from reflection. But the materials for such recognition lie in the intuitive notions together with their ordinary applications.

"Together with" is important. System is not contained in the intuitive notions, but implicit in applying them. The mastery of sub-propositional forms in *using* language or theory is what is systematic. The relation between the intuitive notions and the intuitive mastery of logical form is what contains the materials for a systematic elaboration of semantical structure. That is why I said that an *imperative* toward systematization is conceptually associated with the intuitive semantical concepts. The combination of the intuitive semantical notions and the logical forms that ordinary individuals have intuitively mastered is synthetic, not a matter of containment analysis. But the combination is present in intuitive practice. This point is fully compatible with recognizing Frege

---

Frege 1892 and Frege 1891 for examples of the application of the method. In his conception of logical truth as being entirely general and in his appreciation of the role of sub-propositional semantical structure in all truth, including logical truth, Frege employed an intuitive notion of logical validity. This is so even though he regarded semantical notions as dispensable in a fully formed logic. Frege did not employ the full-blown model-theoretic counterparts of the intuitive notions. Since he regarded the real world (including logical objects) as the only basis for evaluating logical truth, he did not allow domain variation (cf. Appendix II and notes 31, 32). He had a different conception of what constitutes truth explicable in terms of structure than standard modern conceptions of the intuitive concept. He thought that logical axioms carry a commitment to an infinity of objects (cf. note 19). These doctrinal differences are important, but hardly entail that he lacked an intuitive notion of logical validity. His notion of logical truth is closer to modern notions—especially in its structural, non-modal cast, and in its association with a deep conception of sub-propositional semantical structure—than some commentators have allowed.

and Tarski's achievements in formulating this systematization, and the achievements of Skolem, Gödel, Tarski, and others in mathematicizing it.

Now to the third aspect of our answer. The intuitive semantical notions do not contain any specific mathematical systematization of their application. In the first place, the intuitive semantical notions are mathematically inspecific. In the second, no one mathematical semantical systematization seems fundamental. Recognition of any of a number of ways of systematically exemplifying logically relevant structure is what is fundamental to understanding the mathematical aspects of logical validity and logical consequence (cf. note 33). Such understanding is deepened by appreciating relations among different mathematical systematizations.

So the notion of truth in a model is not contained in the intuitive notions *logical validity* or *logical consequence*. The constitutive relations are apriori and necessary, but not "analytic" in any of its senses. Some of these relations are accessible only by acquiring new concepts and discoveries. Whether there are theoretical equivalences for the intuitive notions is an open philosophical and mathematical question. Mathematicization of a semantics for these notions nonetheless indicates constitutive aspects of the notions and of the underlying deductive practice.

I distinguish six levels of understanding in logical practice. Outlining them will summarize my construal of the relation of logic's meta-theory to intuitive logical practice.

There is, first, the understanding involved in minimally competent deductive inference. I think that some non-human animals engage in deductive inference. They have perceptual beliefs, memories, and some simple logical constants. They think according to simple rules of inference. They believe no logical truths, lack a concept of logical validity, and lack a concept of truth. They make valid inferences without understanding what they are doing. Whether this is empirically so about some non-human animals, this level of understanding seems conceptually possible. Understanding at this level involves minimal inferential competence with logical constants.

Second, there is the understanding involved in believing what are in fact logical truths, including general ones. Such understanding includes the previous level, but involves a further capacity for generalization and abstraction. Believing logical truths like "Everything red and round is round" (as distinguished from following the associated inference rule applied to non-general thoughts) requires abstracting from the useful. This second level requires a capacity not only for inference but for being compelled to belief in general logical truths.[38]

Third, there is the understanding involved in the use of schematic generalization. This is an abstraction from any actual assertions or truths. Take the ability to consider and use, apart from any application, "If A is a human and A is male, then A is human", or "If Socrates is such and such and so and so, then he is such and such". One abstracts from any particular name substituting for "A", or from any particular predications of Socrates, and one understands the generality of the schematic usage. Understanding *how* to fill in the schematic elements is distinguishable both from quantification and from having a meta-logical perspective that specifies such fillings-in as such. It is like explicitly considering "that is green" abstracted from any application of "that". One can understand such singular expressions apart from applications to particular individuals or properties by knowing how to use the expressions while explicitly abstracting from specific contextual application. Such minimal schematic abstraction can also be distinguished from an ability to conceptualize the semantical relations of the substituted names and predicates (or applications of demonstratives or indexicals) as such. Whether or not this is a developmentally distinct level, it is notionally distinguishable from the second and fourth levels.[39]

---

38. I think it possible to infer from "That ball is red and round" to "That ball is round", without being able to believe the logical truth "If that ball is red and round, then that ball is round", much less the logical truth "Everything that is red and round, is round". Certainly the capacities are different capacities. Otherwise the deduction theorem would be a tautology.

39. Modern first-order logic is usually formulated with schemas. It is sometimes claimed that first-order logic is distinct from higher-order logics and from the logics of Frege and Russell in being fundamentally *about* sentences and in including a truth predicate (and meta-logical specifications of substitution operations). This claim is mistaken. Certainly, modern model-theory for first-order logic is from a meta-theoretic perspective that has these features. But the schematic formulations of first-order logic allow a perspective within the logic proper (the schematically formulated axioms and the rules of inference) as distinguished from a meta-perspective on the logic. The logic proper is not about sentences and invokes no truth predicate. A minimal non-meta-theoretic understanding of the logic proper involves *knowing how* to fill in forms like "If something is such and such and so and so, then it is such and such" so as to have a logical truth like "If something is red and square, then it is red". It also involves knowing how to fill in schematically stated inference rules so as to make actual non-schematic inferences. This is the third level of understanding. Such

Fourth, there is the understanding involved in using meta-logical concepts. Distinctive of this level is having some conception of logical truth and of arguments' deductively preserving truth.[40] This level requires distinguishing logical truths from others, and deductive arguments from other types. Logical truths and deductive arguments may be conceived as evident, or as necessary, or as provable given rules for using certain "logical" constants. Early formulations of logic are at the third and fourth levels. I leave open whether there are cases of occupying the third level, or even second, without occupying the fourth. The levels are notionally distinct.

Fifth, there is the understanding involved in having and applying the intuitive semantical notions *logical validity* and *logical consequence*. Having them perhaps requires, and certainly historically involved, distinguishing them from other conceptions of logical truth—such as modal conceptions, conceptions of obviousness or certainty, conceptions of proof. The intuitive notions *logical validity* and *logical consequence* associate the specialness of logical truths not only with deductive form and formal structure, but with a very strong type of generality.

Sixth, there is the understanding associated with systematization of these notions in model-theory or related systematic, mathematical, semantical theories. This level of systematic reflective understanding is the level at which mathematicization of logic is necessary.

The view I have argued is this: Engaging in inference does not require having the higher levels of understanding. But understanding is rationally impelled from lower levels to the sixth level, given sufficient conceptual maturity and sufficient reflection purely on relatively elementary deductive inferences. Such inferences harbor the seeds of sixth-level understanding.

---

understanding need not be semantical or otherwise meta-logical. Intuitive and mathematical meta-logic involve ascent beyond the minimal understanding involved in using even modern first-order logic proper.

It might be questioned whether the third level is more sophisticated than the second. Quantification into singular term position is more committal than schematic use of the name. But it seems to me that schematic use of dummy names or unapplied demonstratives is conceptually more sophisticated than existential generalization on the singular position in that it involves an abstraction from natural assertive uses in favor of uses that schematize assertions. The issue invites further exploration. It is not crucial to present purposes.

40. Perhaps there is a level, between the third and fourth levels, at which the ordinary concept of truth is first applied. Some conceptualization of sub-propositional forms and sub-propositional semantical structure would be necessary at such a level.

To outline how sixth-level understanding can be developed out of deductive inference: Making deductive inferences requires having beliefs and conversely. Belief aims at truth; deductive inference aims at truth preservation.[41] Deductive inference is essentially associated with logical truth, inasmuch as a conditional between premises and conclusion of a good deductive inference is a logical truth. Logical truth and deductive inference hinge on sub-propositional form. (I believe that propositional calculus is an abstraction from predicate logic.) Understanding both the nature of truth and the specific nature of logical truth and deductive inference requires understanding sub-propositional semantical structure. Logic has maximally general application. Understanding this generality in combination with the points about semantical structure just made yields intuitive notions *logical validity* and *logical consequence*. The relevance of logic to all permutations of sentences or propositions in inference requires that full understanding of the applications of these notions be systematic. The aim at truth, the form-dependence of deductive inference and logical truth, the connection between all types of truth and sub-propositional semantical structure, the generality of application of logical truth and deductive inference, and the systematic character of logical form are all available to reflection, given conceptual resources appropriate to these essential aspects of deductive inference. The actual problems of systematizing the sub-propositional semantical structure of deductive inference, for relatively simple types of deductive inference available even to adolescent children, force mathematicization.

The development of systematic reflective understanding from reflection on deductive inference is throughout apriori. The connection between the first or second level and the sixth is synthetic, under all three concepts of syntheticity. The sixth level conceptualizes and systematizes constitutive, internal aspects of elementary, non-semantical deductive inference. This fact—not facts about containment—indicates that the commitments of systematic reflective understanding bear on the natures of concepts and inferences involved in lower levels of understanding.

The fact that the concepts used at the higher levels need not be available to individuals with lower-level understanding does not show that the higher-level concepts do not help specify apriori the natures of the lower level ones. Attaining systematic reflective understanding

---

41. I spell out what I mean by "aim" in more detail in section I of Burge forthcoming.

took centuries. This indicates not that the semantical relations plotted in such understanding do not partly constitute the nature of deductive inference. It indicates that attaining the relevant meta-perspective and the conceptual precision needed to fully understand first-level deductive practice, are difficult matters—not only for current logic students, but for humankind through its history.

VII.

Kant thought that logic is analytic under the vacuousness concept and that mathematics and all other sciences are synthetic. He held logic and mathematics to be apriori. Carnap thought that both logic and mathematics are analytic under the vacuousness concept and that only the natural sciences are synthetic. He agreed with Kant that logic and mathematics are apriori. Quine thought that no truths are analytic under the vacuousness concept, and that no knowledge is apriori. Quine was right about analyticity. Kant and Carnap were right about apriority. Quine's empiricism is badly out of keeping with the way that mathematical knowledge is obtained and justified. Since his attack on the vacuousness concept seems to me decisive, I think that there is synthetic apriori knowledge (in the sense of "synthetic" that contrasts with the vacuousness concept). Both logic and mathematics constitute examples.

Quine opens "Carnap and Logical Truth" with flippant reference to Kant's key question:

> Kant's question "how are synthetic judgments a priori possible?" precipitated the *Critique of Pure Reason*. Question and answer notwithstanding, Mill and others persisted in doubting that such judgments were possible at all. At length some of Kant's own clearest purported instances, drawn from arithmetic, were sweepingly disqualified (or so it seemed ...) by Frege's reduction of arithmetic to logic. (Quine 1954, 100)

Contrary to his rhetoric, Quine points out that Frege's purported reduction of arithmetic to logic did not show that arithmetic is analytic under the vacuousness concept. Quine's criticism of that concept shows that both arithmetic and logic are synthetic. How is apriori knowledge of such truths possible? Quine sought to evade Kant's question by maintaining that all knowledge is empirical. As noted, this solution seems unacceptable.

One aspect of Kant's answer to his own question is equally unacceptable. Kant required that synthetic apriori cognition be confined to appearances.[42] He thought that space, time, and number—insofar as they are subject matters for cognition—are mind-dependent structures of our representative powers.[43] He was driven to this view because he thought that one can have apriori cognition only of what one produces. I think that this line is not a serious candidate for the truth.

Kant's question remains. How can one know apriori anything about a subject matter?

The argument of section V. is relevant to giving a partial answer to Kant's question, because of the following point. Logical forms, norms, and structures constitute conditions on the possibility of (propositional) thinking. Thinking is constitutively subject to and informed by logical forms, norms, and structures.[44] Reflection on logic uncovers necessary conditions for thought—conditions involving semantical structure. So by the argument of section V., commitment to mathematics and mathematical entities, in semantical elaboration of logical validity and logical consequence, is part of explaining conditions on the possibility of thinking.

I will not try a full argument for this view here. A sketch depends mainly on additions to the beginning and end of the argument already given: Conditions on the possibility of deductive reasoning are conditions on the possibility of (propositional) thinking. Reflective understanding of conditions on the possibility of deductive reasoning is possible by reflecting only on such reasoning. Such understanding requires the notions *logical validity* and *logical consequence*. It constitutively includes synthetic apriori knowledge—for example, knowledge that certain reasoning is logically valid and that its validity

---

42. I have transmuted Quine's "judgment" into "knowledge". I skate over the important point that Kant was less concerned with knowledge than with *Erkenntnis* or cognition. These issues are not important for present purposes.

43. I gloss over Kant's distinction between transcendental idealism and empirical realism. I do not think idealism plausible from any point of view, transcendental or otherwise. Note that Kant believed in non-logical apriori principles in physics. The track record of such claims has not been good. But the difficulty of the subject may account for this.

44. I leave open whether *full* first-order predicate logic, or something equivalently rich, is necessary to *all* thought. Animals or young children may think but use only fragments of first-order predicate logic. Quantificational structure rich enough to require mathematization in any systematic semantical account of it is necessary in adolescent human reasoning, and in science.

is explicable through semantical structures. Systematization of such understanding is rationally required. Systematic understanding of the semantical structure of relatively elementary forms of deductive reasoning is necessarily mathematical and committed to mathematical entities. Such understanding constitutes synthetic apriori knowledge. Such knowledge is of semantical structures that are conditions on the possibility of relatively elementary deductive reasoning —hence on the possibility of relatively elementary thought. So synthetic apriori knowledge of mathematical entities is possible (though not necessarily available to any given thinker) if relatively elementary thinking is possible. Such elementary thinking is possible. Its possibility can be known apriori by reflexively understanding actual thinking—in *cogito*-like instances of it. So the possibility of synthetic apriori knowledge of mathematics is implicit in conditions on the possibility of relatively elementary propositional thinking. Such knowledge is necessary to explaining conditions on the possibility of such thinking.

This conclusion only partially answers Kant's question. It draws an apriori, necessary connection between the possibility of relatively elementary propositional thought and the possibility of synthetic apriori knowledge of mathematics. It is parallel to the aspect of Kant's answer that claims that synthetic apriori cognition is possible because it is necessary to the possibility of explaining and justifying sense experience.[45]

---

45. Kant fixed on experience because he thought that synthetic apriori cognition is possible *only* through certain complex warranting connections to the structure of experience. I think this view incorrect for cognition in mathematics and in several other cases. Perhaps Kant would not have taken sense experience (and its structure) to be the source of all theoretical warrant if he had not regarded logic as analytic in the vacuousness sense.

The notions of explanation and justification are intrinsic to Kant's enterprise. For him, having cognition (*Erkenntnis*) constitutively involves an ability to explain and justify the cognition. Experience is, on his view, a type of cognition.

The present case (explaining conditions on deductive reasoning) and Kant's case (explaining conditions on experience) seem to me to differ in their bearing on epistemic warrant. It is extremely difficult to understand the sense in which an explanation of conditions which make experience possible might provide a warrant that supplements entitlements to perceptual belief (for example, in the context of scepticism). But I believe that there are relatively robust respects in which such explanations can provide supplementary justification. I think that it is even more difficult to discern a sense in which an explanation of the conditions that make deductive reasoning possible might yield a justification that supplements the justification or entitlement involved in competent deductive reasoning. Any such supplementary justification would inevitably be relatively thin. These are complex matters, best discussed elsewhere.

The conclusion does not replace the aspect of Kant's answer rejected earlier. It does not replace the aspect that claims that synthetic apriori cognition is possible because it applies to appearances (Kant 1787, B xvii–xviii; A 26 ff./B 42 ff.). How to bridge the feared gap between thought and subject matter without causal-experiential relations still needs explanation.

The argument that I sketched suggests an approach to confronting the apparent gap between representation and subject matter that Kant's question insinuates. The argument suggests that connection to a subject matter lies in the conditions that make logical inference possible. The fear of a gap derives from an illegitimately subjectivistic starting point—a conception of thinking that does not inquire into the objective conditions that underlie the possibility of thinking.[46]

The fear of a gap is generated from the question, "How can mere thinking yield warranted cognition in the absence of causal relations to a subject matter?" We can know that more goes into conditions on the possibility of "mere thinking" than the subjectivistic starting point recognizes. I believe that the argument given here can be further developed so as to contribute to understanding how aspects of mentality, those involved in relative elementary deductive reasoning, are constitutively associated with warranted apriori cognition of a mathematical subject matter. I will not try to support this claim here, or confront the many issues that arise for it.

I have also not tried to defend the objective truth of logic or mathematics. I have tried to better understand reflective understanding of what we know.

All rational enterprises presuppose logic. Systematic reflective understanding of deductive inference, of logic, and of logical validity and logical consequence each requires mathematics.[47] Whether or not logic is committed through its axioms to the existence of a subject matter, logic is rationally implicated with a subject matter. This connection is available to systematic apriori reflective understanding of applications of the intuitive notions that conceptualize the point and practice of logic. The connection binds inferential structures and norms

---

But in each case, the reflective account is a type of explanation of possibility—possibility of sense experience and possibility of deductive reasoning.

46. There is further discussion of these matters in Burge 1992a.
47. See Appendix III—Poincaré on the Dependence of Logic on Mathematics.

that are constitutive of what it is to be a mind to a subject matter, that of mathematics, that informs all subject matters. By reflection we can know such a connection apriori. We must be able to know it if we are to reflectively and systematically understand relatively simple deductive inference, hence relatively simple propositional representation as of anything at all.[48]

Appendix I—Logic: First-order? Second-order?

In most of this paper I focus on first-order logic. There is, I think, more to the idea that second-order logic must make existential commitments through quantification on predicate position than to the idea that such commitments are made through quantification on individual variables. Predication prima facie implies something to predicate, even bracketing commitment to individuals (cf. note 21.) This intuition counts against interpreting quantification into predicate position as being committed only to pluralities of individuals (cf. Boolos 1975; 1984; 1985). Such interpretations seem artificial. Pluralities of individuals do not seem plausible candidates for what are predicated.

First-order logic demands first attention. The derivability of its valid principles, absent in second-order logic, gives it a feature traditionally regarded as central to logic.

There is the further problem that validity or invalidity in second-order logic, standardly interpreted, can hinge on difficult and unsettled mathematical questions, such as the truth-value of the continuum hypothesis. My concern about counting second-order logic as logic is not about strong ontological commitment in the meta-theory. As sections IV–VI emphasize, the meta-theory of even first-order logic is committed at least to an infinity of entities—though the meta-theory for second-order logic can be forced into vastly larger commitments. My concern is about the lack of transparency, indeed the opacity, to reason of validity and consequence in second-order logic. Logic has traditionally been thought to codify principles of good deductive inference that can elicit agreement through being open to check by any reasonably mature and competent rational being. Given that validity in second-order logic is not only not derivable but very unevident to reason, and given that consequence in

---

48. I believe that Kant's question demands further answers. I think that the idea that thought is constitutively dependent on connection to mathematical structures is an element in many of them.

second-order logic is equally unevident, it is open to doubt whether it should count as logic. The usefulness of logic in being an arbiter for good reasoning is compromised if what counts as good is as unevident as the truth-value of the continuum hypothesis. Of course, historically, reason has sometimes been slow to recognize what seems retrospectively more nearly evident. And there are different conceptions of logic. My primary argument does not depend on whether second-order logic is counted logic.

For further discussion of these matters, see Shapiro 1991, Jané 1993, Burgess 1993, and Cutler 1997. The latter three give reasons closely related to those just given that in effect support taking first-order logic to be the paradigm logic. Jané and Burgess give further methodological reasons. Cutler emphasizes the completeness theorem more than I do, though I think this consideration very significant. If logical consequence in second-order logic were as rationally transparent as reasoning in intuitive arithmetic, my concern about counting second-order logic as logic would be considerably lessened even though arithmetic is incomplete.

I believe that Jané's gloss of first-order logic as having no "substantive content" is quite mistaken. He gives no non-question-begging ground for it. In fact, the reason he gives is a variant of the first of the three considerations I criticize in section III. I think his characterization of the uses and import of first- and second-order logic is otherwise illuminating.

It should be remembered that the notion of model-theoretic validity is not an autonomous, self-standing conception of logical truth. It depends on an antecedent conception of a logical constant, hence of logic. The notion of model-theoretic validity was introduced as a systematization of an *intuitive* notion, *logical validity* (see below, sections IV–VI). It is thus open to discussion whether truth in all models of second-order logic is *logical* validity. (Here "second-order logic" is a proper name!) Notions of what counts as logic are thus prior to application of the model-theoretic notion *validity*. Of course, the notion *truth in all models* can be used independently of whether it helps explicate any logical notion. But insofar as it is meant to illuminate intuitive logical validity, it presupposes a conception of logic. Indeed, the intuitive notion *logical validity* is guided by an antecedent conception of logic. As I noted, there are probably various legitimate conceptions of logic. I am following what I take to be a mainstream conception that has some claim to being fundamental. These issues are relevant to understanding points made in section IV and in note 28.

Appendix II—A Sketch of the Key Intuitive Notions in the History of Logic

It is at best unclear whether Aristotle had the intuitive notions *logical validity* and *logical consequence*. He surely did not have the theoretical model-theoretic notions. Aristotle worked with a notion of *following-from* (cf. Lear 1980, chapter 1). Aristotle had a broadly semantical notion of truth, a limited notion of logical form, and *perhaps* a commitment to the generality of logic. But it is unclear whether he combined such commitments with a non-modal conception of semantical structure or structure-in-the-world to explicate logical truth or good deductive inference. It is widely doubted that he made use of a notion of formal consequence. His notion of following-from seems to have been modal. His immediate followers concentrated on notions of syllogistic form and modality.

The intuitive notion *logical validity* appears to be present in Abaelard. He understands logical validity for conditional *propositions* non-modally, in terms of containment in virtue of form (Abaelard, ca. 1115, II.iii, 253; 255 f.; III, i, 283 f.). He distinguishes this from the modal conception of the impossibility of a true antecedent and false consequent (ibid., III.i, 271), and understands containment in terms of structural relations in the world. Note that containment is seen as a basis for *explicating* truth in terms of structure. Whereas Abaelard seems clearly to have the notion *logical validity* for propositions, his conception of good deductive inference bears a more equivocal relation to the intuitive notion *logical consequence*. He uses a broad modal notion of following-from to characterize good deductive inference. Since this notion is more liberal than the containment conception of true conditionals, he in effect denies the deduction theorem. For conditionals require containment for their truth, whereas good deductive inferences require only the impossibility of true premises and a false conclusion. So his primary conception of good inference is not in terms of the intuitive notion *logical consequence*, even though he has the intuitive notion *logical validity* for propositions.

Abaelard explicates his notion of formal or *perfect inference*, however, in terms of logical-form-preserving substitution of non-logical terms (ibid., II, iii, 255), a notion later associated with Bolzano and Quine. Abaelard's notion of "perfect" inference joined with his notion of containment gives him an approximation to the notion *logical consequence*. He takes perfect inference to entail the modal "following from". Thus he claims that uniform substitution preserves "consecution" or "following from". This claim mingles structural and modal conceptions. But since he conceives of containment non-modally, he has the resources for a conception of substitutivity of non-logical terms that preserves containment. Containment implies modality but is not explained in terms of it. Such a conception would be a conception of formal logical consequence. Abaelard claims that perfect, formal inferences contrast with imperfect inferences in that the former do *not* hold in virtue of "the nature of things" (*de natura rerum*). This does not mean that they hold independently of factual matters, but rather that they are not grounded in the natures of existing particulars. They are not *de-re-based*, or particular *loci* of modality. They constrain God as well as things (cf. ibid., II, ii, 201; III, 1, 285; 290–305.)

In the twentieth century the Abaelard-Bolzano conception of uniform substitution of non-logical terms is commonly associated with conceptions of logical truth that abstain from explication of truth and truth-preservation in terms of sub-propositional semantical relations to a subject-matter. These are the "relatively syntactic" conceptions discussed in section IV. For Abaelard, containment at the level of propositional content is made true by an analog of containment among states-of-affairs (ibid., III.1, 286 f.).

Unlike Abaelard, Scotus aligns his conceptions of logical truth and good deductive inference. He appears to have both the notion *logical validity* for propositions and the notion (formal) *logical consequence*. He explains these notions in terms of fundamental natural structures of priority in the world. Modality does not appear to be fundamental in these explications. For discussion of Abaelard and Scotus, see Martin 2000 and Martin forthcoming.

Like Abaelard, Buridan has a substitutional conception of formal consequence that bears semantical relations to structures in the world. Buridan explains formal consequence as the impossibility of the conclusion being false if the antecedents are true, under structure-preserving substitution of categorematic terms (cf. Buridan, ca. 1340, I.6.1). He thus mixes modal and structural considerations. But in one place he explains this necessity in terms of the conclusion "never" being false when the antecedents are true—presumably "never" under any substitutions (ibid., VII.4.5). Thus it may be that he sometimes conceives of formal consequence in terms that are fundamentally structural rather than modal (instead of both). He certainly regards the substitutional conception of formal consequence as having a semantical underpinning.

I believe that Leibniz had the intuitive conceptions. But the role of generality in his view is sufficiently complex that a discussion of the issue here would take too much space (cf. Burge 2000, 22 note 23).

Bolzano has the intuitive concepts *logical validity* and *logical consequence*. Like Abaelard and Buridan, Bolzano takes the substitution conception of logical truth to have a semantical underpinning (cf. Bolzano 1837, II, sections 147 f.). For a discussion of the fundamentally semantical character of Bolzano's conception, see Proust 1989.

None of these figures used anything like domain variation in evaluating validity. Domain variation is not necessary to the intuitive notions *logical validity* or *logical consequence*. In fact, Tarski's original paper on logical consequence does not employ domain variation (see Tarski 1936; Etchemendy 1990; Bays 2001).

It must be emphasized that in the history of logic, the intuitive notions *logical validity* and *logical consequence* are sufficiently open-ended to allow for different construals of logicality, of formality, of structure, and of the relevant notion of generality. The intuitive concepts are compatible with various conceptions (cf. notes 23, 33 and 37).

Appendix III—Poincaré on the Dependence of Logic on Mathematics

Poincaré 1908, chapter IV, advances a generically similar point of view as a criticism of Russell's (and by extension, Frege's) logicism. Poincaré argues that since setting up logic requires inductive characterizations of the syntax and of the proof procedures, and since those characterizations presuppose the notion of number, logicism is circular: logic "presupposes" mathematics. Poincaré concentrates on the proof-theoretic aspects of logic. I concentrate on its semantical aspects—those that bear on its synthetic character.

Poincaré's criticism of logicism is not on target, however. There is no definitional or justificational circularity in Frege's or Russell's logicist theory. They did not see the primary justification of a proof, or the reduction of logic to mathematics, as lying at a meta-level in which the syntax or the existence of a proof is specified. It lay for them in the giving of a proof itself. Similarly, the justification of an axiom or theorem lay in the self-evidence of the axioms and the steps of the proof, not in a meta-logical account of logical validity or of logical consequence involved in the proof. Frege's definitions reflect his conception of justification. I make these points in regard to Frege in Burge 1998, without reference to Poincaré. I think a similar point applies to Russell. For a fuller discussion of Poincaré's point, see Parsons 1965 and Goldfarb 2001. Goldfarb also points out what is wrong with Poincaré's objection to Frege. (Although I agree with him on this point, we differ in our construals of Frege's logic and its relation to standard model-theoretic accounts of logic.) The problems for logicism lie not in Poincaré's point but in the question whether what is needed to derive mathematics is in fact logic and in the question whether the relevant derivations constitute an explanation of the *nature* of mathematics.

In any case, the Frege-Russell view of justification seems to me correct.

The primary justification for belief in logical truths lies in logical competence. This is the understanding that I characterized in the text in section VI as second-level understanding—the kind necessary to believe the truths. (Entitlement to deductive inference lies in first-level understanding.) A meta-theoretic account may add supplementary justification. But primarily it deepens understanding (cf. note 45). Inasmuch as the meta-level types of understanding involve concepts not analytically contained in the object-level logical concepts, the logical constants, there is no conceptual circularity. The object-level justifications are autonomous. Poincaré's insight is that a systematic reflective understanding of logic must invoke mathematics. This understanding is synthetic, not analytic.

REFERENCES

Abaelard, Peter, ca. 1115: *Dialectica*, L.M. De Rijk (Ed.), Assen 1956.
Barwise, Jon 1977: "An Introduction to First-Order Logic" in *Handbook of Mathematical Logic*, J. Barwise (Ed.), Amsterdam.
Bays, Tim 2001: "Tarski On Models", *The Journal of Symbolic Logic* 66, 1701–1726.
Bolzano, Bernhard 1837: *Wissenschaftslehre*, Sulzbach.
Boolos, George 1975: "On Second-Order Logic", in *Logic, Logic, and Logic*, R. Jeffrey (Ed.), Cambridge, Mass. 1998.
Boolos, George 1984: "To Be is to Be a Value of a Variable (or to Be Some Values of Some Variables)" in *Logic, Logic, and Logic*, R. Jeffrey (Ed.), Cambridge, Mass. 1998.
Boolos, George 1985: "Nominalist Platonism" in *Logic, Logic, and Logic*, R. Jeffrey (Ed.), Cambridge, Mass. 1998.
Burge, Tyler 1974: "Truth and Singular Terms," *Noûs* 8, 309–325, reprinted in *Philosophical Applications of Free Logic*, K. Lambert (Ed.), Oxford 1991.
Burge, Tyler 1975, "On Knowledge and Convention," *The Philosophical Review* 84, 249–255.
Burge, Tyler 1979: "Semantical Paradox," *The Journal of Philosophy* 76, 169–198.
Burge, Tyler 1979a: "Individualism and the Mental," *Midwest Studies in Philosophy* 4, 73–121.
Burge, Tyler 1982: "Other Bodies," in *Thought and Object*, A. Woodfield (Ed.), London.

Burge, Tyler 1986: "Intellectual Norms and Foundations of Mind," *The Journal of Philosophy* 83, 697–720.
Burge, Tyler 1986a: "Frege on Truth," in *Frege Synthesized*, L. Haaparanta and J. Hintikka, (Eds.), Dordrecht.
Burge, Tyler 1990: "Frege on Sense and Linguistic Meaning," in *The Analytic Tradition*, D. Bell and N. Cooper (Eds.), London.
Burge, Tyler 1992: "Philosophy of Language and Mind: 1950–1990", *The Philosophical Review* 100, 3–51.
Burge, Tyler 1992a: "Frege on Knowing the Third Realm", *Mind* 101, 633–650.
Burge, Tyler 1998: "Frege on Knowing the Foundation," *Mind* 107, 305–347.
Burge, Tyler 2000: "Frege on Apriority" in *New Essays on the A Priori*, P. Boghossian and C. Peacocke (Eds.), Oxford.
Burge, Tyler forthcoming: "Perceptual Entitlement", *Philosophy and Phenomenological Research*.
Burgess, John 1993: Review of Shapiro, *Foundations without Foundationalism*, *The Journal of Symbolic Logic* 58, 363–365.
Buridan, Jean, ca. 1340: *Summulae de Dialectica*, G. Klima (Transl.), New Haven 2002.
Carnap, Rudolf 1937: *The Logical Syntax of Language*, London.
Cutler, Darcy 1997: Review of Shapiro, *Foundations without Foundationalism*, *Philosophia Mathematica* 5, 71–91.
Davidson, Donald 1990: "The Structure and Content of Truth", *The Journal of Philosophy* 87, 279–328.
Etchemendy, John 1990: *The Concept of Logical Consequence*, Cambridge, Mass.
Field, Hartry 1989: *Realism, Mathematics, and Modality*, Oxford.
Frege, Gottlob 1879: *Begriffsschrift*, Halle.
Frege, Gottlob 1884: *Foundations of Arithmetic*, J. L. Austin (Transl.), Evanston, Ill. 1968.
Frege, Gottlob 1891: "Function and Concept", in *The Philosophical Writings of Gottlob Frege*, P. Geach and M. Black (Transl.), Oxford 1966.
Frege, Gottlob 1892: "On Sense and Reference", in *The Philosophical Writings of Gottlob Frege*, P. Geach and M. Black (Transl.), Oxford 1966.
Goldfarb, Warren 2001: "Frege's Conception of Logic" in *Future and Pasts: The Analytic Tradition in Philosophy*, J. Floyd and S. Shieh (Eds.), Oxford.
Hanson, William H. 1997: "The Concept of Logical Consequence", *The Philosophical Review* 106, 365–409.

Jané, Ignacio 1993: "A Critical Appraisal of Second-Order Logic", *History and Philosophy of Logic* 14, 67–86.

Kant, Immanuel 1787: *Critique of Pure Reason*, first edition 1781; second, 1787.

Kant, Immanuel 1800: *Logik Jäsche*, in *Akademie-Ausgabe*, volume IX, Berlin 1923.

Kleene, Stephen Cole 1964: *Introduction to Metamathematics*, Princeton, fourth reprint.

Kreisel, Georg 1967: "Informal Rigour and Completeness Proofs" in *Problems in the Philosophy of Mathematics*, I. Lakatos (Ed.), Amsterdam; reprinted in part with a postscript in *The Philosophy of Mathematics*, J. Hintikka (Ed.), Oxford 1969. Page numbers cited from the reprint.

Lear, Jonathan 1980: *Aristotle and Logical Theory*, Cambridge, England.

Leibniz, Gottfried 1677: "Dialog on Connections of Things and Words" in Leibniz: *Selections*, Philip P. Wiener (Ed.), New York 1951.

Martin, Christopher J. 2000: *Theories of Inference and Entailment in the Middle Ages*, Dissertation, Princeton University.

Martin, Christopher J. forthcoming: "Abaelard's Logic: The Theory of Entailment" in *Cambridge Companion to Abaelard*.

Parsons, Charles 1965: "Frege's Theory of Number" in *Mathematics and Philosophy*, with postscript, Ithaca 1983.

Parsons, Charles 1974: "The Liar Paradox" in *Mathematics in Philosophy*, with postscript, Ithaca 1983.

Parsons, Charles 1995: "Quine and Gödel on Analyticity", in *On Quine: New Essays*, P. Leonardi and M. Santambrogio (Eds.), Cambridge, England.

Poincaré, Henri 1908: *Science et Methode*, Paris.

Proust, Joelle 1989: *Questions of Form: Logic and the Analytic Proposition from Kant to Carnap*, A. A. Brenner (Transl.), Minneapolis.

Putnam, Hilary 1962: "The Analytic and the Synthetic" in his *Philosophical Papers*, volume 2, Cambridge, England 1985.

Putnam, Hilary 1975: "The Meaning of 'Meaning'", in his *Philosophical Papers*, volume 2 Cambridge, England 1985.

Putnam, Hilary 1988: *Representation and Reality*, Cambridge, Mass.

Quine, W. V. 1936: "Truth By Convention" in his *The Ways of Paradox*, New York 1966.

Quine, W. V. 1950: *Methods of Logic*, New York.

Quine, W. V. 1953: "Two Dogmas of Empiricism", in his *From a Logical Point of View*, New York, 1961; originally published 1953, Cambridge, Mass.

Quine, W. V. 1954: "Carnap and Logical Truth" written 1954; large parts first published, in Italian, 1956; first fully published in English 1960; in his *The

Ways of Paradox, New York 1966.
Quine, W. V. 1970: *Philosophy of Logic*, Englewood Cliffs, New Jersey.
Quine, W. V. 1990: *Pursuit of Truth*, Cambridge, Mass.
Shapiro, Stuart 1991: *Foundations without Foundationalism: A Case for Second-Order Logic*, Oxford.
Tarski, Alfred 1936: "On the Concept of Logical Consequence" in *Logic, Semantics, Metamathematics*, Indianapolis 1983.

III.
"TWO DOGMAS" AND BEYOND

"SCIENCE ITSELF TEACHES". A FRESH LOOK AT QUINE'S NATURALISTIC METAPHILOSOPHY

Geert KEIL
Humboldt-Universität Berlin

Summary

Quine famously holds that "philosophy is continuous with natural science". In order to find out what exactly the point of this claim is, I take up one of his preferred phrases and trace it through his writings, i.e., the phrase "Science itself teaches that ...". Unlike Wittgenstein, Quine did not take much interest in determining what might be distinctive of philosophical investigations, or of the philosophical part of scientific investigations. I find this indifference regrettable, and I take a fresh look at Quine's metaphilosophy, trying to defuse his avowed naturalism by illustrating how little influence his naturalistic rhetoric has on the way he actually does philosophy.

0. Introduction

Over and above its attack on the analytic/synthetic distinction, Quine's celebrated paper about the "Two Dogmas of Empiricism" reveals some of his more general views on the relationship between philosophy and empirical science. In the opening paragraph, Quine points to "one effect of abandoning" the two dogmas, viz, "a blurring of the supposed boundary between speculative metaphysics and natural science" (1953, 20). He sees a connection between his misgivings about analyticity and what he will later call his *naturalistic* outlook on philosophy. Just as there is no sharp distinction to be drawn between analytic and synthetic truths, there is no clean-cut difference between philosophy and natural science. As he says many years later: "Naturalism brings a salutary blurring of such boundaries. Naturalistic philosophy is continuous with natural science." (1995a, 256–7, see also 1969, 126–7)

Quine does not use the term 'naturalism' until the late sixties. It is obvious, however, that his line of reasoning in *Two Dogmas* prepares the ground for and even anticipates his naturalism. My paper deals with the question of what exactly Quine's claim means that philosophy is continuous with natural science. For that purpose, I shall take up one of Quine's preferred phrases and trace it through his writings. Strikingly, Quine often introduces tenets usually considered philosophical in nature with the words "Science itself teaches" or "Science tells us". I shall gather some of these claims and evaluate them. Thereafter, I shall bring Quine's broad notion of science into play, and discuss the two continuity theses associated with this sweeping notion of science. Unlike Wittgenstein, Quine did not take much interest in determining what might be distinctive of philosophical investigations, or of the philosophical part of scientific investigations. He was more eager to emphasize what philosophy and natural science have in common. I find this limitation regrettable, and I shall take a fresh look at the few remarks Quine does make to distinguish the philosopher's business. His blurring of the supposed boundary between philosophy and natural science has caused a good deal of alarm among Wittgensteinians and promoters of *a priori* conceptual analysis. Towards the end of this paper, I shall try to defuse Quine's avowed naturalism by illustrating how little influence his naturalistic rhetoric has on the way he actually does philosophy. In evaluating Quine's philosophy of science and his metaphilosophy, we are well advised to try to sort out his scientistic avowals from his philosophy at work.[1]

1. *What Science Itself Allegedly Teaches*

Examples of philosophical assertions passed off as deliverances of natural science abound in Quine's writings.

(a) A prominent example is his claim that "science itself tells us that our information about the world is limited to irritations of our surfaces" (1981, 72). Quine restates this point repeatedly:

---

[1]. In a similar vein, Jonathan Cohen (1987) has suggested "to investigate closely the extent to which Quine's ideas about the method of his philosophical enterprise are coherent with the substance of his philosophical doctrine".

> Science tells us that our only source of information about the external world is through the impact of light rays and molecules upon our sensory surfaces. (1975, 68)

> [I]t is a finding of natural science itself, however fallible, that our information about the world comes only through impacts on our sensory receptors. (1992, 19)

> Science itself teaches that there is no clairvoyance; that the only information that can reach our sensory surfaces from external objects must be limited to two-dimensional optical projections and various impacts of air waves on the eardrums [...]. (1974, 3)

In other words, science allegedly teaches that empiricism is true. The quoted passages are variations on the empiricist credo 'nihil est in intellectu quod non prius fuerit in sensu'. Unlike the classical empiricists, however, Quine does not describe the sensory input in terms of perceptions, sensations or impressions, but as "irradiation patterns" or "impacts on our surfaces", or, recently, as "triggerings of our nerve endings", thus in physiological terms, not in mental ones.

(b) A second example is Quine's view that *science itself motivates skeptical doubts* and helps to dispel them as well. "[T]he skeptical challenge springs from science itself", he says, and "in coping with it we are free to use scientific knowledge" (1974, 3). The second half of the statement is a comment on the charge of circularity against naturalized epistemologies. Not claiming to have found a "firmer basis for science than science itself", Quine feels "free to use the very fruits of science in investigating its roots" (1995, 16). All of this is familiar, and there is no need to go into it.

(c) A third example is his claim that *science tells us what there is*. This view might seem less controversial than the tenets presented above, for most philosophers would admit that there are at least some ways of discovering what there is which are not the philosopher's business. Quine's view acquires a bite when reformulated as a characterization of a joint venture of philosophers and scientists:

> The question what there is is a shared concern of philosophy and most other non-fiction genres. [...] A representative assortment of land masses, seas, planets, and stars have been individually described in the astronomy books [...] What distinguishes between the ontological philosopher's concern and all this is only breadth of categories. Given physical objects

in general, the natural scientist is the man to decide about wombats and unicorns. (1960, 275)

Yet the difference between the philosophical and the scientific parts of the joint venture is only one of degree, as Quine says in the famous passage from *Two Dogmas*:

> The issue over there being classes seems more a question of convenient conceptual scheme; the issue over there being centaurs, or brick houses on Elm Street, seems more a question of fact. But I have been urging that this difference is only one of degree. (1953, 46)

More specific ontological tenets which Quine poses as findings of natural science could be added, for instance, his substitution of coordinates of spacetime regions for physical objects. In his paper "Whither Physical Objects?" he declares the following to be "an outcome [...] of physics itself": that "our physical objects have evaporated into mere sets of numerical coordinates" (1976, 502).

Ontology set aside, there are many further prima facie philosophical insights which Quine ascribes to science. For example, he considers the "question of unity of science [...] a question within science itself" (1995a, 260). His notion that epistemology is "only science self-applied" (1969a, 293) falls into line with (a), i.e., with his scientific justification of empiricism. Similarly, his behavioristic speculations about the process of language acquisition have been dubbed an attempt at "naturalizing empiricism" (Gibson 1999, 461). I shall finish this brief survey, however, in order to make a few comments on the tenets (a), (b) and (c). These comments will be made, for the time being, in disregard of Quine's broad and somewhat idiolectal use of the term "science".

ad (a) As to the first claim about science establishing the truth of empiricism: It is tempting to dig more deeply and enquire *which* scientific discipline has found out that "our information about the world is limited to irritations of our surfaces". It has also been asked how natural science *could* demonstrate that sensory evidence is the only evidence (Koppelberg 2000, 71). This is a good question to ask. After all, to assert that there is no other kind of evidence amounts to a non-existence claim, and non-existence claims are notoriously hard to verify empirically.

It seems to me not quite correct to call it empirical findings that, for example, the phenomena of clairvoyance and telepathy do not exist, or that they are no source of information about the world. The better thing to say would be that there is *no empirical support* for assuming that people with such talents exist, and that we, good empiricists that we are, might *conclude* from the lack of empirical evidence that there are no such phenomena. A conclusion drawn from a lack of evidence is a more indirect discovery than an empirical verification. As soon as someone opens a debate about what *counts* as evidence, though, the empiricist would no longer get away with simply citing what he deems to be evidence. Giving empirical evidence for a claim is one thing, reflecting about what counts as evidence is quite another. It is the latter that empiricism, as a philosophical doctrine, has to deal with. And, while being a scientifically minded person arguably promotes being converted to empiricism, it is certainly not an empirical finding that empiricism is true.

Quine holds, famously:

> The question how we know what there is is simply part of the question [...] of the evidence for truth about the world. The last arbiter is so-called scientific method, however amorphous. (1960, 22–3)

Here, I would suggest that the phrase "the question of the evidence for truth about the world" is ambiguous, in the way just described. As to the question what counts as evidence, it is simply not true that this question can be *settled* by scientific method alone, as the phrase "the last arbiter" suggests. An appeal to scientific method(s), amorphous or unified, plays an important role in such debates, but the relation is less direct than Quine suggests, more of which below.

ad (b) Quine explains his second claim, viz., that "the skeptical challenge springs from science itself", as follows: "The skeptics cited familiar illusions to show the fallibility of the senses; but this concept of illusion itself rested on natural science, since the quality of illusion consisted simply in deviation from external scientific reality" (1974, 3).

This passage invites the reply that not all doubts are skeptical doubts. Even doubts concerning the reliability of our senses need not amount to skepticism proper. If everyone who has become aware of the fallibility of our senses were reckoned to be a skeptic, non-skeptics could only be recruited among very young children. Skeptical doubt, Cartesian or Pyrrhonean, is a more serious affair, and it could well be the case that, while science motivates doubts, it does not motivate skeptical doubts. Furthermore, it is hard to see why the external reality from which illusions deviate should be described as "scientific reality", so that the "concept of illusion itself rest[s] on natural science". Common sense realism as a backdrop should suffice.

When it comes to the question of how the skeptical challenge can be met, it is worth noting how modest Quine's claim actually is. It is one thing to hold that science itself answers skeptical doubts, but it is quite another thing to hold, as Quine does, that in coping with skepticism "we are free to use scientific knowledge" (ibid.). The latter claim is much weaker, and it prompts me to draw the same moral as before, viz. that the connections between scientific findings and philosophical conclusions are not as direct as it initially seems. In particular, Quine's view that skepticism is a pointless exercise with regard to natural science as a whole does not constitute a scientific result, but is rather an upshot of his *philosophy* of science. Quine is known to argue that global skepticism is generally out of place because it rests on the faulty assumption that natural science is "answerable" to "a supra-scientific tribunal" (1981, 72). If science is not in need of a philosophical justification or foundation in the first place, the skeptic's worry that this foundation is crumbling turns out to be pointless. Whatever the merits of this line of reasoning, it is clearly philosophical in nature.

ad (c) As Quine urges in *Two Dogmas*, determining what there is should be seen as a joint venture of philosophical ontology and natural science because the difference between the conceptual issue over there being classes and the empirical issue over there being unicorns is only one of degree. To him, the difference between philosophical ontology and empirical science boils down to a difference in the breadth of the categories involved.

In general, it is unrewarding to dispute continuity claims in philosophy. They sound so wise and serene, and they are very hard to refute. Even the distinction between a heap and a non-heap seems to admit of degrees. On the other hand, nobody denies that different methods are employed for tracking down unicorns than for deciding whether there are classes. Russell once tried to convince his student Wittgenstein that there is no rhinoceros in the room. Wittgenstein, who held, at that time, that nothing empirical is knowable, would not admit this. "In later life Russell made great play of these discussions and claimed he had looked under all the tables and chairs in the lecture room in an effort to convince Wittgenstein that there was no rhinoceros present " (Monk 1990, 40). You can bet that Wittgenstein, whose sense of humour was underdeveloped, was not amused. A familiar way of expressing the misgivings about Russell's verification procedure is to say that "for Wittgenstein the issue was metaphysical rather than empirical" (ibid.). Now let us assume that on Wittgenstein's making such a claim, Russell would had retorted that this difference is only one of degree. Wittgenstein would have gone wild, understandably enough.

Quine's claim that ontology differs only gradually from empirical science exploits an ambiguity in the question of what there is. In the case of rhinoceros, or of brick houses on Elm Street, the question is whether physical objects of a given kind are to be found in a certain place, the answer being a matter of betaking oneself to go there and to have a look. In the case of classes or numbers, the question is whether to include a certain category in one's ontology or not. Establishing the existence of numbers would amount to a *justification* of an ontological commitment. Both such justifications and empirical discoveries about the presence of brick houses or rhinoceros may count as answers to the question 'what there is'; yet in calling the difference only a matter of "breadth of categories", Quine deliberately ignores the more significant differences.

In general, calling a difference one of gradation does not smooth out the difference. Rather, it indicates the speaker's reluctance to regard the difference as relevant to the present context. We must distinguish, of course, between differences and distinctions, the former residing in the world, the latter being drawn in language. Every difference is as big as it happens to be, and how many degrees there are in between depends on how many distinctions one is prepared to draw, i.e., how many predicates one finds in order to draw finer distinctions. (Besides, there may be distinctions without a difference, but this is not what Quine seems to have in mind when he calls the difference between ontology and empirical science one of degree.) In view of this consideration, it seems wise not to attach too much importance to the question whether the difference between philosophy and the rest of science is one of degree or one in kind. In a way, every difference admits to gradation, and in another way, everything is *sui generis*, if the genera are cut to a suitable size.

In order to reach firmer ground again, let us turn to Quine's more specific claim about replacing spacetime regions for physical objects, since physics itself has done so (cf. 1976, 502). On closer examination, Quine's ontological revision is not *motivated* by the fact that matter goes by the board in modern physics. His real argument is that if we specify the wormlike region of four-dimensional spacetime that a certain physical object takes up in the course of its career, we have fixed the object uniquely. Therefore, he thinks, we are well advised to *identify* the object with the region in order to avoid "the inelegance of a tandem ontology: matter and space" (1974, 133). Quine admits that the identification "is artificial, but actually it confers a bit of economy, if we are going to have the space-time anyway" (1995a, 259). In other words: *It's economy, stupid.* It goes without saying that physicists may *adopt* this policy of not multiplying entities sine necessitate. This fact, though, makes neither Occam's maxim nor Quine's worries about a heavily overpopulated universe a result of physics.[2]

2. Quine's Sweeping Notion of Science

Hitherto, I have disregarded Quine's unusually wide use of the term 'science'. It is now time to make up what I have missed.

It is instructive to contrast Quine's views on the relationship between philosophy and science with Wittgenstein's. In his middle period, Wittgenstein used to say things like these:

> Philosophers constantly see the method of science before their eyes, and are irresistibly tempted to ask and answer questions in the way science does. This tendency is the real source of metaphysics, and leads the philosopher into complete darkness. (Wittgenstein 1972, 18)

This remark of Wittgenstein's seems to contrast sharply with Quine's views that philosophy is continuous with science, and that the last arbiter is always scientific method. But wait. When Wittgenstein speaks of 'science', or 'Wissenschaft', he has in mind *the sum total of the natural sciences*, which he considers to be equivalent with "the totality of true propositions" (*Tract.* 4.11). In the *Tractatus*, Wittgenstein makes it clear that "[p]hilosophy is not one of the natural sciences" (4.111). Nobody would take exception to this, not even Quine. Philosophy is not physics, nor is it biology, chemistry, etc.

---

2. A closer look also reveals that Quine's move from a three-dimensional to a four-dimensional conception of physical objects is not motivated by the theory of relativity with its spacelike treatment of time, but rather by age-old philosophical puzzles such as Zenon's paradoxes and Heraclitus' problem about stepping into the same river twice. See Quine 1960, 171–2.

When Quine looks upon philosophy as part of the scientific enterprise, he employs a different notion of science. When he uses 'science' in the singular, the term is not a collective name for a bunch of scientific disciplines. Rather, it is supposed to mean 'our scientific world view' or 'our overall theory of the world'. This shift in meaning changes the situation considerably. In the face of Quine's embracing notion of science, the issue over a certain assertion's being scientific or philosophical in character tends to lose its point, and it becomes hard to understand why I was making such heavy weather of Quine's assertions about "science itself" telling us all these things.

Previously, I asked *which* science has found out that our information about the world is limited to irritations of our surfaces, and I suggested that no theory of physics and no biological theory could ever discover what *counts* as evidence for our beliefs about the world. Expecting otherwise, however, rests on a tendentious interpretation of Quine's empiricist tenet. For if the term 'science', here and in related places, stands for 'our overall theory of the world', it should come as no surprise that Quine has no particular scientific theory up his sleeve to substantiate his claim. Given his sweeping notion of science, "science has found out" does no longer mean "*a* science has found out". I hasten to add that, by the same token, Quine's formulations are stripped of their naturalistic bite. The same holds true for his slogan "Philosophy of science is philosophy enough": Against whom is this slogan directed if science includes philosophy?

A characteristic passage goes like this: "Even our appreciation of the [...] under-determination of our overall theory of nature is not a higher-level intuition; it is integral to our under-determined theory of nature itself, and of ourselves as natural objects" (1969, 303). Only on an uncharitable reading does Quine suggest here that even the underdetermination thesis is written in the Book of Nature, or that it is a finding of natural science. This passage is perhaps not very fortunate, but clearly enough it invokes once more the inclusive notion of 'our overall theory of nature' which excludes nothing but "higher-level intuitions", whatever this may be. Quine's terminological strategy is different from Wittgenstein's. He uses the term 'science' in a sense so wide that it covers the cognitive enterprises of both the natural scientist and the philosopher. They are both in the same boat, as Quine so often says. To him, science is not even to be identified with a set of true propositions, as Wittgenstein would have it. Rather, he sees science as an ongoing truth-seeking enterprise, being defined by the procedures it employs rather than by the propositions it yields.

In his last book, Quine has something to say about the "softer sciences, from psychology and economics through sociology to history", to which he adds in parentheses: "I use 'science' broadly" (1995, 49). I wish to go into the last sentence only. Using 'science' broadly could mean different things. In the given context, the issue is which academic subjects count as sciences. Quine's broad notion of science indicates his willingness to accept the so-called soft sciences as sciences. "It is awkward", he says, "that 'science', unlike *scientia* and *Wissenschaft*, so strongly connotes natural science nowadays" (2000, 411). His own liberal use of 'science' is in line with his "casual attitude toward the demarcation of disciplines. Names of disciplines should be seen only as technical aids in the organization of curricula and libraries" (1981, 88). In his view, "all sciences interlock to some extent" (ibid., 71), and his main reason for this view has always been that all sciences "share a common logic and generally some common part of mathematics, even when nothing else" (ibid.). Of the three recalcitrant 'M's (modality, the mental, and mathematics), only the last is indispensable to Quine, since it is indispensable to theory in physics.

Yet there is a further sense of "using 'science' broadly", which is associated with the shift from plural to singular, i.e., from 'the sciences' to 'science' in the sense of 'our overall scientific world-view'. What is sometimes overlooked is that there are *two distinct continuity theses* concerning science in Quine's work. Both are to be found already in *Two Dogmas*. Firstly, there is his claim to continuity between philosophy and natural science, which I quoted at the beginning. Secondly, Quine holds that "[s]cience is a continuation of common sense" (1953, 45, see also 1966, 220). I submit that his sweeping notion of science in the sense of 'our overall theory of the world' reflects this latter continuity. Drawing his holistic conclusions in the final section of *Two Dogmas*, Quine speaks of "the totality of our so-called knowledge or beliefs" which constitute "a man-made fabric which impinges on experience only along the edges". This fabric is what he refers to as "total science" (1953, 42).

Quine's sweeping notion of science has some odd consequences. It has been remarked, for example, that "[i]f I want to know what time the meeting begins, or where I left my copy of *Word and Object*, what I am concerned with is very oddly described as a question of 'science'.

Quine accepts this oddity, however" (Hylton 1994, 265–6). We may safely reckon that most truths ever discovered were not discovered by professional scientists. So when we hear a Quinean credo such as: "We naturalists say that science is the highest path to truth" (1995a, 261), his words should be still ringing in our ears that "science is self-conscious common sense" (1960, 3). Elsewhere, Quine comments on the scientific or proto-scientific character of common-sensical investigations as follows:

> The scientist is indistinguishable from the common man in his sense of evidence, except that the scientist is more careful. This increased care is not a revision of evidential standards, but only the more patient and systematic collection and use of what anyone would deem to be evidence. (1966, 233)

A good example of how the common man and the scientist share evidential standards is provided by the quarrel between orthodox and alternative medicine. An adherent of natural healing may declare: 'I don't care what the orthodox medical practitioners and their scientific studies say. The herb has cured my aunt, that's enough for me.' The disagreement here is not as sharp as it seems. Both parties plausibly do care for the effectiveness of a drug. It is merely that the scientist is not so easily convinced. The fact that aunt Mary recovered after taking the herb does not exactly meet the standards of evidence-based medicine. Strikingly, non-scientists often draw conclusions on an extremely narrow inductive base. But even for an adherent of natural healing, *post hoc* is not the same as *propter hoc*. Witnessing the next time that aunt Mary recovers without being treated at all will make him suspicious. It is just as Quine says: Both the common man and the scientist do care for evidence, but the scientist is more careful and systematic.

While Quine's views about the continuity between philosophy and natural science are characteristic of his *naturalism*, his view that science is a continuation of common sense is very much in the spirit of American *pragmatism*. Some writers, though, regard the latter continuity thesis as a defining feature of naturalism as well.[3] This view is unfelicitous. Plausibly, the naturalist's distinguishing trait is his reac-

---

3. "Naturalism, as a philosophy, is a systematic reflection upon, and elaboration of, the procedures man employs in the successful resolution of the problems and difficulties of human experience." (Hook 1961, 195)

tion in the case of *conflict* between common sense and science. Since the Quinean naturalist holds that "science is the highest path to truth" (1995a, 261), scientific investigations must in some way be *superior* to common-sensical ways of determining truths about the world. As Danto saliently points out:

> Science reflects while it refines upon the very methods primitively exemplified in common life and practice. [...] Should there be a conflict between common sense and science, it must be decided in favor of science, inasmuch as it employs, but more rigorously, the same method that common sense does and cannot, therefore, be repudiated without repudiating common sense itself. (Danto 1967, 448)

For the naturalist, science is not only a continual extension of common sense, but at the same time its better half. Everything that common sense can find out science can find out as well, but science is more reliable and more accurate. Besides, scientists have special methods and tools at their disposal when things get complicated. This is why science has the last word in cases of conflict.

I return to the first continuity thesis, the naturalistic claim about science and philosophy. As explained above, it is always hard and unrewarding to dispute continuity claims. In a way, everything is a matter of degree, and every distinction can be questioned, if necessary by Sorites arguments. The issue over there being a gradual difference or a difference in kind between philosophy and science is ill-defined. Being pressed to choose between the two, I would prefer not to. Wittgenstein and Quine may both have points here. It is just that Quine always focuses on what philosophy and the rest of science have in common, while Wittgenstein is tremendously interested in determining what is *distinctive* of philosophical investigations (or of the philosophical part of scientific investigations, in Quinespeak). Unquestionably, this is a natural and legitimate concern for a philosopher. For Quine, however, it seems to be a matter of indifference.

"If Quine is right, then philosophy is an extension of science [...]. If Wittgenstein is right, then philosophy is *sui generis*." (Hacker 1996, 33) This brusque way of confronting both philosophers seems a bit simplistic to me. Ideologies set aside, nothing prevents us from investigating both the similarities and the differences between philosophy and the rest of science. Moreover, nothing prevents us from confronting Quine's naturalistic rhetoric with the way he actually does philosophy.

For there is a serious problem with Quine's sweeping notion of science. Wittgenstein's insistence on the non-scientific character of philosophy is a trivial consequence of his narrow and stipulative definition of 'science' as "the sum of the natural sciences". But if the word 'science' is supposed to have any determinate meaning, it must neither be used too broadly. *Omnis determinatio* being *negatio*, Quine should be prepared to explain what his inclusive notion of science does exclude. Simply declaring that "demarcation is not my purpose" (1995a, 252) will not do, since the intelligibility of his naturalism hinges on such a demarcation. Quine famously holds that "[t]he world is as natural science says it is, insofar as natural science is right" (1992a, 9). Elsewhere: "We naturalists say that science is the highest path to truth" (1995a, 261). Clearly, these declarations do not contribute to distinguishing science from non-science, but rather presuppose such a distinction. What is needed is a positive characterization of the notion of science invoked in Quine's naturalistic creeds. And, he must resist the temptation to leave it up to "science itself" to tell us what science is.

Others have not resisted this temptation. Arthur Fine, for example, holds that science will take care of itself in every respect. He advocates a "natural ontological attitude" which abstains from any "essentialist premises about the 'nature' of science" (Fine 1996, 175). Fine recommends to take science at its face value, rejecting "the mistaken idea that one must add distinctively philosophical overlays to science in order to make sense of it" (ibid., 188). We may say that his anti-essentialistic scientism boils down to the maxim: *Wherever science leads, I will follow*.[4]

Now, it is not easy to distinguish between the scorning of "essentialist premises about the 'nature' of science" and the refusal to explain what one is talking about. Even avowed anti-essentialists should be prepared to clearly articulate what they mean with the words they use. Surely, Fine would not accept as science just any cognitive endeavour that anyone has ever *called* science. His maxim, "follow good science as far as science goes but do not demand that science do more" (Fine 1996, 184) at least indicates that he feels able to tell apart good science from bad science. Presumably, he would advise us to ask the good scientists about what good science is. But a charlatan or a fraud, passing himself off as a scientist, would not shy away from passing himself off as a good

---

4. Cf. Keil and Schnädelbach 2000, esp. 20–31.

scientist. We may hope that in the long term, he will not be accepted by the scientific community, but if he is clever enough in faking and cheating, it may take some time until he gets unmasked. What about his status up until then? Is he a good scientist just as long as the majority of his research group accepts him as a peer? Or worse yet: What if one of the next 'science wars' is won by the social constructivists, so that the 'good scientists' Fine relies on find themselves in a minority?

For a naturalist, it is not advisable to regard membership in the scientific community as a *brute* sociological or institutional fact. The truth is that the peer group has reasons for accepting or not accepting someone as a member. And such reasons will be needed as soon as the charlatan takes the university to court because of his dismissal. Fine's defeatism regarding the definability of the science game would simply leave the scientific community empty-handed in such quarrels.

Another scientifically-minded philosopher who has not resisted the temptation in question is Stephen Stich. Stich takes exception to a widespread "puritanical naturalism" in the philosophy of mind. The search for a naturalistic criterion of acceptable properties or predicates, as carried out in the various armchair projects of naturalizing the intentional, is "misunderstanding the way that science works", Stich says (1996, 198). According to him, there is no way of identifying the naturalistically acceptable predicates in advance, i.e., independent of the role they play in science as practiced. "What 'legitimates' certain properties (or predicates, if you prefer) and makes others scientifically suspect is that the former, but not the latter, are invoked in successful scientific theories. [...] [B]eing invoked in a successful science is all that it takes to render a property scientifically legitimate" (ibid., 199).

Just as Fine speaks of "good" science, Stich speaks of "successful" science. And just like Fine, Stich becomes quite taciturn when pressed for an explanation of what being a successful science amounts to. He says: "I don't claim to have an account of what it takes to be a successful scientific theory. Indeed, I suspect that that, too, is a pluralistic, open-ended, and evolving notion." And as to "the question of whether successful science can be constructed using intentional categories [...], it is working scientists [...] who will resolve this question, not philosophers of the puritan persuasion" (ibid.).

Again, this result is disappointing. Stich, too, seems to resort to the maxim: *Wherever science leads, I will follow*. But whatever the philosophical merits of anti-apriorism and anti-essentialism are, the advice

'Ask the working scientists!' cannot settle the question what counts as good or successful science. Abstaining, for fear of apriorism, from setting any methodological standards or criteria that distinguish science from humbug and charlatanism leaves us with nothing but a sociological notion of science: *Everything that can be studied at a university is a science.* Or: *Science is what professors are paid for.* Or: *Science is what you can get money for from the National Science Foundation.* But, as is well-known, weird things are taught at universities, for example that science is just another genre of literature, or that reality is but a social construction. Naturalism cannot be so liberal as to embrace these claims as *scientific* doctrines, just because they are taught at universities by tenured professors. Quine's tenet that "the world is as natural science says it is" assumes a more ambitious, non-institutional account of what (natural) science is, even if some naturalists are reluctant to spell this out. After all, the doctrines taught at universities include apriorist epistemologies, and *ex hypothesi*, such doctrines cannot be reconciled with Quinean naturalism.

Quine once defined his naturalism as the "abandonment of the goal of a first philosophy prior to natural science" (1981, 67), and as "the recognition that it is within science itself, and not in some prior philosophy, that reality is to be identified and described" (ibid., 21). Late in his career, he acknowledged that "these characterizations convey the right mood, but they would fare poorly in a debate" (1995a, 251). That's what I say as well. Eventually, Quine seems to have an inkling of how vaguely he has always described his naturalism. At last, he puts the appropriate questions: "How much qualifies as 'science itself' and not 'some prior philosophy'? [...] What then *have* I banned under the name of prior philosophy?" (ibid., 251–2)

3. *Philosophy as Conceptual Analysis Within the Framework of Science: A Fresh Look at Quine's Alleged Naturalism*

I shall now take a fresh look at Quine's job description for naturalistic philosophers. In a survey article from the 90s, he asks himself, after giving a short description of his naturalistic epistemology, whether "this sort of thing" is "still philosophy". His answer is that

Naturalism brings a salutary blurring of such boundaries. Naturalistic philosophy [...] undertakes to clarify, organize and simplify the broadest and most basic concepts, and to analyze scientific method and evidence within the framework of science itself. (1995a, 256–7)

With suitable omissions, the passage reads: 'Naturalistic philosophy clarifies the most basic concepts and analyzes scientific method'. This is a remarkably traditional job description for philosophers. Philosophy seems to be, in a word, conceptual analysis, though "within the framework of science itself". What precisely this addition means is anything but obvious. Does it, for example, make Quine's job description incompatible with inherited conceptions of philosophy as involving conceptual analysis of the aprioristic kind? Quine's earlier explications of his naturalism suggest that the addition "within the framework of science itself" is chiefly made in opposition to the epithet 'a priori'.

The expression 'conceptual analysis' is not a registered trademark. There are so many kinds of conceptual analysis. Regarding Quine, the main challenge is to harmonize his job description for philosophy with what he considers to be the defining mark of the scientific enterprise, namely that it yields empirically testable predictions. For unlike Fine and Stich, Quine has a robust empiricist account of what it takes to participate in the game of science. The *prediction of observations* is the name of the game:

[W]hen I cite predictions as the checkpoints of science, I do not see that as normative. I see it as defining a particular language game, in Wittgenstein's phrase, the game of science, in contrast to other good language games such as fiction and poetry (1992, 20; see also 1987, 159–162).

So, in Quine's view, the fixing of empirical checkpoints is *constitutive* of the science game. Now philosophy is supposed to be part and parcel of the science game as just defined, while at the same time it is said to clarify, organize and simplify the most basic concepts, and to analyze scientific method. This double job description creates a certain tension, for arguably, the clarification of concepts and the analysis of methods do not provide empirical checkpoints of their own.

To be sure, there are varieties of conceptual analysis which do bear relations to empirical checkpoints. Strawson (1959, 9) describes his "descriptive metaphysics" as "aiming to lay bare the most general features of our conceptual structure", and as "describ[ing] the actual structure of our thought about the world". In Austin's linguistic phenomenology, the empirical bearings are even more obvious. Austin used to check his philosophical claims against the actual usage of the terms in question by nonphilosophical speakers. These kinds of conceptual analysis license the remark that "[q]uestions about the actual structure of our concepts are *in principle* as empirical as questions about the actual structure of iron" (Bishop 1992, 269). The same point has recently been made by Frank Jackson:

> It is an empirical fact that we use a certain term for the kinds of situation and particulars that we do in fact use it for, and the conclusions we come to on the subjects are fallible—as Gettier made vivid for us when he showed us that fine conceptual analysts like Ayer and Chisholm got it wrong in the case of the word 'knowledge'. (Jackson 1998, 47)

Seen this way, there is a fairly direct connection between conceptual analysis and empirical checkpoints, the empirical data being the linguistic behavior of ordinary speakers.[5] Of course, this approach is not Quine's. Ironically, it's just his own reservations about ordinary language philosophy which set off his preferred kind of conceptual analysis against the partly empirical project just described. Instead, Quine advocates what he calls *don't-care analyses*, which he explains thus:

> We do not claim synonymy. [...] We do not expose hidden meanings, as the words 'analysis' and 'explication' would suggest; we lack supplies. We fix on the particular functions of the unclear expression that make it worth troubling about, and then devise a substitute, clear and couched in terms to our liking, that fills those functions. Beyond these conditions of partial agreement [...] any traits of the explicans come under the head of 'don't cares'. (1960, 258–9, cf. 182)

It is, in other words, the *stipulative* or *legislative* character of Quine's explications and paraphrases that prevents him from substantiating his continuity thesis in a straightforward manner. It is, of course, far from me to make Austin's way of integrating the philosopher's business into the science game palatable to Quine. He has good reasons to think of

---

5. Strawson, by contrast, speaks of "the actual structure of our thought about the world", which might, after all, "not readily display itself on the surface of language" (1959, 10). This is why conceptual structures, unlike linguistic ones, are hardly ever reckoned empirical data. Strawson says that the descriptive metaphysician "must abandon his only sure guide when the guide cannot take him as far as he wishes to go" (ibid.). It is doubtful, however, whether a fact's being less accessible makes it less empirical.

the way in which conceptual analysis contributes to testable predictions as being more devious.

The tension between the way Quine describes the science game and his job description for scientific philosophy is still unresolved. Which role exactly does the clarification, organization and simplification of our most basic concepts play for the business of predicting observations? To find an answer to this question, I wish to return to Quine's remarks about the so-called soft sciences in his last book:

> In softer sciences [...] checkpoints are sparser and sparser, to the point where their absence becomes rather the rule than the exception [...]. Observation categoricals are implicit still in the predicting of archaeological finds and the deciphering of inscriptions, but the glories of history would be lost if we stopped and stayed at the checkpoints. (1995, 49)

Quine makes it clear that even theories in the soft sciences have *some* testable consequences. Empirical checkpoints are sparser here, but still there are some. Elsewhere, he puts it in a nutshell: "[T]he softer the science the sparser the tests" (1995a, 258).

It should be noted that the empiricism contained in Quine's characterization of the science game relates only to the output, not to the input. This is why he surprisingly is prepared to accept, in his later writings, even telepathy and clairvoyance as "scientific options, however moribund. It would take some extraordinary evidence to enliven them, but, if that were to happen", then this "collapse of empiricism would admit extra input by telepathy or revelation, but the test of the resulting science would still be predicted sensation" (1992, 21). This is a remarkable passage. Taken as a theory about the input, empiricism would be falsified if it turned out that some information about the world reaches us via other channels than impacts on our sensory receptors. The immediate question is, though, what the "extraordinary evidence" for telepathy could consist of. What does Quine have in mind here? In order for us to *accept* any evidence for the existence of telepathic phenomena, it seems that our views about what counts as evidence must have changed beforehand. As long as the triggering of sensory perceptors is the only thing that counts as a source of information, scientific evidence for telepathy is simply ruled out from the start. In Quine's view, empiricism as a scientific doctrine is itself "fallible and corrigible" (ibid.). But, the trouble with accepting any findings as "extraordinary evidence" for telepathy is that such acceptance would at the same time change our views of what *counts* as evidence. It is difficult to see how both revisions could be undertaken with a single blow. Quine's liberalism seems to be caught up in a methodological circle.

Let us return to what Quine has to say about the soft sciences. We are told that theories in economics, sociology or history, do have some testable consequences. But now for the big question: What about philosophy? How soft a science is philosophy? Clarifying, organizing and simplifying our most basic concepts, and analyzing scientific method —which testable consequences do these activities have? Are the tests so sparse here that philosophy is even softer than, say, sociology?

This is an odd suggestion. Philosophy plays a part in the science game, but its role seems to differ in kind from the role that sociology or economics play. A parallel to the role of logic and mathematics is more easily drawn. According to the Quinean picture, logic and mathematics do contribute to the fabric of total science, but not by fixing the edges, i.e., not by supplying additional checkpoints. Rather they contribute by enabling us to knit the fabric more closely. The same could hold true for philosophy: It does contribute, but it does not contribute additional checkpoints. Therefore, *even if* philosophy is part and parcel of the scientific enterprise, and *even if* prediction of observations is the name of the game, philosophy does not belong to *that* part of science which is subject to direct empirical test. This is in principle Quine's own picture, which is sometimes obscured by his needlessly bold and crude naturalistic avowals.

In *Two Dogmas*, he famously holds that the fabric of science "impinges on experience only along the edges" (1953, 42). Yet, if we take the criterion of distance from the checkpoints at face value, mathematics and logic come out as much softer sciences than even sociology does. This result cannot be welcome to Quine. I suggest, anyway, that we do not attach too much importance to the determination of the grade of hardness of a science. The systematic significance of the soft/hard distinction as applied to scientific disciplines seems rather limited. Calling a science "hard" or "soft" is more a matter of exploiting dubious connotations.[6] There may be kindred distinctions which are more useful, for example that between exact and inexact sciences, or that between sciences which invoke intentional notions and those which do not.

---

6. In the hard sciences, hard-working people discover hard facts, while soft scientists are probably soft characters, perhaps even soft in the head ...

As Quine's use of the fabric metaphor shows, the yielding of testable predictions is not a *conditio sine qua non* for participation in the science game, contrary to his suggestion in *Pursuit of Truth*. The question, *in which way* the clarification and analysis of our most basic concepts and methods contributes to our weaving the fabric of total science, is still without a positive answer.

The parallel between philosophy and mathematics is very instructive, particularly since Quine changed his view about the empirical content of mathematics late in his life. While in *Pursuit of Truth* he still held that "[h]olism lets mathematics share empirical content where it is applied" (1992, 55–6), he writes in his last book that

> the participation of mathematics in implying the [observation] categoricals [...] does not confer empirical content. The content belongs to the implying set, and is unshared by its members. I do, then, accept the accepted wisdom. No mathematical sentence has empirical content, nor does any set of them. (1995, 53)

In other words, no mathematical sentence has the capacity of turning a semantic mass into what Quine dubs a critical semantic mass. Regarding the results of conceptual analyses, would therefore an analogous concession be appropriate? This much is certain: the fact that words mean what they mean contributes to the *truth* of empirical statements, in the obvious way: "The statement 'Brutus killed Caesar' would be false [...] if the word 'killed' happened rather to have the sense of 'begat'" (Quine 1953, 36). Or, if I make a random guess at the number of coins in my pocket, and the guess turns out to be correct, it would be false, according to the standard analysis, to say that I *knew* the right number. If, however, 'knowledge' happened to have the sense of 'true belief' instead of 'justified true belief (plus x)', then it would have been true that I knew the number.[7]

This kind of affecting truth value, however, does not by itself confer empirical content to analytical definitions. Nor does the fact that word meanings are subject to historical change, as it has been the case, for example, with the German word "Junggeselle". The fact, emphasized

---

7. As to the notion of knowledge: Quine's own view, that "for scientific or philosophical purposes the best we can do is give up the notion of knowledge as a bad job and make do rather with its separate ingredients" (1987, 109), is motivated by his insight that "knowing is a hybrid of warranted belief, which is mental, and truth, which is not" (2000, 415). This insight is clearly a result of good-old-fashioned conceptual analysis.

by Quine, that "no statement is immune to revision" (1953, 43) has no relevance whatsoever to the issue of analyticity. A change in meaning cannot retrospectively deprive a sentence of its analytical character. Quine himself conceded in his later years that analyticity must be dissociated from incorrigibility (cf. 2000, 415).

In a way, the results of conceptual analyses do make a difference to the truth-value of synthetic statements. However, they do so because they *reflect* semantic facts, not because they *generate* them. Conceptual analyses can only *reveal* facts about meaning which have been previously established by the speech community.[8] Or facts about usage, as Quine and Wittgenstein would prefer to say: Conceptual analysis well-understood is a matter of "fluctuant usage to be averaged out", not of "intrinsic meanings to be teased out" (Quine 1992, 55). And, of course, an analytical definition alone never *implies* a synthetic truth. It is just as Quine says with respect to mathematics: "No conjunction or class of purely mathematical truths, however large, could ever imply a synthetic observation categorical. [...] Every critically massive set of truths has some nonmathematical members." (1995, 53)

Recognizing the difference between yielding testable predictions and merely belonging to an implying set is crucially important to the re-evaluation of Quine's tenets about the deliverances of science. The clarification and analysis of our most basic concepts may be viewed as part and parcel of the scientific enterprise, if we embrace Quinespeak, but still it does not belong to that part of science which directly faces the tribunal of experience.[9] It belongs to the more general and more abstract part of science which some non-naturalist philosophers like to call *a priori*. The empirical checkpoints being miles away (below the horizon, as it were), philosophers have to *give arguments* for their claims instead. As Quine has put it: "Having reasonable grounds is one thing, and implying an observation categorical is another" (1994, 497). Devising "reasonable grounds" is essential to the philosopher's business, while coming up with analytical definitions is little more than

---

8. See Hanjo Glock's contribution to this volume, sct. 5, where he rephrases what Yablo has called "the Lewy point" as the insight that conventions and meanings do not *create* truths.

9. This line of reasoning assumes that the epistemological holism from *Two Dogmas* is an exaggeration, as Quine himself often granted in later years: "Excessive holism surfaced only back at midcentury in my pioneer 'Two Dogmas', in a regrettably eloquent passage that readers never tire of quoting" (1997, 572).

preparatory work in this business. A philosopher's job is by no means accomplished when he has framed a sentence like 'Knowledge is justified true belief', or 'An action is a bodily movement caused in the right way by rationalizing beliefs and desires'. After having written down such a definition, the philosopher's job has only just begun. He has to argue in its favour, defend it against competing proposals, coordinate it both with the linguistic data and with speakers' intuitions about "what we should say when" (Austin) and check its implications for previously accepted analyses of other concepts. Sometimes, he may even have to explain why some basic concepts, perhaps 'truth', 'identity', or 'existence', are too elementary as to admit of analytic definitions. Whatever the fate of analytic definitions proper, conceptual analysis in a wider sense will continue to be a major part of the philosopher's business, which is a business of devising reasonable grounds for claims abstract enough to count as philosophical in nature.

Quine's talk about "science itself telling us" remains puzzling because it covers up the difference between being *an empirical finding* and being *a reason which has some bearing on science*. One last example from ontology will illustrate my point: As to the similarities between existence statements such as 'There are tigers' and allegedly philosophical existence statements such as 'There are numbers', Quine says:

> Existence statements in this philosophical vein do admit of evidence, in the sense that we can have reasons, and essentially scientific reasons, for including numbers and classes or the like in the range of our variables. [...] Numbers and classes are favoured by the power and facility which they contribute to theoretical physics and other systematic discourse about nature. (1969, 97–8)

Saying that "we have reasons, and essentially scientific reasons" for accepting numbers and classes sounds much better than taking it from "science itself" that such entities exist. But still: In which sense are the reasons scientific ones? A moment's reflection reveals an ambiguity in calling a reason 'scientific'. A scientific reason might be *a justification which is somehow related to scientific purposes*. This is obviously what Quine has in mind here.[10] A scientific reason could as well consist of

---

10. In general, Quine is far from maintaining that all questions about what there is are questions of empirical fact. Rather, the "issue over there being classes" is aligned with "the issue over there being brick houses on Elm street" in the name of "a more thorough prag-

a direct appeal to an empirical finding, that is, to a fact discovered by empirical science. While it's clearly the former that Quine has in mind, it's the latter that everyone thinks of, and rightly so, when getting informed that science itself tells us this and that, or when being told, as we are in *Word and Object*, that it's "the business of scientists" to determine "what is real", and that "scientific method is the last arbiter".

So, more attention must be paid to the difference between *citing an empirical finding* as if it spoke for itself, and *giving an argument* which is somehow *related to scientific purposes*. (Some philosophers go so far as to call facts themselves reasons, but that is another story. I adhere to the view that scientific findings and facts are never justifications by themselves, though they can, of course, be *appealed to* when *giving* a reason, in philosophy and elsewhere.) I find Quine's declaration unobjectionable that in coping with philosophical problems we are always "free to use scientific knowledge", when interpreted along these lines. "All scientific findings" he says, are "as welcome for use in philosophy as elsewhere" (1969, 127). This avowal stems from his paper "Natural Kinds", where he appeals to Darwin's natural selection as "a plausible partial explanation" (ibid.) of the fact that human beings are innately disposed to make, by and large, inductions which are correct. On closer scrutiny, however, his appeal to the findings of evolutionary theory plays a minor role than it seems. Quine does refer to innate similarity standards, but the crucial argument in his paper is about the *projectibility of predicates*, thus "entirely philosophical in character", as Susan Haack noticed: Quine "proposes a solution—that only natural kind predicates [...] are projectible—which involves no appeal to evolution (or to any scientific work), but is entirely philosophical in character" (Haack 1993, 133).

Hence, Quine's appeals to 'scientific findings' and 'scientific reasons' are in need of a careful interpretation. More often than not, these appeals do not consist in merely citing an empirical finding, but are embedded in a philosophical argument which is in some way related to scientific purposes.

---

matism", since ultimately, *all* kinds of entities "enter our conception only as cultural posits" (1953, 46 and 44). At the same time, he accepts all entities posited by science as "utterly real denizens of an ultimate real world" (1995a, 260). To him, the posits are nonetheless real. Quine sees no clash between his constructivist pragmatism and a robust realism. Ontological questions inevitably being answered from within a scientific theory, calling the entities posits and calling them real is just a matter of changing the perspective.

4. Conclusion

Hence, as long as we keep aware of the difference just explained, we need not be intimidated by Quine's frequent appeals to "science itself". It sometimes may look as if Quine appealed to the authority of natural science to establish philosophical tenets, but this impression is due to a superficial reading, one which is encouraged, though, by some bold formulations of Quine's.[11]

Quine holds that the yielding of empirically testable predictions is constitutive of the science game, and that nonempirical truths are scientifically respectable if and only if they belong to sets of truths that imply observation categorials. This view is of course not a deliverance of empirical science, but rather stems from his *philosophy* of science, a philosophy which even the formula "Empiricism without dogmas" is not an adequate expression of. For when it comes to the question whether and how nonempirical disciplines such as mathematics or philosophy contribute to our overall scientific picture of the world, *empiricism itself* is a dogma. Quine's concession that some distance from the checkpoint is allowed does not change the situation, because the concession, and his reasons for it, are not by themselves empiricist tenets. If any -ism is called for, they are more rationalistic than empiristic in spirit.

I have argued that, given Quine's inclusive notion of science, his addition "within the framework of science itself" to the job description for philosophy has an innocuous reading, which at the same time strips his avowed naturalism of real bite. In general, Quine's notion of naturalism is not as elaborate as, say, his notion of observation sentence. He regarded names of philosophical positions as "a necessary evil" (1995a, 251), and he "tend[ed] to be impatient with the quest for

---

11. Here I agree with Pihlström and Koskinen (2001, 14) who suggest "a more modest interpretation of the metaphilosophical implications of [Quine's] naturalized epistemology". They characterize Quine's naturalism as "a holistically empiricist metaphilosophical view about the nature and role of philosophical knowledge" (ibid., 2). In particular, they discuss the issue of *normativity*, which I have neglected. In case we are forced to revise our web of belief in the face of recalcitrant experience, Quine is known to appeal to the principles of *simplicity* and *conservativism*. Both are clearly normative principles, which cannot be read off from the descriptive content of scientific theories. Quine's rejoinder that this normative element "gets naturalized as a chapter of engineering: the technology of anticipating sensory stimulation" (1992, 19) simply misses the point, for it cannot answer the crucial Humean question of where on earth the normative 'ought' is to be taken from.

precision in the names for disciplines and schools of thought: in asking what really counts as naturalism, epistemology, physics" (2000, 411). We should not, however, let him get away with this nonchalance, given the huge impact his naturalistic avowals had on the scientific community. When Quine defined naturalism as "abandonment of the goal of a first philosophy prior to natural science", it was far from clear what he did ban under the name of prior philosophy. He did not ban speculative metaphysics, nor conceptual analysis per se, nor the soft sciences. What one finds are mainly tendentious and polemical formulations such as having "higher-level intuitions" (1969a, 303), speaking from a "cosmic exile" (1960, 275) or establishing "a supra-scientific tribunal" (1981, 72). (The last remark might be an misconceived allusion to the Kantian metaphor of the court of reason.)

The upshot of my discussion is that Quine's naturalistic rhetoric does not show him at his best. There are not many philosophers left at whom Quine's criticism of philosophical apriorism could be aimed. Hardly any first-rank philosopher does appeal to "higher-level intuitions" when making *a priori* assertions—neither did Leibniz, nor Kant, nor Wittgenstein. On the other hand, Quine's own writings clearly belong to philosophy and logic, and not to some other scientific discipline. Even if names of disciplines should be nothing but "technical aids in the organization of libraries" (1981, 88), librarians know pretty well on which shelf Quine's books are to be placed. "Why not settle for psychology?", he suggestively asks in "Epistemology Naturalized" (1969, 75). Now, did he settle for psychology? Did he accord "a physical human subject [...] certain patterns of irradiation in assorted frequencies" as an "experimentally controlled input", so that his epistemology "simply falls into place as a chapter for psychology, and hence of natural science" (ibid., 82–3)? No, he settled for philosophical speculations about what behavioristic psychology *might* find out about the roots of reference.[12]

---

12. This has been noted before: that "Quine's attempt to trace a path from stimulation to science is carried out with almost no concern for the psychological reality of the process, that is, with almost no references to empirical investigations of how language is actually acquired. [...] Quine's inspiration comes from the library, not the laboratory. [...] Launched from a starting point of debatable empirical significance—observation sentences taken holophrastically—Quine's program proceeds with almost no contact with the empirical checkpoints central to doing philosophy in a naturalistic spirit" (Fogelin 1997, 561–2).

Steve Stich has emphasized that "Quine offered a new job description for philosophy".[13] I agree with him only under the qualification that changing a job description is one thing, while providing somebody with a new job is quite another. Quine's celebrated blurring of the boundary between philosophy and natural science is a piece of naturalistic rhetoric which fortunately had little effect on the way he actually did philosophy. The real tension exists between his empiricist definition of the science game and the non-empirical nature of mathematics, logic, and major parts of philosophy. These parts of the scientific enterprise enable us to knit our web of belief more closely without contributing additional empirical checkpoints.

REFERENCES

Bishop, Michael 1992: "The Possibility of Conceptual Clarity in Philosophy", *American Philosophical Quarterly* 29, 267–277.

Cohen, L. Jonathan 1987: "The Importance of Quine", *London Times Literary Supplement*, Nov. 1987.

Danto, Arthur C. 1967: "Naturalism", in: Paul Edwards (Ed.), *The Encyclopedia of Philosophy*, Vol. V, New York/London, 448–450.

Fine, Arthur 1996: *The Shaky Game*, 2nd Ed. Chicago/London.

Fogelin, Robert J. 1997: "Quine's Limited Naturalism", *Journal of Philosophy* 94, 543–563.

Gibson, Roger F. 1999: "Quine", in: R. L. Arrington (Ed.), *A Companion to the Philosophers*, Oxford, 459–464.

Haack, Susan 1993: *Evidence and Inquiry*, Oxford.

Hacker, Peter M. S. 1996: "Wittgenstein and Quine. Proximity at Great Distance", in: R. L. Arrington/H.-J. Glock (Eds.), *Wittgenstein and Quine*, London/New York, 1–38.

Hook, Sidney 1961: *The Quest for Being (and Other Studies in Naturalism and Humanism)*, London.

Hylton, Peter 1994: "Quine's Naturalism", in: Peter A. French et al. (Eds.), *Philosophical Naturalism* [= *Midwest Studies in Philosophy* 19], Notre Dame, Ind., 261–282.

---

13. Princeton University Memorial, Apr. 14, 2001 [see www.wvquine.org/wvq-obit5.html#PPSS]

Jackson, Frank 1998: *From Metaphysics to Ethics. A Defence of Conceptual Analysis*, Oxford.
Keil, Geert and Herbert Schnädelbach 2000: "Naturalismus", in their *Naturalismus. Philosophische Beiträge*, Frankfurt am Main, 7–45.
Koppelberg, Dirk 2000: "Was ist Naturalismus in der gegenwärtigen Philosophie?", in: G. Keil and H. Schnädelbach (Eds.), *Naturalismus. Philosophische Beiträge*, Frankfurt am Main, 68–91.
Monk, Ray 1990: *Ludwig Wittgenstein. The Duty of Genius*, London.
Pihlström, Sami and Heikki J. Koskinen 2001: "Philosophical and Empirical Knowledge in the Program of Naturalism", in: *Explanatory Connections. Electronic Essays Dedicated to Matti Sintonen*, Helsinki [www.valt.helsinki.fi/kfil/matti/].
Quine, Willard Van Orman 1953: *From a Logical Point of View*, Cambridge, Mass.
— 1960: *Word and Object*, Cambridge, Mass.
— 1966: *The Ways of Paradox and Other Essays*, New York.
— 1969: *Ontological Relativity and Other Essays*, New York/London.
— 1969a: "Replies", in: D. Davidson/J. Hintikka (Eds.), *Words and Objections*, Dordrecht, 292–352.
— 1974: *The Roots of Reference*, La Salle, Ill.
— 1975: "The Nature of Natural Knowledge", in: S. Guttenplan (Ed.), *Mind and Language*, London, 67–81.
— 1976: "Whither Physical Objects?", *Boston Studies in the Philosophy of Science* 39, 497–504.
— 1981: *Theories and Things*, Cambridge, Mass.
— 1987: *Quiddities*, Cambridge, Mass.
— 1992: *Pursuit of Truth*, 2nd Ed. Cambridge, Mass.
— 1992a: "Structure and Nature", *Journal of Philosophy* 89, 5–9.
— 1994: "Responses", *Inquiry* 37, 495–505.
— 1995: *From Stimulus to Science*, Cambridge, Mass./London.
— 1995a: "Naturalism; Or, Living Within One's Means", *Dialectica* 49, 251–261.
— 1997: "Response to Haack", *Revue Internationale de Philosophie* 51, 571–572.
— 2000: "Quine's Responses", in: A. Orenstein/P. Kotatko (Eds.), *Knowledge, Language and Logic: Questions for Quine*, Dordrecht/Boston/London, 407–430.
Stich, Stephen P. 1996: *Deconstructing the Mind*, New York/Oxford.
Strawson, Peter F. 1959: *Individuals. An Essay in Descriptive Metaphysics*, London.

Wittgenstein, Ludwig *Tract.*: *Tractatus logico-philosophicus* [1921], London 1961.
— 1972: *The Blue and Brown Books*, Oxford.

QUINE'S EXTERNALISM

Donald DAVIDSON
University of California at Berkeley

Summary
In this paper, I credit Quine with having implicitly held a view I had long urged on him: externalism. Quine was the first fully to recognize that all there is to meaning is what we learn or absorb from observed usage. This entails the possibility of indeterminacy, thus destroying the myth of meanings. It also entails a powerful form of externalism. There is, of course, a counter-current in Quine's work of the mid century: the idea of stimulus meaning. Attractive as this choice of empirical base is compared to such options as sense data, appearances, and percepts, it has serious difficulties. In general, an externalism which ties the contents of observation sentences and perceptual beliefs directly to the sorts of situations that usually make them true is superior to those forms of empiricism which introduce intermediaries between word and object.

In the summer of 1950 my then wife and I were bicycling through France. Having made it from Cherbourg to the Riviera we decided to rest for a month in Cagnes-sur-Mer, where we rented a five-story stone house (one room per floor) for a dollar a day. Quine and his new wife Marge came to visit, and we spent the warm days swimming, biking to the neighboring hill towns, and talking. Quine had the manuscript of *Two Dogmas of Empiricism* with him, and we discussed it. I was familiar with Quine's rejection of the dogmas, having heard about them in a seminar at Harvard a decade earlier. What was new to me, and exciting, was the sketch of a new, and positive epistemology to go with Quine's holistic view of language. But I was critical, then as now, of what I considered a relic of empiricism, a relic that showed up in the metaphor of a conceptual scheme facing the tribunal of experience, and the claim that ordinary physical objects are 'posits', constructions based on something more fundamental.

Quine did not write *Two Dogmas* as he wrote almost everything else, as the result of inner promptings. Word had been getting around of Quine's new take on epistemology, and he was asked to read a paper on the subject at the annual late December 1950 meeting of the American Philosophical Association. His son Douglas, with whom Marge was pregnant when we were biking around the Riviera, was born on December 20th, and a few days later Quine read *Two Dogmas* to the Association. It was printed the next year.

It was old stuff to Quine, who had been discussing the supposed analytic/synthetic distinction with Carnap, Tarski, Morton White, and Nelson Goodman for ten years. I once asked Quine how his views on analyticity and related matters had developed so rapidly between 1934, when he had delivered three entirely uncritical lectures on Carnap at Harvard, and a few years later, when the thoughts expressed in *Two Dogmas* were firmly set. When I asked, Quine had no answer. But later, when both those early lectures on Carnap and the Quine-Carnap correspondence were published, Quine discovered to his surprise that he had argued in correspondence with Carnap about analyticity almost from the time of their meetings in Prague.

The attention *Two Dogmas* attracted, both positive and negative, made Quine realize that the metaphors and hints in the last section of his paper should be backed by a more explicit development. The development appeared in print in 1960. It was *Word and Object*. By another stroke of luck I was in on the late stages of its composition. Quine spent the academic year 1958–59 at the Center for Advanced Study in the Behavioral Sciences on the Stanford University Campus. Fellows at the Center were allowed to bring an informal assistant, and Quine asked me to read the manuscript of *Word and Object*. I had the year off from teaching at Stanford, and gladly accepted.

Quine has often replied to criticisms of *Two Dogmas* by pointing out that in *Word and Object* he had replaced what was left implicit or nebulous in *Two Dogmas* with an explicit statement of his views, and he wished his views could be discussed on the basis of the book. This is why I intend in this paper to treat those two seminal works as a unit. I think that in spite of all the attention they have received, they contain theses that are still underappreciated.

It seemed natural to many philosophers in the first half of the last century to think that one central project in the philosophy of language was to try to define the expression 'x means y'. If and only if—what? The attempts to fill in this blank were, it is clear in retrospect, hopeless, worse, if possible, than the endless attempts to define justice or the good or truth. Multiple failures did discourage the attempts at defining 'x means y' (except, perhaps, in Australia), but the idea persisted that meanings are entities connected in some way with words on the one hand and aspects of the world on the other.

Of course everyone agreed that language is a human construct. Somehow languages evolved, and somehow each of us has learned one or more of them. Hypotheses were floated about how these events may have taken place, but the end of the story in each case was: meanings did get attached to words and sentences; those who learned a language learned what meaning was attached to each word (or what word was attached to each meaning) of a preexisting language. It is hard to exaggerate the extent to which the assumption that there are eternal entities—ideas, intensions, meanings—attached to words was, and still is, taken for granted. This Platonic notion was fundamental to the work on language of Frege, Russell, Carnap, and many others. Prompted by Frege, they were clear that meanings were not mental states, which would make them private, but rather entities that any number of people could grasp and which they had to grasp if they were to communicate. Frege, Russell, and Carnap didn't argue for or against the idea of fixed meanings: they assumed their existence. Many philosophers still do.

But what is wrong with the assumption? The objection can't be that meanings are abstract objects, since we cannot begin to spin a theory of meaning without talk of abstract objects (such as words, sentences, etc.). Nor will I bother with the complaint, justified as it is, that meanings are not well individuated. It is enough simply to wait until they are shown to be convenient or necessary in the explanation of verbal communication. They would be needed, for example, if the project of defining 'x means y' or 'the meaning of x is y' were to get off the ground.

Wittgenstein pointed in a better direction, though vaguely, when he asserted that meaning is use. There is no good reason to assume from the start that words have meanings, and that our only task is to say how to attach the right meaning to each word or phrase. The place to begin is with the jobs speech helps us perform. It is surprising to reflect now on what a fresh breeze this idea brought with it; but what exactly was the message borne by that breeze? One difficulty is that there are myriad uses to which we put language and they need to be sorted out before we can base any sort of theory on the notion of use. The trouble is not so much that each utterance may be for the sake of a different end as that each individual utterance answers to many intentions. If I utter the words "You will drop that gun", I intend you to interpret my utterance as one that is true if and only if you drop the gun, I do that with the intention that you take my utterance as a demand or order, I do that with the intention of getting you to drop the gun, I do that with the intention of countering what I perceive as a threat to my welfare, and so on. One action, many intentions. But each realized intention constitutes a use to which I am putting those words. Which use is the one we should identify with meaning? If we pick what Frege called the force of my utterance—in this case the force of an order or demand—we will have difficulty in relating force directly to grammatical mood, for "You will drop that gun" is in the indicative mood, not imperative, though I am making a demand. The relation between grammatical mood and force is far too complex to lend itself to serious, or at any rate precise, theory. My further intentions, for example to get you to drop the gun, seem often to be the sort of uses Wittgenstein had in mind (remember "Block" and "Slab"), but it is surely optimistic to expect to find any explicitly formulable relation between such ulterior purposes and the literal contents of utterances.

Because it was unclear how to harness Wittgenstein's insight, it was hard to view Wittgenstein's later work as leading to a coherent view of the general structure of language. As a result much of the work he inspired led to a dead end. Nevertheless, the basic idea is right: meaning *is* use; what is needed is to take this in, and apply it to the right use.

One lead is obvious: the sort of uses that are relevant are first of all the uses of sentences. Words have no use except as they contribute to the uses of sentences. Frege was on to this when he wrote in the *Grundlagen* that "it is only in the context of a sentence that a word has a meaning". After the *Grundlagen* Frege unfortunately came to treat sentences as names, and the distinction between sentences and singular terms was lost—"a retrograde step on Frege's part", Dummett remarks (Dummett 1973, 7).

Word and Object undid Frege's mistake. The ordinary language philosophers called our attention to the various ways in which language is put to work, but the main effect was to discourage the systematic study of language through failure to distinguish clearly among the ways. Austin, in *How to Do Things with Words* (1962), made an impressive start at sorting out the varieties of use, but by then Quine was on his way.

Whatever there is to 'meaning', whatever it is about speech that makes it useful for communication, has to be conveyed by the publicly observed behavior of language users. This is true no matter how much of the human language instinct is genetically given. Quine was, of course, deeply interested in showing that the analytic/synthetic distinction could not be taken for granted. He urged that if we abandon the assumption of meanings simply there to be learned by the beginner we will realize that nothing in what we can observe in the linguistic behavior of others justifies the postulation of meanings. What we have to go on is observed usage, and usage reveals no neat boundaries.

Starting with whole sentences Quine sketched the process by which we can abstract out the repeatable, replaceable parts of sentences, thus mastering the rules of combination that make the creativity of language possible. If we start from usage, the only possible methodology takes sentences as basic and treats words as useful constructs.

Quine had a solution to, or a way around, the problem of the multiple uses or intentions implicit in any speech act. He did this by introducing the concept of prompted assent. What the learner of a new language may plausibly be expected to recognize is occasions on which some stimulus is observed by the interpreter to have caused an alien speaker to assent to an utterance. The stimulus must therefore be mutually observed. If such occasions can be discriminated the problem of multiple uses has been solved in a way that picks out from among the many reactions of the speaker just those that are of direct interest to the theorist of meaning. This is an awesome assumption, since it supposes both that a response of assent can be distinguished from other responses, and that those assents are, often enough, to a sentence taken literally rather than, say, to the informant's intent to amuse, confuse, metaphorize, or implicate. Awesome or not, I think the assumption is justified. Both adults and three-year-olds are uncannily skilled at distinguishing the serious from the jocular, the sly from the straight, the honestly instructive from the devious. If they were not, it is hard to see how they would ever uncover meaning at the level at which interpretation must begin.

Quine has sometimes been criticized for employing the concept of assent as the empirical basis for his theory of radical translation, given his distaste for such psychological concepts. It is true that if Quine ever dreamed of a behaviorist, non-mentalistic, definition of prompted assent, he certainly never came up with such a definition. But protocols recording prompted assents are not intensional; they are not mentalistic in the sense of requiring a non-extensional analysis. One can miss this point because a sentence of the form "A assents to the proposition that p"

clearly is intensional, and can be attributed to an agent only by someone who thinks he can individuate the propositional attitudes of that agent. But Quine's concept of prompted assent relates agents to *uninterpreted* sentences, and so is extensional: the truth value of sentences of the form "*A* assents to utterance *u*" does not depend on how *A* and *u* are described. (This claim is not defeated if we describe the relation between speaker and utterance thus: "*A* assents to *u* as an utterance of a sentence of his language taken literally".) Interpretation is the *aim*; it isn't assumed. The product of the successful translator is the ability to translate, and hence understand, a speaker's words. A concomitant outcome is a view of the speaker's beliefs, for given an interpretation of the sentences to which the speaker honestly assents, beliefs are revealed. Quine's method doesn't demonstrate how to go from a description of behavior in the terms of the natural sciences to an understanding of utterances and of beliefs, but it does show how a learner starting from an extensional perception of speakers interacting with the world can come to understand those speakers. This is an intermediate variety of reduction, and an extremely illuminating one. For subtle as assent is to analyze, it is not hard to believe that we are equipped by nature to discriminate the human reaction of assent, and Quine has shown how this special gift would suffice to work one's way into the realm of thought and speech. No doubt we would not get everything right at the start. No harm would be done: no coherent picture of world or language would emerge, for it is not in the cards that we would end up with a coherent but false picture. Human curiosity, need, and ingenuity can be counted on to make us persevere until we get it right. Once we come close, the rest will flood in.

Quine has also been criticized for not making use of all the evidence available to a radical translator. I don't think he ever claimed that he had. But if one wants to add to the evidence, one should be sure that the added evidence meets the standard of extensionality. Otherwise there will almost certainly be a circle. Consider the various attempts to define meaning on the basis of intentions. Even if such an approach succeeded it would beg the issue at hand if it depended on an independent ability to individuate intentions, for the ability to individuate intentions sufficiently finely is surely dependent on linguistic competence. In any case there was no reason for Quine to resist evidence in the form of information about other attitudes than assent to sentences, such as wanting a sentence to be true or preferring that one sentence be true rather than another. I think this last may be a valuable addition since, as I tried to show, it can be used to uncover relations of evidential support between sentences as judged by the speaker (Davidson 1990b). This is a form of the "interanimation of sentences" (Quine's term) which Quine never developed. Without such a measure, "analytic hypotheses" for translating theoretical sentences can take any form which accommodates the data concerning sentential logic and the translation of observation sentences. But given degrees of evidential support, it is possible to put constraints on the translation of theoretical terms and the sentences containing them.

Now I turn to the process of radical interpretation as Quine describes it. It is here that I would locate the key to the essential breakthrough in the theory of meaning. Radical translation depends on three devices. The first delivers tentative translations of observation sentences with indices to time and place, sentences like "This is red" and "Here is a table". Quine made a number of attempts to define the notion of observation sentence, but in fact defining the notion is unnecessary from the point of view of the translator. He will start, of course, with sentences to which his chosen speaker assents only in the presence of some relatively ephemeral, and easily observed, phenomenon: the occurrence of a color, or of a snow storm, or the brief appearance of a familiar person, or the sighting of a dangerous beast. Given the extent to which sense organs and other built-in recognition abilities are similar from person to person, first guesses are often going to be right. But no matter if they are not: further discoveries will lead to improvements here, and at every stage that follows.

The second act concerns the logical constants. The basic idea is simple and revealing. Patterns of assents and dissents will identify the pure sentential connectives. Simple, since what else could there be to go on in deciding that a connective should be translated by the word "and" than that the speaker assents to two sentences conjoined by that connective iff he assents to each of the sentences alone? I shall speak of what this reveals about Quine's methodology in a moment.

In a further phase of radical translation, sentences are translated which combine predicates whose empirical content was discovered independently, sentences which are not themselves observational: "Snow is white" is an example. Theoretical terms and sentences containing them are translated in such a way as to preserve their relations with sentences containing more observational terms, a guiding principle being to translate in a way that maximizes intelligibility.

I am reminding you of what you long ago absorbed from *Word and*

Object. I want it to be fresh in your mind now, when I come to what is so importantly novel, and may go unnoticed. A few sentences back I said that patterns of assents and dissents will allow the radical translator to identify the pure sentential connectives. This wording suggests the very idea that I was scouting at the start, the idea that words have a fixed meaning to be identified or discovered. How has Quine departed from that dogma? Consider the case of translating observation sentences. From the translator's point of view, the process differs little from ostensive learning. There is, indeed, one difference. In ostensive learning, we think of the learner using his natural powers of induction to use a certain word (really sentence) to tag objects, qualities, events as belonging to a certain class. The radical translator already has his word (sentence) for these same situations, so he is not learning a new classification, just using an old one for the purpose of translation. This difference is mainly illusory. *All* the translator knows about the use to which the alien is putting his sentence the translator has picked up from observed causal interactions between the world and the alien. We have been thinking of the translator then asking himself what sentence of his own language he would use in the same situations. But we do better to say he is acquiring the alien's sentence. For him, this new sentence has been baptized, given a content, by the situations in which he has been working at translation. If the interpreter were to use the sentence himself, it would mean just what these situations have contributed to it (plus, of course, whatever has been contributed by observed relations to other sentences, etc.), but no more. With luck, few situations will arise in which the alien's sentence and the translator's translating sentence will fail of mutual applicability; the two users' dispositions to use their sentences will be nearly enough alike to serve. The postulation of a 'meaning' shared by alien and translator is neither needed nor justified by this procedure.

The point is easily missed because of our natural way of thinking about translation. We are told it preserves meaning, and so we summon up visions of meanings learned and then shared. But there is nothing shared except the common world of objects and events about which we communicate. We think of ostension and other forms of inculcating language as providing no more than *evidence* for meanings. But in fact they provide the communicative charge our words have. *The process of acquisition confers meaning; it doesn't identify a preexisting meaning.* If we do not see this at once, it is because evolution has shaped us so nearly alike. We recognize faces, though seen in different lights and at different distances and angles; moving animals against a background; shapes and objects and colors are distinguished in much the same ways. No wonder it seems as though nature itself comes classified, and it is up to each of us merely to notice the distinctions already there, and to put names to them as Adam did. Learning the words assigned to nature's divisions, we learn what everyone in our language group already knows. The myth of meaning comes naturally.

Nevertheless, it is a myth. At the bottom reaches, your words and my translations of them (perhaps the very same words) do pretty nearly divide nature at the same joints. But this is the gift of a common genetic heritage, not the work of shadowy meanings. Meanings, like sense data, are intermediate entities between the mind and what it knows and thinks about, and they are philosophers' inventions. It is better to think of our language not as a tool we have borrowed from the common store, but as an organ each of us develops for dealing directly with other people and the world.

The so-called principle of charity (so-called by Quine, following Neil Wilson) is best seen as an acknowledgment of this direct connection between utterances (and the thoughts they express) and what they are about. Consider the prime example: observation sentences. Their translation invokes charity because it requires the translator to translate an observation sentence as made true by what the translator observes and takes the speaker to be observing, thus making the speaker correct if the translator is. Thus the translator is constrained by how he knows language operates to translate so as to make the speaker speak and think what the translator takes to be true. Of course error on either or both sides is possible. The translator may on occasion find his informant assenting to the query "Gavagai?" when there is only a papier-maché rabbit in sight. If all past assents to "Gavagai" utterances were geared (as far as the translator has observed) to real rabbits, the translator may well take the present case to be a mistake on the informant's part. It also might be a mistake on the translator's part, since gavagais may include papier-maché rabbits. Further observations can straighten this out. In any case, charity does not mean the translator never finds his informant in error, but it does mean he is not in a position to attribute error with confidence until he has accumulated a considerable backlog of evidence.

Charity mates the responses of translator and informant just as it does the responses of the learner of a first language and that learner's linguistic environment. But it should be clear that at the primitive level of assents to observation sentences, there is no way most assents can fail to be mostly correct. Since the situations that typically trigger such assents constitute the contents of those assents, they also constitute the contents of the utterances to which assent is won. Wittgenstein makes a point of the fact that the learner of a new word through ostension is not in a position to doubt that the word (embedded in a sentence, pronounced "Dog" or "That's a dog") truly applies in those situations. The teacher may be wrong, in that the teacher, having a word already employed in a network of a language, may not be applying it correctly according to his own standards. But the learner has no other standards to go by than those provided by the ostensions: for him, the word correctly applies in the ostended situation, at least until he learns better. To say the learner has made a mistake when he applies a locution just when the teacher does is to miss the point: the learner may not fit into an intended linguistic society (including, perhaps, that of the teacher), but his newly learned bit of language could be understood by anyone patient enough to learn it in turn.

It may seem that there is no real difference between the two pictures of language I have been trying to contrast. According to one picture, there is a social enterprise ("game", Wittgenstein misleadingly calls it) which the learner of a first or second language learns to engage in. This is certainly how the learner, and society, consisting of teachers and parents and friends, see it. According to the alternative picture, the learner is acquiring a new language more or less closely modeled on that of others, a language that is apt to be pushed more and more nearly into socially acceptable shape by exposure. The difference seems vanishingly small because in the first scenario as well as the second perfection isn't there at the start; both stories reveal a learner usually anxious to be as much in the social swim as possible. But there is a difference, which is that *only on the second story is there an indissoluble connection between words and what they are about.*

The aspect of Quine's theory of meaning in *Word and Object* which I have been stressing is a form of externalism, though the word was not used this way, as far as I know, until later. The idea that Quine was an early externalist is apt to surprise, and Quine himself was surprised when I told him this, so I shall spend most of the rest of this paper defending this suggestion. I depend on two things: the role ostension plays in radical translation, and the emphasis on the fact that all there is to empirical meaning is what is picked up in such situations (aside from what we learn from the interanimation of sentences). In the first paragraph of *Word and Object* we read,

> Each of us learns his language from other people, through the observable mouthing of words under conspicuously intersubjective circumstances. Linguistically, and hence conceptually, the things in sharpest focus are the things that are public enough to be talked of publicly, common and conspicuous enough to be talked of often, and near enough to sense to be quickly identified and learned by name; it is to these that words apply first and foremost (Quine 1960, 1).

Quine stresses that "uniformity comes where it matters socially; hence rather in point of intersubjectively conspicuous circumstances of utterance than in point of privately conspicuous ones" (ibid., 8). Then comes a wonderful topiary comparison:

> Different persons growing up in the same language are like different bushes trimmed and trained to take the shape of identical elephants. The anatomical details of twigs and branches will fulfill the elephantine form differently from bush to bush, but the overall outward results are alike (8).

The first sentences of the Preface to *Word and Object* read as follows:

> Language is a social art. In acquiring it we have to depend entirely on intersubjectively available cues as to what to say and when. Hence there is no justification for collating linguistic meanings, unless in terms of men's dispositions to respond overtly to socially observable stimulations (ix).

There you have it. As I shall argue, Quine's account of ostension plus the insistence that what is acquired in ostensive situations as it filters through the web of language is all there can be to meaning, add up to a subtle form of externalism which (alone, I would say) can constitute the basis of a satisfactory theory of meaning.

There is, of course, a counter-current in Quine's work of the period; the source of the counter-current is the idea of stimulus meaning. The work expected of stimulus meaning in characterizing the translation of observation sentences does not fit well with the passages I just quoted. Quine wanted a starting point for his project of answering the question: "Given only the evidence of our senses, how do we arrive at our theory of the world?" (Quine 1974a, 1). He wanted something that could serve as an ultimate source of the contents of our empirical beliefs, and abjuring sense data as hopelessly vague, he turned to the stimulations of the sense organs. But whatever serves to give content to empirical beliefs must also give content to the observation sentences that express those beliefs. Quine put it this way when summing up what he called the two "cardinal tenets of empiricism": "One is that whatever evidence there *is* for science *is* sensory evidence. The other ... is that all inculcation of meanings of words must rest ultimately on sensory evidence." (Quine 1969, 75) The stimulus meaning of a sentence is the ordered pair of patterns of sensory stimulation that would prompt a speaker to assent to the sentence and the patterns that would prompt dissent (all of this relative to a time interval). If observation sentences match in stimulus meaning, one can serve as translation of the other, since all the evidence relevant to their meaning is contained in their stimulus meanings.

Attractive as this choice of empirical base is compared to such options as sense data, appearances, percepts, and the like, it has serious difficulties. Quine was worried from the start that different people might have different stimulus meanings for what intuitively were the very same scenes. In any case he abandoned the earlier dependence on stimulus meaning (Quine 1996). The objections were weighty; it is good that Quine changed his mind. There is a further reason to give up stimulus meanings, and this goes to the tenets of empiricism they were designed to satisfy: stimulus meanings depend on private events, not in the sense that these events are mental, but because they are on or in the skin and flesh of the individual. As elements from which to construct meanings or thoughts, they are too much like sense data. They are less mysterious than sense data, but they are not the level at which one can start to build either a theory of meaning or an epistemology, no matter how naturalistic. But I depart from my theme: it is unclear whether Quine would have agreed with this conclusion, particularly in the case of epistemology. His remarks that physical objects are "posits" or "nodes" whose function is to systematize and predict further experiences suggest both the problem I see, and why we did not see eye to eye on the matter.

Whatever drawbacks stimulus meanings may have as a basis for meaning and empirical knowledge, they do indicate that Quine was from the time of *Word and Object* an externalist, at least if we understand this term in one natural way. The natural way is this: a theory or position is externalist if it entails that a person's beliefs and what he means by what he says are not completely determined by the physical state of his brain. Since much goes on between skin and thought, there is no reason to assume a perfect correlation between the stimulus meaning of an utterance (or the thought it expresses) and states of the brain. If one starts with stimulus meanings, then thoughts and meanings "ain't in the head". That is how Hilary Putnam famously put it in "The Meaning of 'Meaning'" (Putnam 1975) in order to shock us. Strictly speaking, this isn't quite right: the point isn't that thoughts and meanings are not in the head, but that the entities or events that individuate thoughts and meanings are not all in the head. As an externalist, Quine was fifteen years ahead of Putnam.

Starting in 1958–9, when I read *Word and Object* in manuscript, I urged Quine, first in conversation, and then in a series of papers, to become an all-out externalist, and anchor meanings of observation sentences to the objects, events, and situations they are about (Davidson 1974; 1990a; 1995). He was already an externalist (without knowing it); it was just a matter of moving the cause of the mental state that helped identify it from the stimulated skin out to the relevant distal stimulus. It was not clear that this had not always been his position. The passages quoted above from *Word and Object* seem to take the distal line (the "conspicuously interpersonal circumstances"), and there is much more of the same in that book and others that followed. In section 10 of *The Roots of Reference*, for example, he writes, "Ostensive learning is fundamental, and requires observability. The child and the parent must both see red when the child learns 'red', and one of them must see also that the other sees red at the time". It is red things that both child and parent observe, not nerve endings. A strong statement of the distal position is in a talk Quine gave in Oxford in 1974:

> ... consider the case where we teach the infant a word by reinforcing his random babbling on some appropriate occasion. His chance utterance bears a chance resemblance to a word appropriate to the occasion, and we reward him. The occasion must be some object or some stimulus source that we as well as the child are in a position to notice. Furthermore, we must be in a position to observe that the child is in a position to notice it ... the fixed points are just the shared stimulus and the word ... the occasions that make the sentence true are going to have to be intersubjectively recognizable (Quine 1974b).

It is clear that the stimulus here is the distal stimulus, for it is shared, and can be noticed by teacher and child.

The form of externalism implicit in *Word and Object* is not to be found in those philosophers who came later and called the idea externalism or anti-individualism. Putnams's externalism in "The Meaning of 'Meaning'" is far more special, being limited primarily to sortal predicates, and involving a questionable debt to essentialism. By contrast, Quine's externalism extends to the entire empirical thrust of the language, and does not depend on supposing that something isn't properly called water unless it is H_2O. For Quine, such questions are settled, when they need to be settled, by repeated, interlocking ostensions, and the interanimation of sentences. Quine's externalism is social, but despite his emphasis on the importance of speakers being coaxed by parents, teachers, and society to make the same sounds in relevantly similar situations, he never suggests, with Tyler Burge, that even someone who is mistaken about what most people mean by a word nevertheless means, all unwittingly, what they do. The social element in Quine's picture enters in a far more fundamental way: it concerns agreement, not on sounds (which is why translation plays the role it does) but on the external circumstances which prompt the sounds.

Quine's externalism combines a form of what I call perceptual externalism with a form of social externalism, and together they make a powerful team. The contribution of perceptual externalism to the learning and interpreting of language is obvious, as Quine points out, in the primacy of ostension. The contribution of social externalism is less obvious, though its role in ostension is clear. The additional force of the social is best brought out by posing two questions to those who have promoted perceptual externalism without linking it to the social (I think here of those who have followed Russell, like Gareth Evans and John McDowell). One question is this: where, in the infinite causal chains that lead to the sense organs, should we locate the elements that give content to our observation sentences and their accompanying perceptual beliefs? The short answer is that the location is given by two or more observers whose simultaneous interactions with each other and the world triangulate the relevant stimulus. This is something one person alone cannot do.

The second question is this: what, in the process of acquiring a first language and propositional thought, gives us the idea of error (and so of truth)? Society provides the clue to the possibility of error. Under good conditions, the observations of different observers will agree: these are the observations Quine characterized as being of the things in sharpest focus, the things that are public enough to be talked of publicly, common and conspicuous enough to be talked of often, and near enough to sense to be quickly identified. And, as he added, the things we are programmed by evolution to classify, through our responses, as similar. Most observations will agree, but from time to time some will not, due to poor lighting, an obscuring tree, or failing eyesight. At the start, such deviations show us the possibility of error and the distinction between belief and truth, without which we do not have the idea of an objective world independent of us.

Externalism which ties the contents of observation sentences and perceptual beliefs directly to the sorts of situations that usually make them true is superior to those forms of empiricism which introduce intermediaries between thought and thing, word and object, for such externalism is immune to the threat of skepticism. If all we have as ultimate evidence are sense data, appearances, or even sensory stimulations, the question is bound to arise how we know there is anything beyond. At one time, Quine was inclined to say, So What? We would never know the difference, so long as our stimulations remained organized. "What", asked Quine, "does our overall scientific theory really claim regarding the world. Only that it is somehow so structured as to assure the sequences of stimulations that our theory gives us to expect" (Quine 1981, 474). I am suggesting that to the extent that Quine accepted the externalism which ties the content of observation sentences to their distal stimulus, he had a better answer.

I have said nothing about what many, including perhaps Quine himself, took to be the most important single thesis of *Word and Object*, the indeterminacy of translation: "[M]anuals for translating one language into another can be set up in divergent ways, all compatible with the totality of speech dispositions, yet incompatible with one another." In *Word and Object* Quine believed that observation sentences would diverge "less drastically" (27), but even this was to change with the later discovery of the inscrutability of reference. Once one has given up the myth of meanings, indeterminacy should seem a relatively minor point, like the fact that length can be measured in feet or meters. The cases are, after all, exactly analogous. The structure required for the measurement of lengths can be stated precisely, and its empirical primitives such as the relation 'x is at least as long as y' and 'x added on to y' given empirical interpretations. When this has been done, one can apply the theory to objects. It turns out that if one wants to assign numbers to keep track of lengths, this is possible, but any set of numbers that keeps track of the relations of length among objects can be converted into another equally good set by multiplying all the original numbers by any positive constant.

This is the 'indeterminacy of length' (but better called a Uniqueness Theorem). In the case of language, logic (and semantics, I would add) provide the structure, and the method of radical translation gives the empirical interpretation. Within these constraints, there will be endless different ways of assigning my sentences to yours as translations.

Some forms of indeterminacy can, perhaps, be reduced further than Quine thought. It hardly matters. For suppose it turned out that acceptable structural and empirical constraints reduced indeterminacy to zero, not as a matter of principle, but as an empirical discovery. This would do nothing to diminish the importance of Quine's attack on the myth of meanings. Radical translation leads to the recognition of the possibility of indeterminacy, and this is enough to destroy the myth. Quine was the first fully to recognize that all there is to meaning is what we learn or absorb from observed usage. This entails the possibility (in fact, the infinite likelihood) of indeterminacy, thus destroying the myth of meanings. It also entails a powerful form of externalism.*

REFERENCES

Davidson, Donald 1974: "On the Very Idea of a Conceptual Scheme", in: Donald Davidson, *Inquiries into Truth and Interpretation*, Oxford, 183–198.

Davidson, Donald 1990a: "Meaning, Truth and Evidence", in: *Perspectives on Quine*, ed. by R. B. Barrett and R. F. Gibson, Oxford, 68–69.

Davidson, Donald 1990b: "The Structure and Content of Truth", *The Journal of Philosophy* 87, 279–328.

Davidson, Donald 1995: "Pursuit of the Concept of Truth", in: *On Quine*, ed. by P. Leonardi and M. Santambrogio, Cambridge, Mass., 203–220.

Dummett, Michael 1973: *Frege: Philosophy of Language*, London.

Putnam, Hilary 1975: "The Meaning of 'Meaning'", in: *Language, Mind and Knowledge*, ed. by K. Gunderson, Minneapolis, 131–193.

Quine, W. V. 1960: *Word and Object*, Cambridge, Mass.

---

* This paper (except for some opening paragraphs) was read at a mini-conference at Boston University on 21 January, 1998. The organizer and other speaker was Jaakko Hintikka, and Quine was the chairman and impromptu commentator. Slightly tongue-in-cheek, I here credit Quine with having implicitly held a view I had long urged on him. He remained an explicit internalist.

Quine, W. V. 1969: *Ontological Relativity and Other Essays*, New York.

Quine, W. V. 1974a: *The Roots of Reference*, La Salle, Illinois.

Quine, W. V. 1974b: Unpublished manuscript.

Quine, W. V. 1981: "Reply to Stroud", *Midwest Studies in Philosophy* 6, 473–5.

Quine, W. V. 1996: "Progress on Two Fronts", *The Journal of Philosophy* 93, 159–163.

Philosophische Analyse
Philosophical Analysis

Hrsg. von / Edited by
Herbert Hochberg • Rafael Hüntelmann • Christian Kanzian
Richard Schantz • Erwin Tegtmeier

Andreas Bächli / Klaus Petrus (Eds.)

Monism

ontos verlag

Monism is not a particular theory or even a school. However, monistic intuitions or doctrines are grounded in many different ways of philosophizing. For instance, one may argue that there is ultimately only one thing, or one kind of thing, or that there is only one set of true beliefs, one truth, one type of action, one sort of meaning, one way of analysing, explaining and understanding; or, alternatively, one may pursue the project of the unity of knowledge or even that of the unity of science. Taken in this broad sense, monism is often opposed to varieties of pluralism or numerous versions of dualism, since so much philosophical debate has focused on the question whether there are two different kinds of thing, mind and matter, or only one. The aim of the present volume is to discuss some of these aspects historically and systematically.

With original contributions by Scott Austin, Andreas Bächli, Alex Burri, Thomas Grundmann, Herbert Hochberg, Mark A. Kulstad, E.J. Lowe, Eduard Marbach, Alex Mourelatos, Klaus Petrus, Matjaz Potrc, Wolfgang Röd, Richard Schantz, Ralf Stoecker, Karsten R. Stueber, Leonardo Tarán, and Jean-Claude Wolf.

ontos verlag 2003
ISBN 3-937202-19-6
340 pages / Hardcover € 70,00

Starting with the roots of the analytic tradition in Frege, Meinong and Bradley, this book follows its development in Russell and Wittgenstein and the writings of major philosophers of the analytic tradition and of various lesser, but well known and widely discussed, contemporary figures. In dealing with basic issues that have preoccupied analytic philosophers in the past century, the author notes how analytic philosophy is sometimes transformed from its original concern with careful and precise formulations of classical issues into the dismissal of such issues. The book thus examines the change that came to dominate the analytic tradition by a shift of focus from the world, as what words are about, to a preoccupation with language itself.

Herbert Hochberg is Professor for Philosophy at the University of Texas at Austin. He "has emerged as one of the most distinctive and throroughgoing of contemporary ontologists" (Grazer Philosophische Studien).

ISBN 3-937202-21-8
280 Seiten, Pb. € 22,00
ISBN 3-937202-14-5
Hardcover € 40,00

Herbert Hochberg

Introducing Analytic Philosophy

Its Sense and its Nonsense
1879 – 2002

ontos verlag

ontos verlag
P.O. Box 61 05 16
60347 Frankfurt
Germany
www.ontos-verlag.de
info@ontos-verlag.de

ontos verlag

Frankfurt ■ London